ARCHIVING warhol

an illustrated history by gerard malanga

CREATION

credits

ARCHIVING WARHOL
An Illustrated History by Gerard Malanga
ISBN 1 84068 076 8

Published 2002 by Creation Books
www.creationbooks.com
Design: The Tears Corporation

Front cover image: Andy Warhol and Gerard Malanga as they appeared, winter 1963, in Gerard's Photomaton series. Copyright © by Gerard Malanga

Inside covers: Andy Warhol solarized photomaton portrait by Gerard Malanga, 1965, mixed media. Copyright © by Gerard Malanga

contents

For
Charles Henri Ford...
who first introduced me to Andy

by Gerard Malanga

POETRY
3 Poems For Benedetta Barzini (1967)
Prelude To International Velvet Debutante (1967)
The Last Benedetta Poems (1969)
Gerard Malanga Selbsportrait eines Dichters (1970)
10 Poems For 10 Poets (1970)
chic death (1971)
Wheels Of Light (1972)
The Poetry Of Night, Dawn And Dream/Nine Poems For Cesar Vallejo (1972)
Licht/Light (1973, bilingual)
Incarnations: Poems 1965 – 1971 (1974)
Rosebud (1975)
Leaping Over Gravestones (1976)
Ten Years After: The Selected Benedetta Poems (1977)
100 years have passed (1978)
This Will Kill That (1978)
Three Diamonds (1991)
Mythologies Of The Heart (1996)
No Respect: New & Selected Poems 1964 – 2000 (2001)

PHOTOGRAPHY
Screen Tests/A Diary, in collaboration with Andy Warhol (1967)
Six Portraits (1975)
Good Girls (1994)
Seizing The Moment (1997)
Resistance To Memory (1998)
Screen Tests Portraits Nudes 1964 – 1996 (2000)

SELECTED COMPILATIONS
Transatlantic Review #52 – An Anthology of New American Poetry (1975)
Little Caesar #9/"Unprecedented Information" (1979)
Angus MacLise Checklist 1959 – 1979 (1981)
UP-TIGHT: The Velvet Underground Story (with Victor Bockris, 1983)
Scopophilia: The Love Of Looking (1985)
A Purchase In The White Botanica: The Collected Poetry Of Piero Heliczer (with Anselm Hollo, 2001)

COMPACT DISCS
48 Cameras & Gerard Malanga, *Three Weeks With My Dog*, Besides 006 (1999)
Gerard Malanga, *Up From The Archives*, sub rosa SR170 (1999)

ARCHIVING
warhol

preface
now by way of then

Not long ago a newspaper reporter came to interview me on the work I had done with Andy Warhol, and at one point in the conversation asked, "How come your work doesn't resemble the work you were doing with Warhol?" To which I replied, "Simple. I was thinking that way for Andy. I could never think that way for myself."

Yet I was surprised, when I began dredging the files for this book, to discover just how much I had given thought to Andy over the years. At the very beginning and for the several years we worked and travelled together, I'd given no thought to where all this would lead, committed as I was to helping Andy achieve his goals. To me it was second nature in what I set out to do, and in seeing the magic unfold.

In retrospect I think these pieces and transcripts were to satisfy a curiosity about how one can become unintentionally involved with history. Yet, deep down I intuited that I was very much involved with something that some day would be looked upon with great importance – what Charles Henri Ford, the gentleman responsible for introducing me to Andy, refers to as my "archival consciousness", being active in that sense. But to what extent, I had no way of really knowing; I was having too much fun.

–gm
29:xii;01

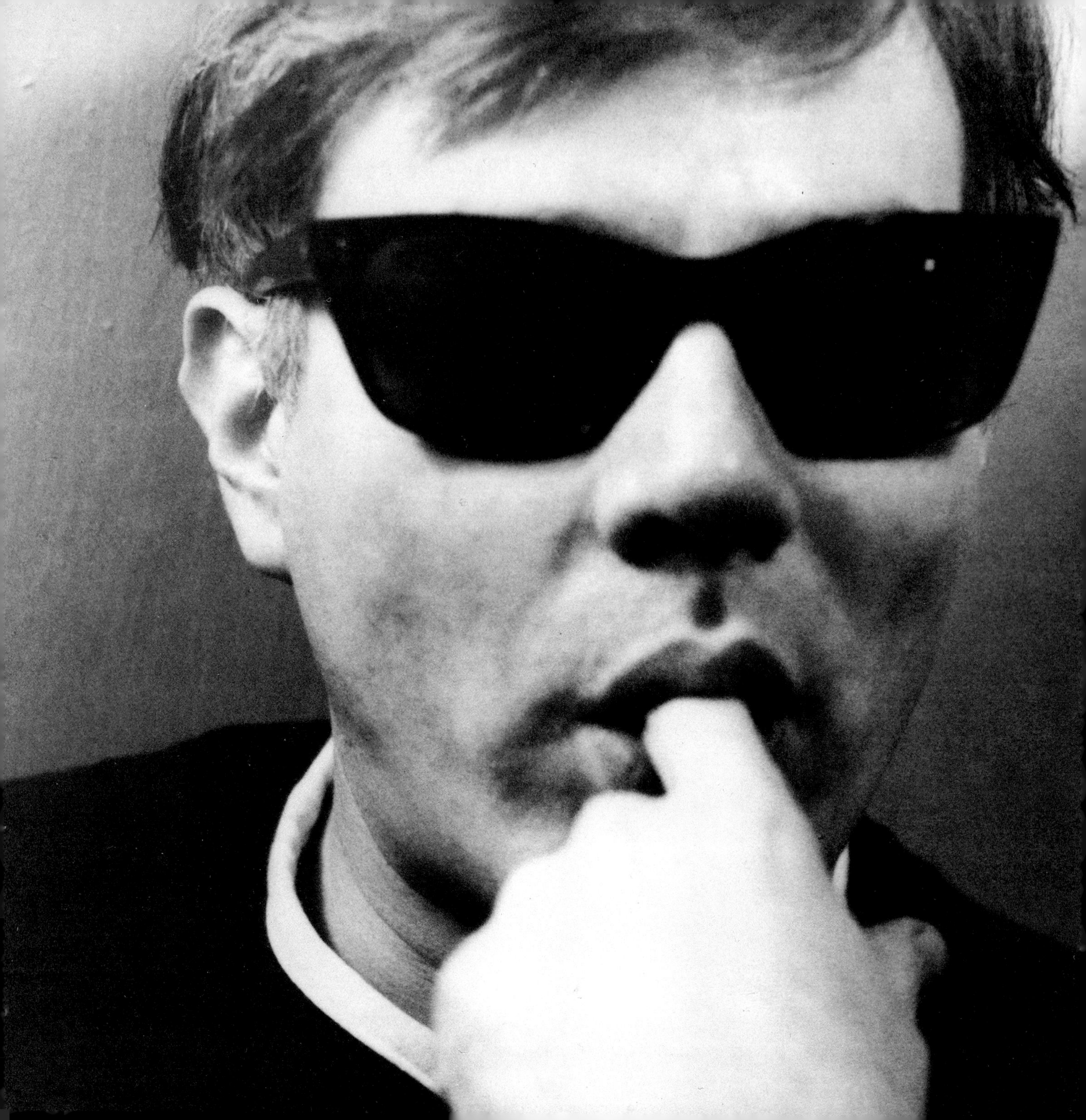

one

andy warhol interviewed

Q. What is your name and address?

A. My name is Andy Warhol. I live on Lexington Avenue in New York. Actually I spend most of my time a couple of blocks away on East 87th Street. It's an abandoned firehouse I rent from the city.

Q. Where were you last employed?

A. The Miller Shoe Salon.

Q. What is your profession?

A. Factory owner.

Q. Do you have a secret profession?

A. Commercial artist.

Q. Do you have a secret profession?

A. Yes.

Q. If so, what?

A. I can't think of it.

Opposite: Andy Warhol, 1963

Q. Why aren't you doing what you should be doing?

A. Because I'm making films.

Q. Are you allowed to do what you should by circumstances?

A. No.

Q. What is beyond your control?

A. What's that mean?

Q. Why should anyone hire you?

A. Because I'm dependable.

Q. Does society owe you anything?

A. Yes.

Q. If you are happy doing what you do, should you be paid for it?

A. Yes.

Q. If so, why?

A. Because it will make me more happy.

Q. And how much?

A. As much as I want.

Q. Are you human?

A. No.

Q. Why do you answer what you answer?

A. Because I'm sensitive.

Q. If you are unhappy, should you be paid for this?

A. Yes.

Q. Who should not be allowed to be paid?

A. Talented people.

Q. Why?

A. Because they can do it so easy.

Q. If you were very stupid, could you still be doing what you are doing?

A. Yes.

Q. If so, why do you do it?

A. Because I'm not very smart.

Q. If not, should you be compensated for this?

A. Yes.

Q. Should very stupid people be compensated?

A. Yes.

Q. How?

A. Because, sometimes, when I put on some weight from eating too much I get depressed.

Q. What do you need?

A. Nothing.

Q. Where should what you need come from?

A. From God.

Q. What are you?

A. A man.

Q. What do you know?

A. Nothing.

Q. Are you glad you know this?

A. Yes.

Q. How much?

A. Nothing.

Q. Should it pay?

A. Yes.

Q. What would you like to forget?

A. Everything.

Q. Who are you glad you are?

A. I don't know.

Q. How does this affect our educational standards?

A. It doesn't.

Q. Is it more wonderful than awful to know the right people?

A. Yes.

Q. Why?

A. Because they're right.

Q. Who do you know?

A. Almost no-one.

Q. Are you sure you know them?

A. I'm not sure of anything.

Q. Could you be hired on this basis?

A. It's not what I'm not certain of, it's what I can do that counts, I suppose.

Q. How can you help?

A. I can help by doing everything right.

Q. Who do you want to help?

A. Those whom I know that deserve it.

Q. Is there any necessary connection between wanting to help and a potential value in helping?

A. No.

Q. Why not?

A. Because wanting to help does not necessarily lead to actually helping; therefore no potential value can exist.

Q. Do your answers to the above make you useful to people?

A. It's not that I am made useful to people, it's those people who are made useful to me.

Q. Do your answers to the above make you some kind of Communist?

A. No. But I've been referred to as a Platonist.

Q. Please tell me about yourself.

A. I already have.

—1963 at The Firehouse.

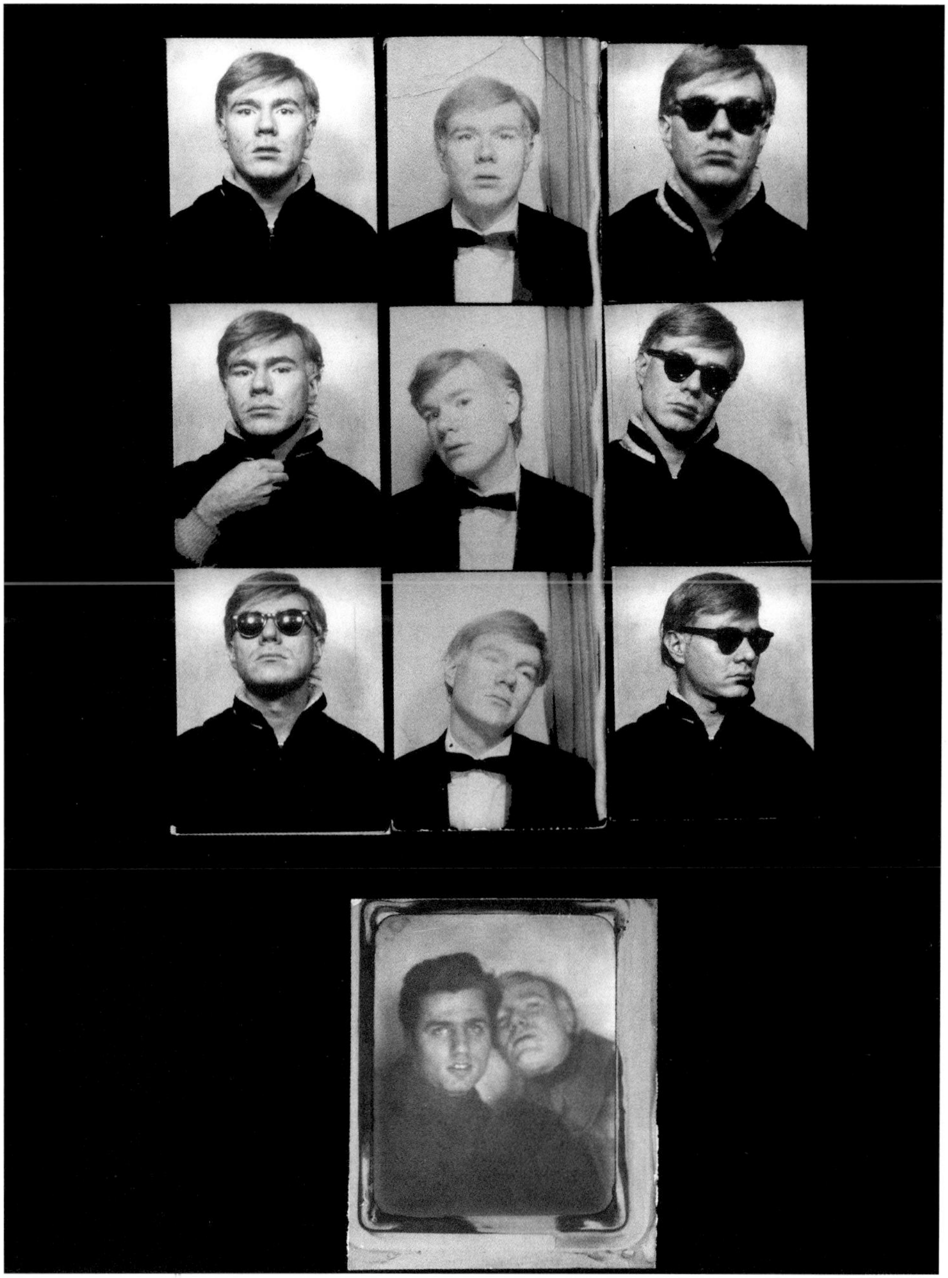

Andy Warhol in photomat, ca. 1964, from Photomat Archival Series by Gerard Malanga.

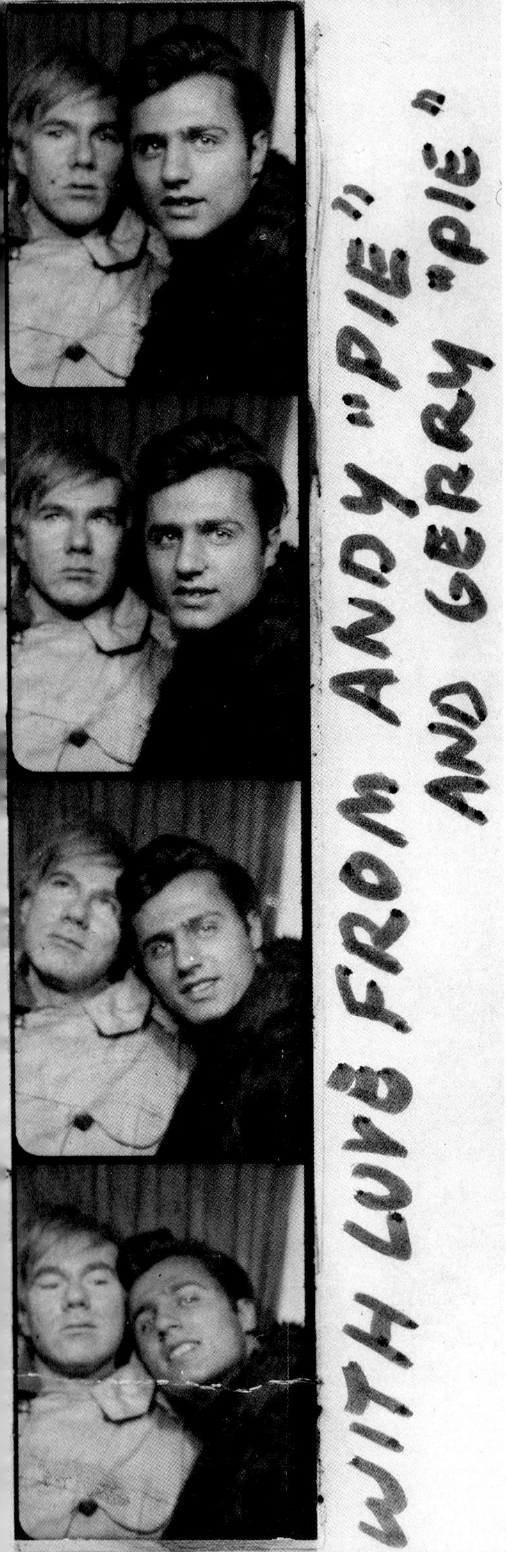
WITH LOVE FROM ANDY "PIE"
AND GERRY "PIE"

two
notes from a non-literary life

It's a bitter-cold night – new snow blanketing the old snow – early December 1963. Andy and I come out from seeing a double feature at the Empire on Forty-second Street. On the way to hailing a cab, I pull him into the Playland Arcade and suggest we send a photobooth Christmas card to Charles... Charles Henri Ford. Andy agrees and I drop a quarter into the slot. Huddled together in the warmth of our coats, changing expressions slightly with each turn of the flash, we stare directly into the camera, like a couple of teenagers. We anxiously wait the three minutes it takes for the finished photostrip to develop. We take turns looking at it, holding it in our hands, joking about each other's expression. My identity (now confirmed by my image with Andy) recalls the way we might have looked to others at the time.

I pocket the strip and take it home; I'm living with my mom in the Fordham Road section of the Bronx. The next day I fasten the strip to a sheet of oaktag and write up along the side, calligraphy pen dipped in red India ink – *With love from Andy "Pie" and Gerry "Pie"*, nicknames Charles had adopted for Andy and me. I seal the strip in a manila envelope and send it off to Charles, not thinking I'd ever see it again. Several months earlier he had brought Andy Warhol and me together in what would amount to a friendship that would forever change my life. The gift is a gesture of thanks.

Opposite: Andy Warhol and Gerard Malanga in the earliest known photomaton together, ca. November 1963, with inscription to Charles Henri Ford.

1955 was a signal year for me in the deveopment of my consciousness. When kids my age were passing time idolizing baseball players, I was discovering Orson Welles, mesmerized as I was by the first telecast of *Citizen Kane*, on Channel 9's "Million Dollar Movie". An only child, I spent many hours reading *Screen Stories* (a magazine specializing in Hollywood screenplay synopses), and compiled scrapbooks of the *Daily News* Coloroto column. “New York’s Changing Scene”.

School trips to the Metropolitan Museum of Art didn’t hold my attention for long. My earliest recollection of an art that would widen my field of vision was standing before Thomas Cole’s sequence of five paintings, *The Course Of Empire*, at the New York Historical Society one Sunday afternoon. His vision stimulated me. I would go back several times to see it.

My parents enrolled me in an after-school art class at the neighbourhood YWCA, and while students were busy drawing landscapes and still lives, I would tape sheets of paper into one extended scroll, creating a continuous detailed cross section of New York City’s subways and elevated lines from memory.

My art teacher thought I was “overgifted”. I didn’t know exactly what that meant. A book on her desk caught my eye, *Metropolis: An American City In Photographs*. I would spend entire sessions in a corner of the classroom turning its pages, reading the texts, making elaborate sketches from a few of the pictures, enchanted by a bygone time that somehow didn’t seem all that different from the present. At some point (I’m not sure when) I realized the pictures were from the early 1930s, only twenty years earlier. This was my first aesthetic experience with photography. At the end of the workshop semester I charmed the teacher into letting me have the book. *Metropolis* proudly has its place in my library.

For as long as I can remember, I sensed that the experience of my childhood would be ephemeral, so when news reached me that the Manhattan section of the Third Avenue El would be put out of service, I recognized that its passing symbolized the end of a part of my childhood. A few months earlier, I had received a Kodak Brownie 2.25 camera for my twelfth birthday. So I made the decision to imitate the pictures I had admired in *Metropolis*, and set out to preserve what I could on film for my private amusement. I had no idea at the time that such an undertaking would help focus my perception of things to come.

It came as no surprise to my father when I told him of wanting to

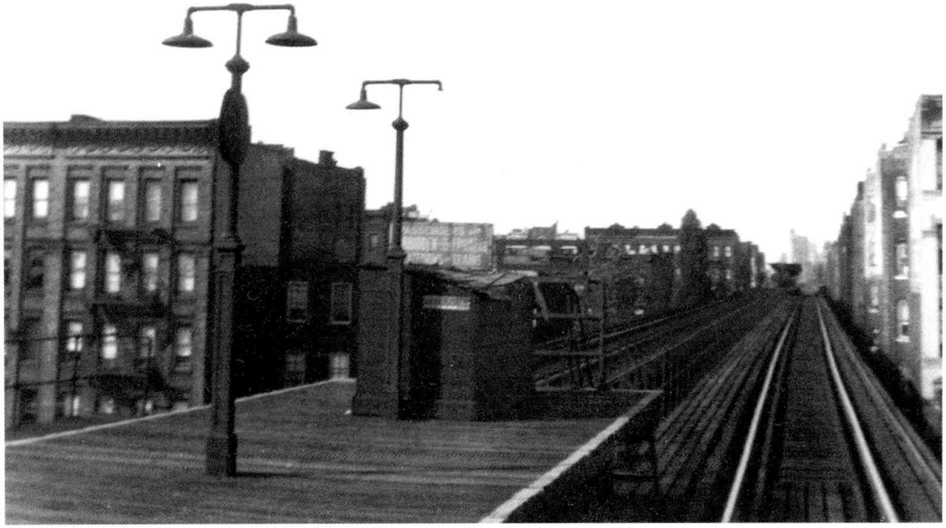

photograph the El, to remember what it would look like after it ceased to exist. He agreed to accompany me. On the very last day that the El was in service we embarked at Fordham Road and took the ride as far south as 125th Street. I photographed the 125th Street station with its Venetian gables from street level. We then returned to the uptown platform and boarded the train back to the Bronx, not knowing that at that moment it was the last official train in service, closing forever each station it stopped at and passed. As we made our way to the front cab window of the six-car train, we found the aisle crowded with passengers, but for some reason I found myself pressed to the door window next to the motorman's cab, which gave me the perfect vantage point for making my pictures. The train had already pulled out of the station when I realized I would not have much time to photograph all that I remembered from my previous commutes, nor would I be able to make a second trip; the line was officially closed up to the 149th Street station by the time the train pulled out of 125th Street. A group of newspaper photographers crowded and hovered over me taking pictures. They seemed sympathetic to my mission and made room for all

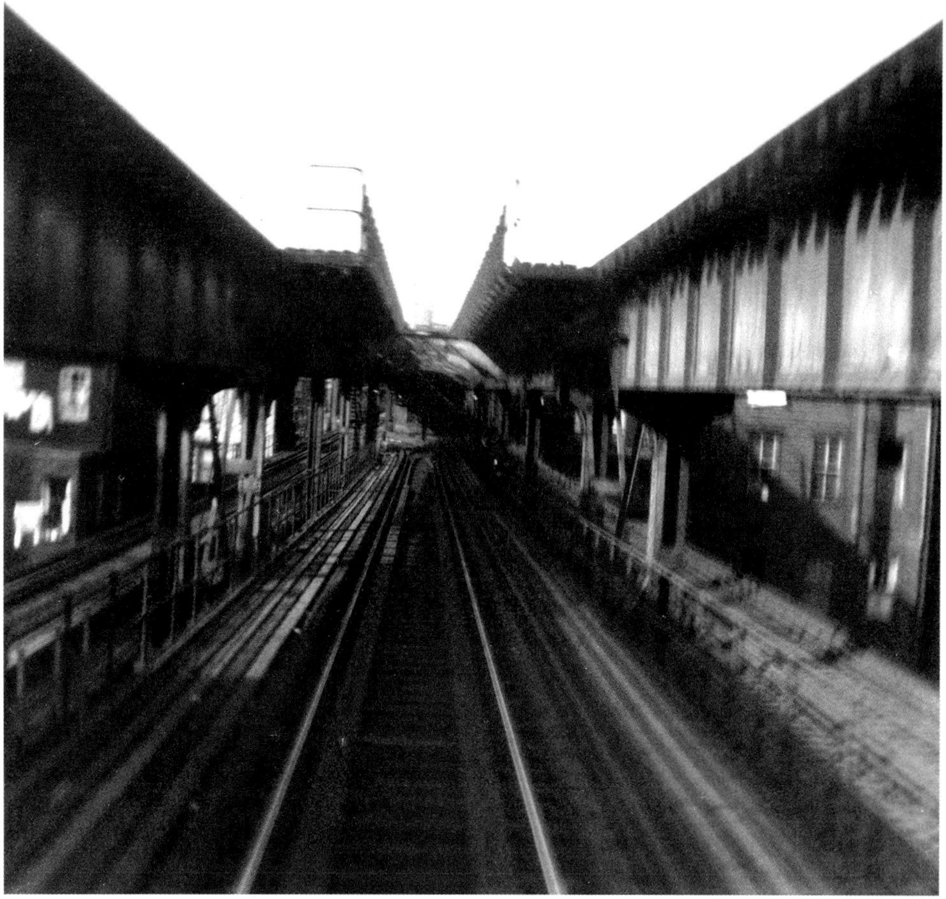

four feet, eight inches of me by the window. The first picture I snapped was of a southbound train – the last to make the downtown run. Our train wound its way north through the narrow corridor between apartment tenements in Mott Haven and I clicked off a twelve-frame black-and-white roll. The last two pictures depicted our approach into the 149th Street station.

Whereas Andy Warhol led a sheltered childhood in Pittsburgh, I grew up a street hood in the Bronx. Yet there are parallels here: both of us had traditional Catholic upbringings. We were first generation Americans and our parents were considerably older than the parents of our friends. We learned to draw at an early age. We were fascinated by the movies – not just movies but movie posters, movie stars, and movie studios. At one point I even took out a subscription to *Boxoffice*, a trade publication not found on any newsstand. Years later I would give all my back issues to Andy. The first book I remember reading on the movies was Bosley Crowther's *The Lion's Share*, a history of MGM studio.

Never had I considered that one didn't make one's living as a poet. I thought it was something that one just did. I continued my interest in poetry as a freshman at the University of Cincinnati, where I first met and studied with Richard Eberhart in the spring of 1961.

I dropped out at the end of my freshman year, unable to return as my father could no longer afford to pay for my schooling. I was eighteen at the time. Not knowing what I wanted to do with my life – except to write poetry – and not seeing much point participating in a structured system of any predictable kind, I occupied my time with just sort of thinking about things, reading anything I could get my hands on that dealt with poetry, exchanging ideas with other people, and sharing poems with friends and poets I came to know along the way. I was without means of support.

Willard Maas, a poet and professor of English at Wagner College in Staten Island, with his wife (filmmaker Marie Menken) – early admirers of my poetry – realizing my plight, were instrumental in securing a fellowship anonymously established to further my literary abilities and education. I was enrolled in Wagner College two weeks after classes began, in early October 1961.

What to give the poet who has everything? A pair of argyle socks, someone suggests. Argyle socks, it is. As my memory serves me right, the engraved card reads... *Chester Kallman requests the pleasure of your company at a 57th birthday gathering for Wystan Hugh Auden, February 21st, 8pm, at 77 St. Mark's Place*. The year is 1963.

Wystan could probably be considered one of the first modern poets

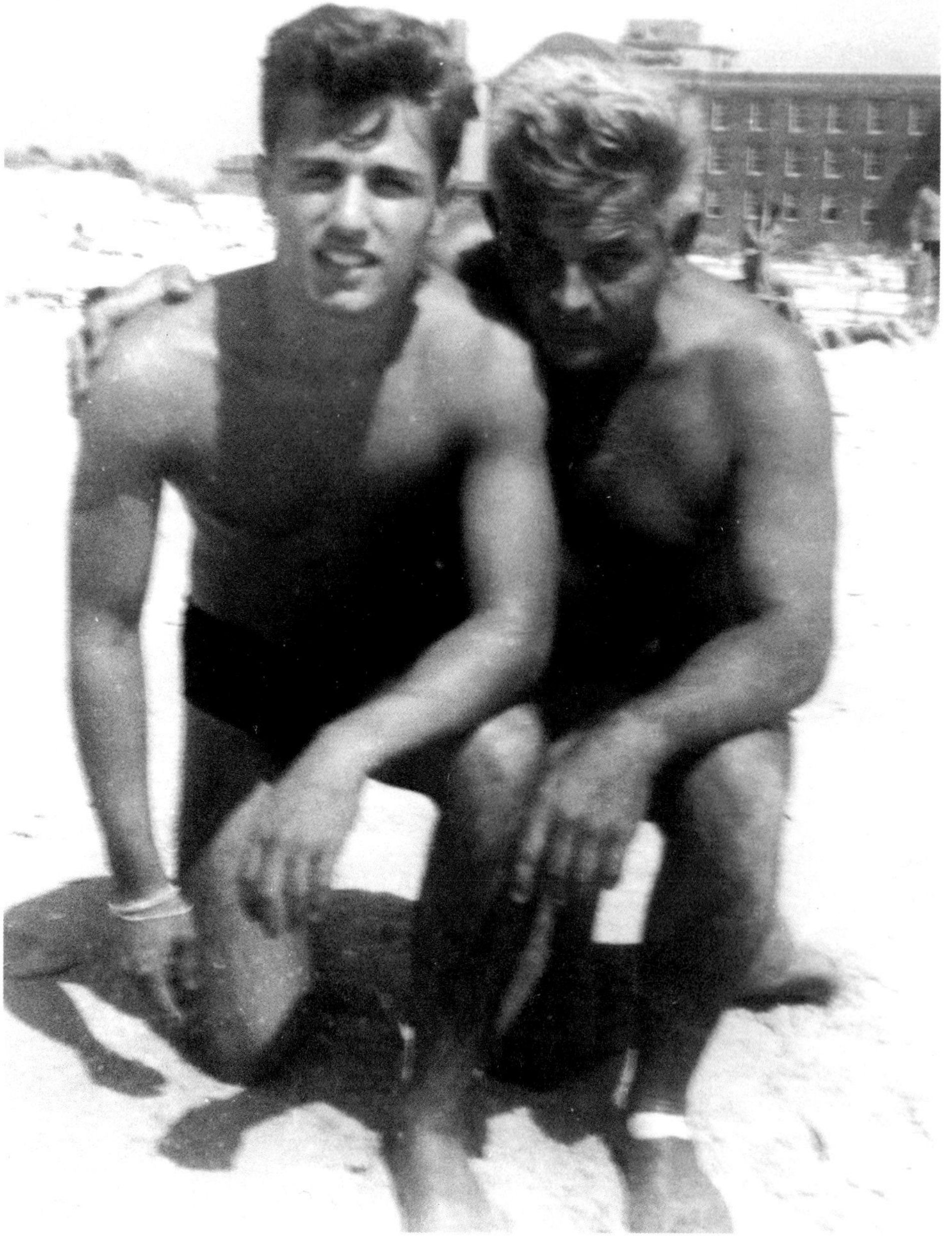

Gerard Malanga and Willard Maas, Summer 1960, Jacob Riis Park beach, Queens, NY.

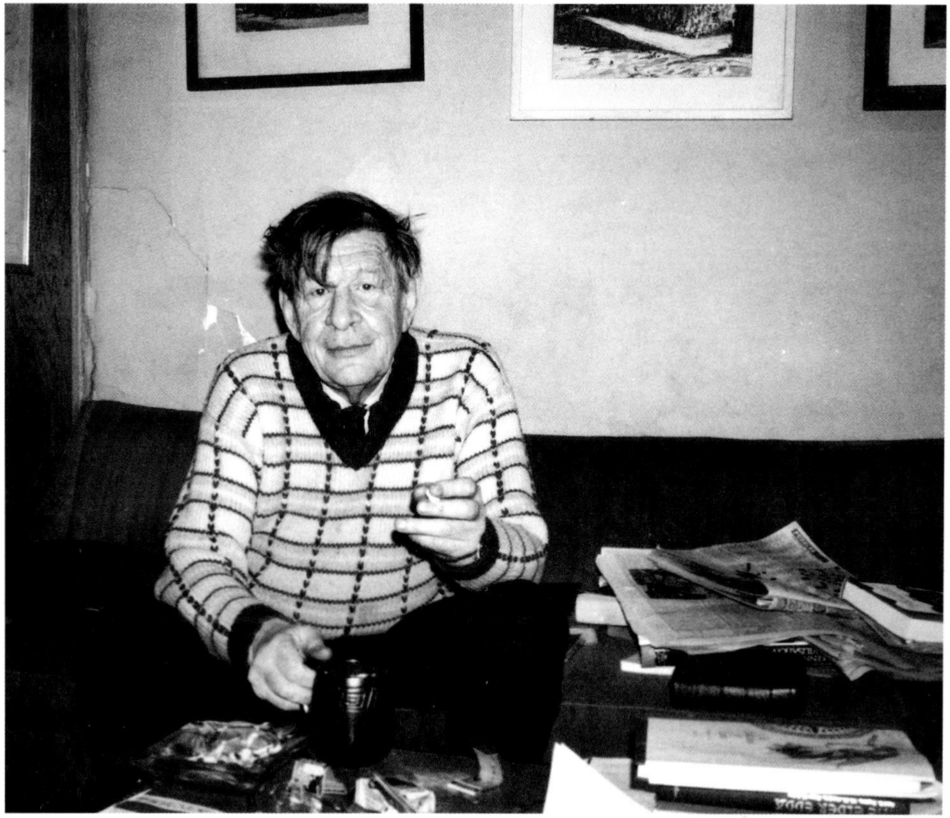

W.H. Auden.

to homestead the East Village in this regard. For a teenager (I would turn twenty a month later) there was nothing more glamorous to my mind than a party filled with poets. But this had to be the exception! You couldn't go much higher. I could only fantasize at who might be present. Charles Henri Ford was there, flitting from room to room, throwing a friendly glance in my direction, but I could not know at the time he would in a few months be the catalyst bringing Andy Warhol and me together.

The one person who did make a lasting impression was William Meredith. Who could not be impressed with "Love Letter From An Impossible Land".... opening:

Combed by the cold seas, Bering and Pacific,
These are the exile islands of the mind.
All the charts and history you can muster
Will not make them real as the fog is real
Or crystal as a certain hour is clear
If you can wait.
Write to me often, darling.

I first read this poem in *The War Poets*, so-called "An Anthology Of The War Poetry Of The Twentieth Century" by its editor, none other than Oscar Williams, anthologist *extraordinaire*. My copy had been given me by Willard Maas (my English professor at Wagner College), also included. Poems by Rukeyser, Jarrell, Spender and Eberhart, William Abrahams, Dylan Thomas, Ben Maddow, Weldon Kees, and F.T. Prince – favourites I would return to again and again.

The contributor's note listed Meredith, then Lieutenant, USNR, as having entered naval aviation, receiving Navy wings and commission in October 1942, and then serving as pilot in the Pacific area. He had already one book of poems to his credit, *Love Letter From An Impossible Land*. The photo of Meredith, most likely a public relations shot from when he was a non-commissioned officer attached to the Army Air Force public relations, was striking nonetheless. So, here I was sitting at the feet of William Meredith, "war poet" as I had remembered him, now forty-four.

A few weeks earlier I had submitted poems and been accepted to participate in an undergraduate poetry reading competition – the Irene Glascock Memorial Poetry Contest – held annually at Mount Holyoke College, South Hadley, Massachusetts. Judges for the contest were Meredith, then an associate professor at Connecticut College, John Sweeney of Harvard, and Andrews Wanning of Bard College. A press release stated that well-known poets who had read for the prize as undergraduates included Muriel Rukeyser and Robert Lowell. I felt honoured to be in such distinguished company. The first prize would be one hundred dollars. The date: 19th April. Meredith said he would be on the lookout for me. I felt reassured.

I'd never been to Mount Holyoke. Even reading a map I had no idea how to get there... didn't even have enough money for the bus. Two friends

– Mr. Clean (I never knew his real name), a wealthy Argentinean whose visa had apparently expired, and John MacDermott, both looking for adventure – offered to chauffeur me to South Hadley. We tuned up Mr. Clean's 1952 white Cadillac convertible and off we went. It would be my first time in the Commonwealth of Massachusetts – a kid from the Bronx. We had enough methamphetamine hydrocholoride to last us the weekend. I'd packed a three-piece tripler for the occasion, but together we looked anything but presentable. My hair had grown way past my ears. Mr. Clean wore a sweatshirt with the sleeves ripped out.

We got lost on the way – after taking a wrong turn – and, having arrived late for lunch, I missed out on the group photo opportunity arranged by the *Springfield Union-News*.

I was greeted by my official Mount Holyoke student chaperon, Martha George. Since the rooms for the other contestants had already been assigned, Martha arranged a room for me in one of the girl's dorms – Mandelles Hall, Room 103. The boys and I chuckled at this turn of events, for it was like putting the fox in the henhouse. We proceeded to unpack our bags and relax for a bit before the night's event. We immediately got into our stash, so relaxing was out of the question. We were wired and ready to go.

The contest was to be held at 8:00pm, Friday, in the Bookshop Inn, in South Hadley, near the campus. Martha came to escort us to the reading. We arrived at about fifteen minutes prior to the event. The audience consisted mostly of female students and a smattering of teachers. Meredith gave me the nod. As each contestant was allotted ten – maybe fifteen – minutes at most, I'd already timed myself to read only two poems.

Somehow I was last on the roster. The first poem I read, titled "Yellow", was, as I recall, unlike anything else read that night. The poem was an exercise suggested by Kenneth Koch, whose workshop I'd been attending at the New School on a fellowship. The assignment was to write a poem using a comparison in every line – "Yellow is like..." or "Yellow is when..." For the first time that night the audience applauded between poems. My second poem, much longer, "When Youth Shall This Generation Waste" was both inspired and influenced by the rapid-fire rhetoric I had assimilated from reading Auden's poetry, with a little bit of George Barker thrown in. The poem alluded to a relationship I'd fantasized between two lesbians. (Two years later this poem would appear in the fifth issue of *Art And Literature*, edited by John Ashbery). The audience response was the most effusive, exceeding any expectation I might have anticipated, clearly demonstrating I was the winner. It was in the bag, as they say.

Martha escorted me and my buddies to a party held in honour of the contestants at the home of an English professor. We made a beeline for the bathroom to give a boost to our nostrils. We were now in high gear. The party was festive enough. I'd spoken a bit with Meredith, reminiscing about Wystan's birthday soirée and getting into a rap with Martha. I noticed that while the students were being served apple juice, the adults were sneaking off into the kitchen and returning with alcoholic beverages. I gave a nod to the boys that we attack the source of supply. We raided the fridge and downed a few beers and stashed a reserve in our duffel bags for when it came time to split.

As the party was winding down, Martha led us back to the dorm. We agreed to meet up next morning for breakfast. Meredith was to give a reading, scheduled for precisely 11:10 and he would also announce the first prize.

We finished off the beers, took a few snorts, smoked some j, and decided to redecorate Room 103. We turned the furniture around, removed the pictures from the walls and threw the mattress on the floor, remembering how the Beats had done it from some photos I had seen published in *Life*. Actually, our real intent was to duplicate the surroundings of the Bond Street loft we'd been living at in the city. We were so much involved in our antics, we didn't take note of the ruckus we were causing. The dorm mother reported the disturbance and within minutes the campus police arrived to investigate – searchlights in hand – and I was told that the room was reserved for me only. They were to escort my friends to the power plant located way the other side of campus. Martha came by in the morning and when we all joined up I discovered John and Mr. Clean were given cots without blankets or pillows. I vowed we'd get even somehow.

After breakfast, Martha took us over to where Meredith would be reading on campus – the New York Room, as it was called. To my utter dismay I learned that I was not the winner of the prize. Bill had voted my work second place and while Andrews Wanning voted me third, Sweeney refused to rate me at all. I was not amused. I gather he wasn't either. Based on the audience's unanimous enthusiasm the night before I felt the prize was stolen out from under me, but I was helpless to turn it around. It made not the slightest difference whatsoever that Auden, months earlier, had remarked of my work: "These are the best poems I have ever read of anyone under twenty-five writing in America today." A lot of help that did. (Ironically, or perhaps not so ironically, not one of the contestants was ever heard from again, in terms of poetry.)

Nearly 1:00 now. A bright, spring breezy day. Martha and I exchanged phone numbers. We would see each other a year or two later in New York when she'd come visit at the Warhol Factory. The boys and I headed for the grassy knoll adjacent to the scene of our ruckus the night before. We took off our shirts and stretched out on the sloping lap. A number of students were spread out on blankets and sheets, with books and clipboards, T-shirts modestly riding up, oblivious to our presence – that is, until I stripped down to my Rudi Gernrich bikini and suddenly, looking around, all heads turn. The prize was lost but the day was mine. A copy of the *Springfield Union-News* Martha had given me lay by my side – its banner read "Young Poets Compete Friday In Mount Holyoke Poetry Contest." In a day – in a matter of a few hours – the event had become old news, but it would be the first of many, many disappointments I'd experience in the course of my one true vocation at the hands of the poetry elite.

After about an hour of hanging out talking non-stop in what us A-heads called "amphetamine rapture", the speed was beginning to wear off. We decided to chuck it and Mount Holyoke, too, and head back to New York. Along the way, as the sun silhouetted the overall landscape, Auden's adage stuck in my head, "The poem is not completed. It is abandoned".

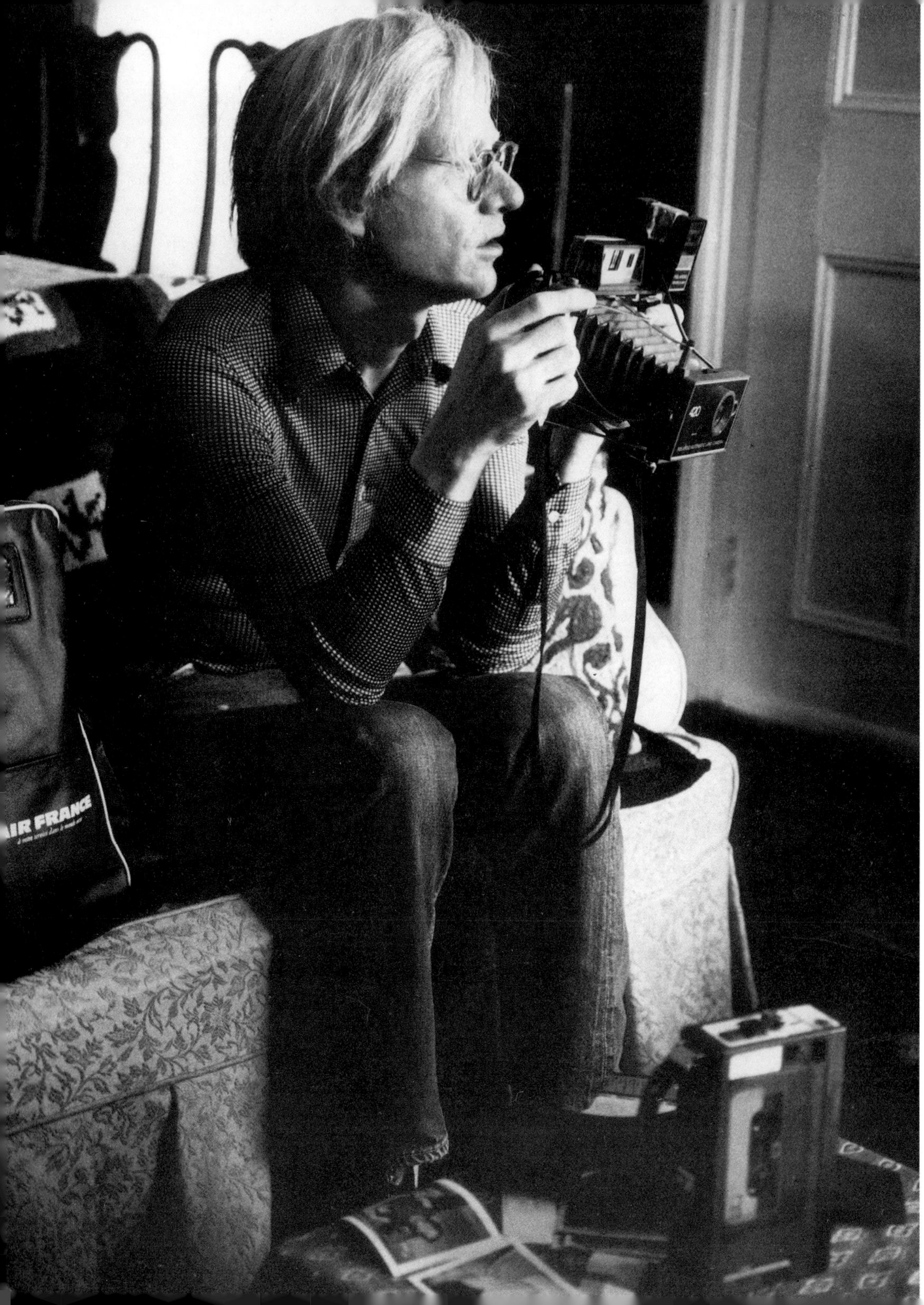

Andy Warhol with
Polaroid camera, 1971.

The Assistant: Working With Warhol

Established as a poet with a string of publications (*Paris Review, Partisan Review, Poetry, The New Yorker,* etc), I was one year short of graduating when I met Andy Warhol, an encounter that was to have a major impact on the direction my life and work would take for the next several years, during which time I collaborated on all major artworks Warhol would produce.

Early on I was busy with the "translation of pictures" in the Warhol Factory, as well as the researching of all photo concepts and the application of the silk-screen process, onto canvas or paper – images for the most part originating from newspapers and magazines.

After working with Andy for nearly a year, I decided not to go back to school for my last year. There was just too much excitement happening for me to suddenly give it up and return to the classroom. Seduced by Andy's access to a world of experience for which no formal education could ever prepare me, I dropped out of school again, to the chagrin of Professor Maas. Ezra Pound has commented about people who make such decisions as "strugglers in the desert" – artists willing to risk everything for what they believe as true to their vision. I agreed with Pound: being thirsty is better than being bored.

I worked with Andy during arguably his most important period. The very first painting I screened was a 40 x 40 inch silver Elizabeth Taylor portrait at a shutdown firehouse that Andy rented from the city for one hundred dollars a year. In making the Elizabeth Taylor painting, masking tape was shaped to the contours of the face directly on the canvas to create a stencil that followed the lines of a transfer-rubbing originating from the acetate-positive. Then we would fill in the flesh tones, eyebrows, and lips by hand with Liquitex paint, and when it was dry, the masking tape was peeled off, resulting in shaped colours. Andy remarked to me once that his paintings looked more like Alex Katz paintings before the silk screen was applied. The last step in the process was to screen in the black paint. The paintings were a step-by-step transformation of photography into painting.

Andy loved all sorts of machines and gadgets, embracing new techniques and technologies, working with tape recorders, cassettes, Polaroid, Thermofax, but the heart of all this experimentation had as its central focus photography and the silkscreen for making a painting; this was by extension his love for the machine because the screen process was very machine-like. Andy's reasoning was that the silkscreen would make it as easy as possible to create a painting. Ironically, the process relied directly on manual application.

When the screens were very large, we worked together; otherwise, I was pretty much left to my own inventiveness. I had a first-hand knowledge of silkscreen technique, having worked for a summer as intern to a textile chemist in the manufacture of men's neckwear, so I knew what I was doing from the start.

Andy and I would lay the screen down on the canvas, trying to line up the registration with the marks we made where the screen would go. Then oil-base paint was poured into a corner of the frame of the screen, and I would push the paint with a squeegee across the mesh surface. Andy would grab the squeegee still in motion and continue the process of putting pressure on pushing the paint through the screen from his end. We'd lift the screen, and I would swing it away from the painting and start cleaning it with paper towels soaked in a substance called Varnolene. If not done immediately, the remaining paint would dry and clog the pores.

After work was completed, we would go over to Andy's house. The firehouse was three blocks from where Andy lived with Julia, his mother, a seemingly frail but hearty woman who was then in her seventies. She would make lunch for us, which usually consisted of a Czechoslovak-style hamburger stuffed with diced onions, sprinkled with parsley, and always on white bread, and with a 7-Up on ice.

Sometimes, he would have people over to view the work. The paintings were for the most part rolled up in the corner of a very cluttered living room. He couldn't store the art at the firehouse because there was no electricity or running water – no conveniences of any kind. The firehouse was basically a shell of a space. There was an opening in the floor where the slide-pole used to be. However, all this would shortly change.

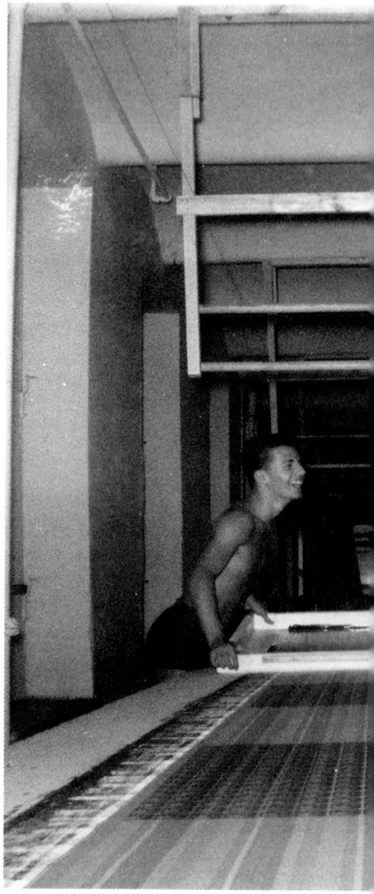

Gerard Malanga apprenticed as a silkscreen technician to Charles Singer, textile chemist, NYC – Summer 1960.

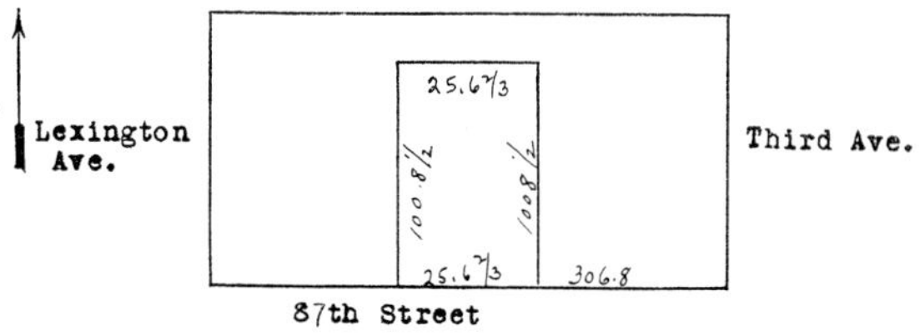

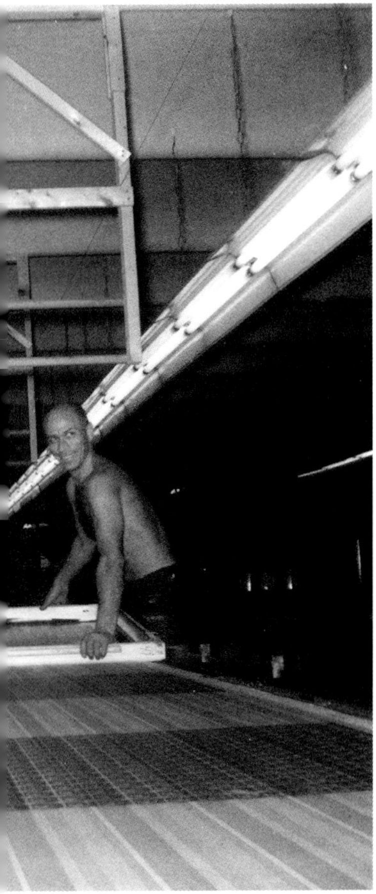

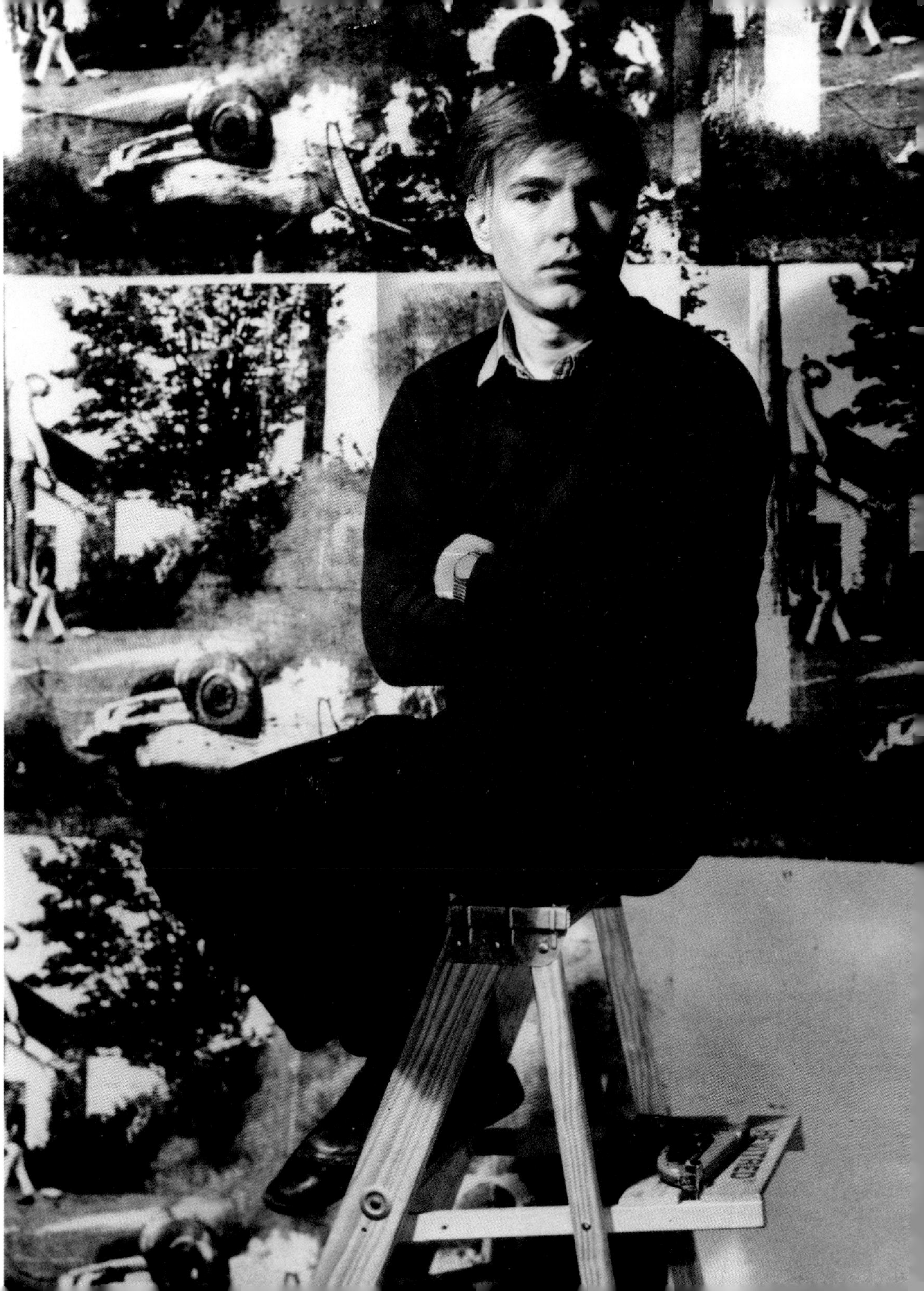

Andy Warhol, posing in front of one of his paintings from the *Death & Disasters* series, in the living room of his townhouse at 1342 Lexington Avenue, NYC – 1963.

In September of '63, he was notified that the building would be put on the auction block. We went hunting for a space. We spent two months looking for a space throughout the city. We covered Hell's Kitchen and Little Italy. The move forced Andy to get a better working space. Upon moving into the new studio, which had previously been a hat factory, all socializing at Andy's home pretty much ceased. When this happened, his work schedule changed because once he'd leave the house for the day he was out for good. There was no returning home for lunch or anything. We were now in midtown on the East Side. Andy would arrive at the Factory, as it was now called, noon or thereabouts. We would work on and off until 5:00 or 6:00 pm and then go out to party.

The first works created at the Factory were a series of food boxes. Andy was fascinated by the shelves of foodstuffs in supermarkets and the repetitive, machine-like effect they created. Andy wanted to become totally mechanical in his work the way a packaging factory would normally silkscreen information onto cardboard boxes. He wanted to duplicate the effect but soon discovered that the cardboard surface was not feasible. I located a carpenter in the East Sixties, and Andy hired him out to build plywood boxes that we would then paint and screen, to create the illusion of the real thing.

The brand names chosen consisted of two versions of Brillo, Heinz Tomato Ketchup, Kellogg's Corn Flakes, and Mott's Apple Sauce. We obtained cardboard-box samples of each of these products either from a grocery store or, in the case of the Brillo box, directly from the manufacturer. I'd deliver the cardboard box, at this point flattened out, to the silkscreen manufacturer Harry Golden, who made all of Andy's screens. Specifications were drawn up according to size and density of the screen. In this case, we went for the total black-and-white contrast to complement the original we were working from.

We were able to get at least two sides done in a day. A hundred or more were produced in a period of a month. They were literally three-dimensional photographs of the actual products.

The ambience was one where we talked about registration marks. In making a painting, the conversation would go something like, "Let's move it over this way." When we were working on the Elvis Presley series, I remember suggesting the superimpositions that we tried and successfully

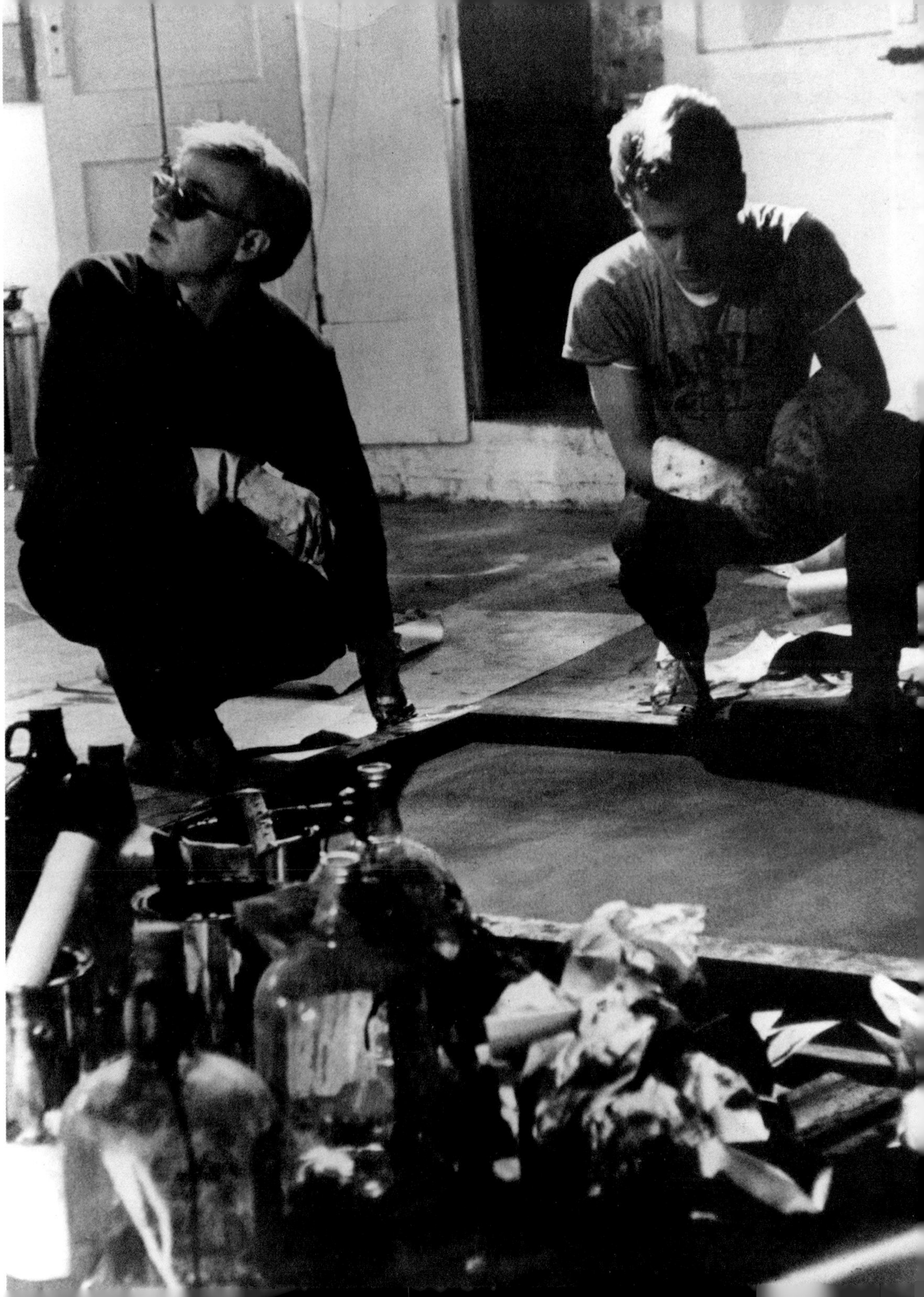

Andy Warhol and Gerard Malanga silkscreening a painting at the Factory, 1964.

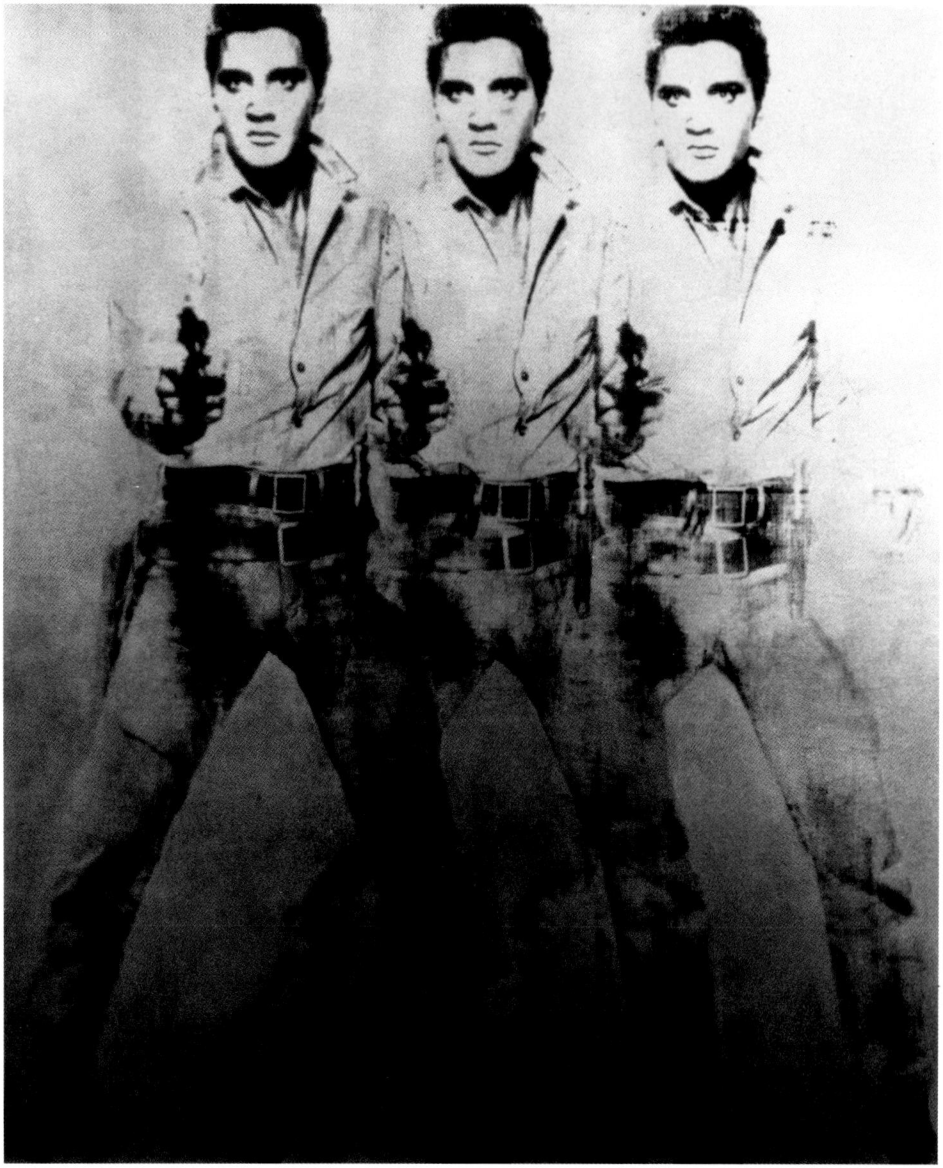

Large Triple Elvis (1963). Synthetic polymer paint and silkscreen ink on canvas, 82" X 82".

realized, and that's why these paintings exist the way they do. It was a very creative period for both of us.

Sometimes, we'd go off-register when making a painting, and there'd be a flaw. Andy accepted all that. I think it can be boiled down to one statement, "Embracing the mistakes" – accepting that which occurs spontaneously.

Andy embraced his mistakes. We never rejected anything. In other words, if we were in the process of making a series of paintings and all of a sudden one painting went off a bit, or the image inadvertently overlapped the previous image, we kept right on moving along. We'd keep it, or, as Andy would say, "It's part of the art". The flaws were part of the art. It was as if he possessed an almost Zen-like sensibility.

Warhol was really one of the first since Duchamp and the dadaists to embrace this seemingly casual attitude towards art. Rather than create art by hand, he made art by the decision of accepting and discarding. Appropriative selection, as it were. Andy would make decisions about how a certain thing would go in the screen. We would discuss the possibilities and what they would propose. He would turn the acetate one way, then another. A decision would be reached to go with a halftone or stick with the contrast. We would agree, "Yeah, that's great". The screen would be ordered.

The early paintings from 1961–62 were made from screens absent of any halftone layering. He would draw from actual photos, and the drawing would be converted into a screen that was photographic by nature to recreate the drawing as a photographic image in silkscreen application. But a year or so later, he eliminated the drawing altogether and appropriated the photo head-on and turned it into a screen. I was sometimes Andy's photo researcher. We would discover images in newspapers and magazines, and I would search out photos in out-of-the-way, second-hand bookshops or bring something in from home.

He was still making art during the period when he started making films. In July 1963, poet-artist Charles Henri Ford and I took Andy shopping at Peerless Camera and helped him select his first movie camera, a 16-mm Bolex with thru-the-lens focusing complete with motordrive that allowed for a one-shot three-minute take.

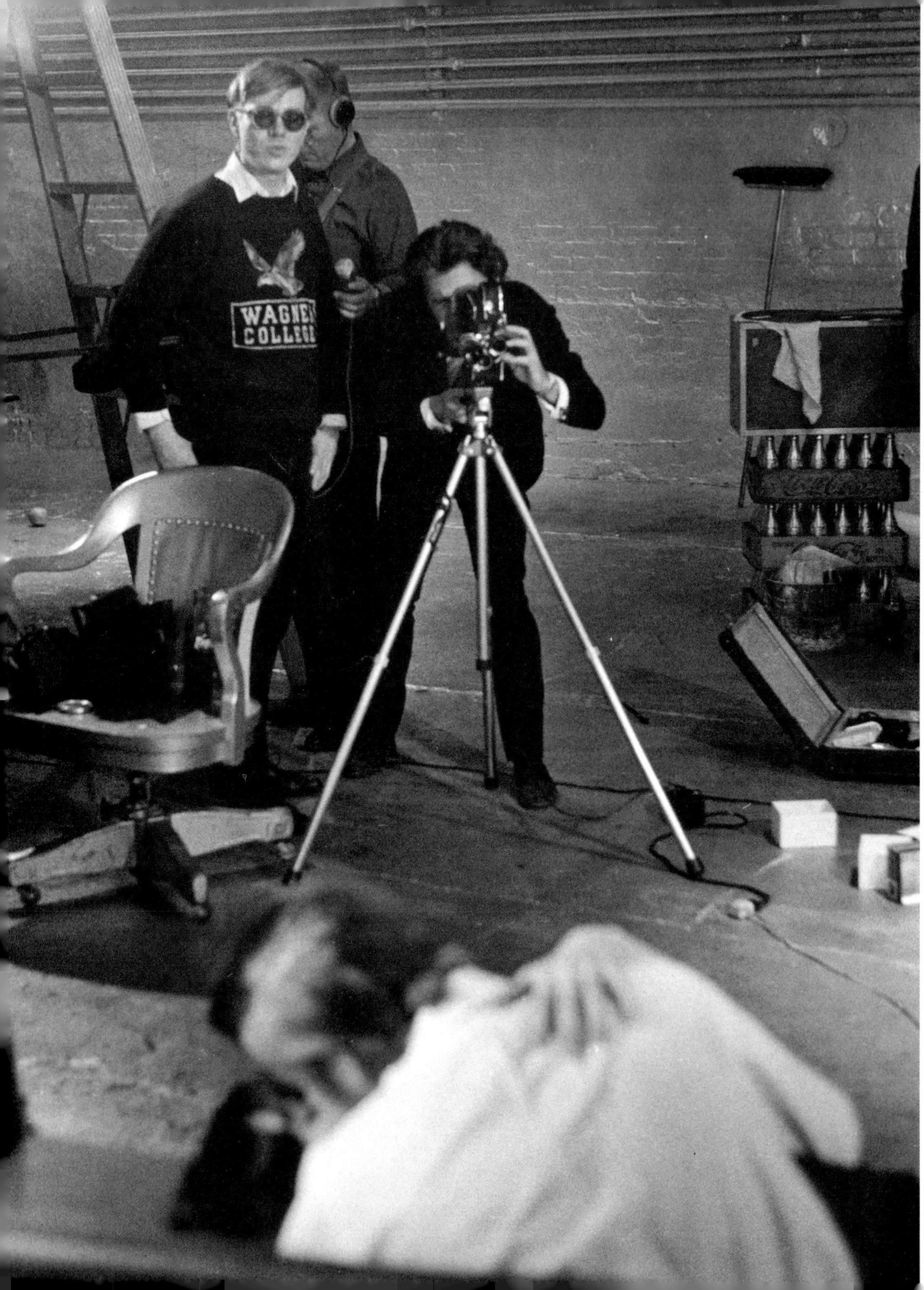

Gerard Malanga shooting a sequence for Warhol's film *Couch* as Andy looks on – 1964.

Sleep was Andy's first and indisputably his most famous film. Perhaps it was famous, too, as a film that few if any ever sat through. Andy conveyed this idea to me – and this was before he actually owned a movie camera – of wanting to make a film of Brigitte Bardot sleeping for eight hours. He said something to the effect that you could get to know everything there is about a person by watching him sleep. He wanted to know what it would be like to watch a movie star sleeping. Obviously the concept was more essential to the realization than was the identity of the protagonist, and knowing Bardot was simply out of his league, he settled for a friend, John Giorno, who was a natural for not waking up.

John gave Andy a key to the flat, and Andy would let himself in. The Bolex was already set up with the lights in place. Andy would turn on the lights and camera, and this activity was repeated for about two weeks.

Sleep runs approximately six-and-a-half hours of equivalent shooting time. Andy duplicated an additional ninety minutes from an equal ninety-minute section of the film to stretch it out to eight hours to approximate the scientifically accepted length of time for normal sleep.

The film *Empire* was also shot mostly at night, in summer 1964. We started shooting around 6:00pm – it was still daylight – and completed around 1:00am. The first two reels are over-exposed because Andy was metering for night light, but it was all guess work. What happens in the course of the first two reels, and partway through the third, is that the building slowly emerges from a twilight haze, balancing out the exposure from the darkness that slowly blankets the sky. The Empire State Building was already a star or sorts when it was featured in *King Kong*, but Andy wanted to make the building an even bigger star!

The films are very similar in style in that they treat time in a one-to-one ratio. Both *Sleep* and *Empire* are in black-and-white, no sound, shot at night, and the camera never moves. The only major difference between the two films is that *Sleep* was shot with the Bolex using 100-foot/three-minute film rolls, and *Empire* was shot with a rented Auricon equipped to shoot 1,200 feet of film for thirty-five minutes non-stop. Andy would have probably filmed *Sleep* with the Auricon had he known of the camera's existence. He was learning as he went along, mimicking the progress of Hollywood without knowing it.

It was John Palmer who came up with the idea for *Empire*. Andy had the resources to get the concept realized finally, so essentially Andy was producer, but he got the billing – Andy Warhol's *Empire*. Andy barely touched the camera during the entire time the movie was being shot. John, Jonas Mekas, and I changed the reels for him. The machine would do all the work, Andy thought. So there's a direct connection between the silkscreen, which is a photographic and mechanical process, and the movie camera, which also creates a photographic-type image.

Photography has always been the underlying theme consistent to Andy's work. If you were to take a strip of 16-mm footage of *Sleep* and examine the frames horizontally, there appears a sameness of repetition that also occurs in his headshot paintings of Marilyn Monroe and Elvis Presley.

I remember once – this happened so many different times and in varied contexts – we were attending the premiere screening of *Empire* at the Bridge Cinema in lower Manhatten near a street that leads onto the Brooklyn Bridge. We were standing in the rear of the auditorium. Andy was observing the audience rather than the film, and people were walking out or booing or throwing paper cups at the screen. Andy turned to me, and in his boyish voice said, "Gee, you think they hate it... you think they don't like it?" *Empire* was a seven-hour movie where nothing happened except how the audience reacted.

Andy was not overly conscious of how an audience might respond to one of his films. In his mind, he was realizing a concept that was perhaps less original than the decision ultimately to put that concept in motion. He extended an already minimal and appropriative vocabulary to include the kind of decision-making he applied to his painting. The only way his films would be accepted or criticized was through their reliance on an audience to see them; otherwise, they would remain concepts in a can.

Andy is often commented about as being a voyeur. He's generally characterized as someone who liked to watch. Watching takes time. You just don't look and turn away. It's a matter of optic absorption. One of the ways Andy expressed obsessive looking was through the movie camera. His silent films were mostly about approximating the same amount of time it would take to make the film as to watch it. A voyeur needs a window frame, or a blind, as a frame of reference to inhabit a situation in a secretive way, which amounted to Andy's fascination with someone having to sit through

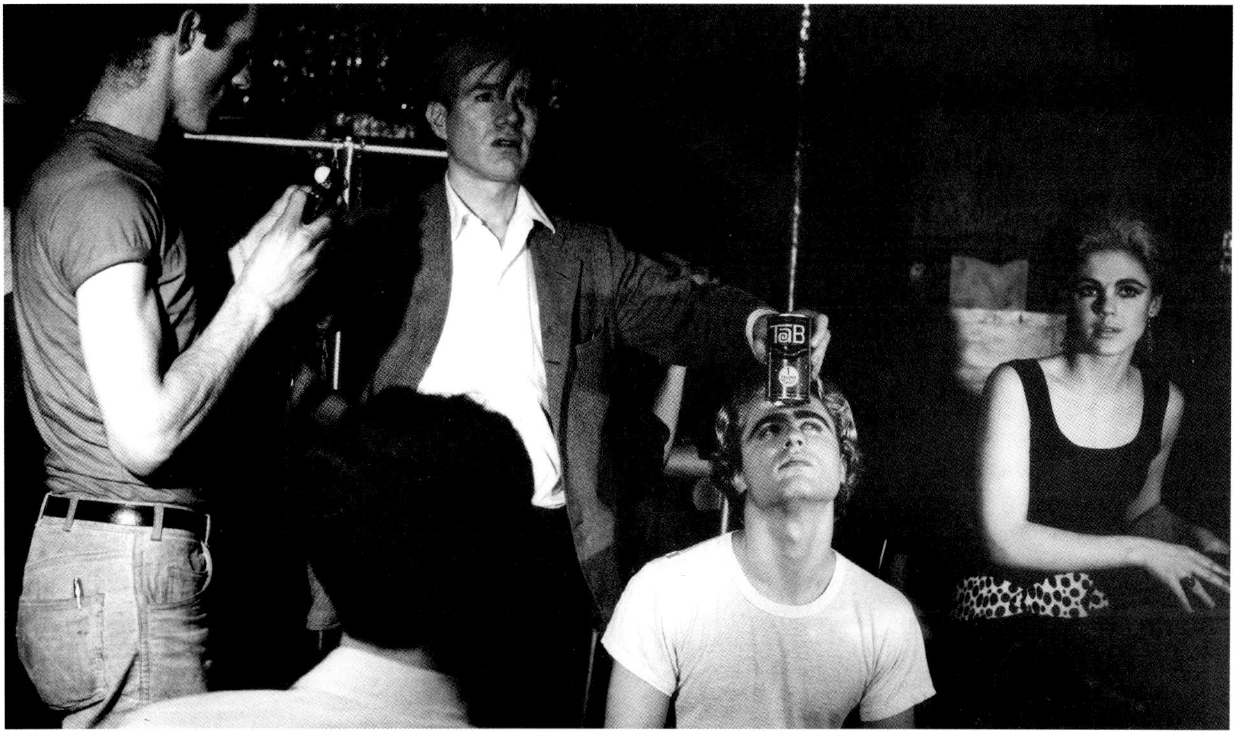

Edie Sedgwick's first appearance in a Warhol movie – *Vinyl* (1965).

it all in the dark. It implies power over a person who is unaware of being watched, like someone sleeping, for instance. Andy's desire for power was initially realized through the voyeuristic tendency of distancing himself from what he was watching with the use of a movie camera.

His desire to make films evolved because he loved Hollywood, and this was his way of getting as close as possible to the allure, magic, and mystery he felt as an adolescent. He wrote to film companies for photos of his favourite stars, which he drew from for hours on end while withdrawing deeper into his fantasies of the rich and famous. So twenty years later in 1965 when Andy met Edie Sedgwick for the first time, it was the closest he'd ever come to someone who possessed the aura of a Hollywood starlet in the flesh.

Edie was not career-orientated at the time she met Andy. Edie was a blue blood. She had no active goals other than to enjoy herself to the

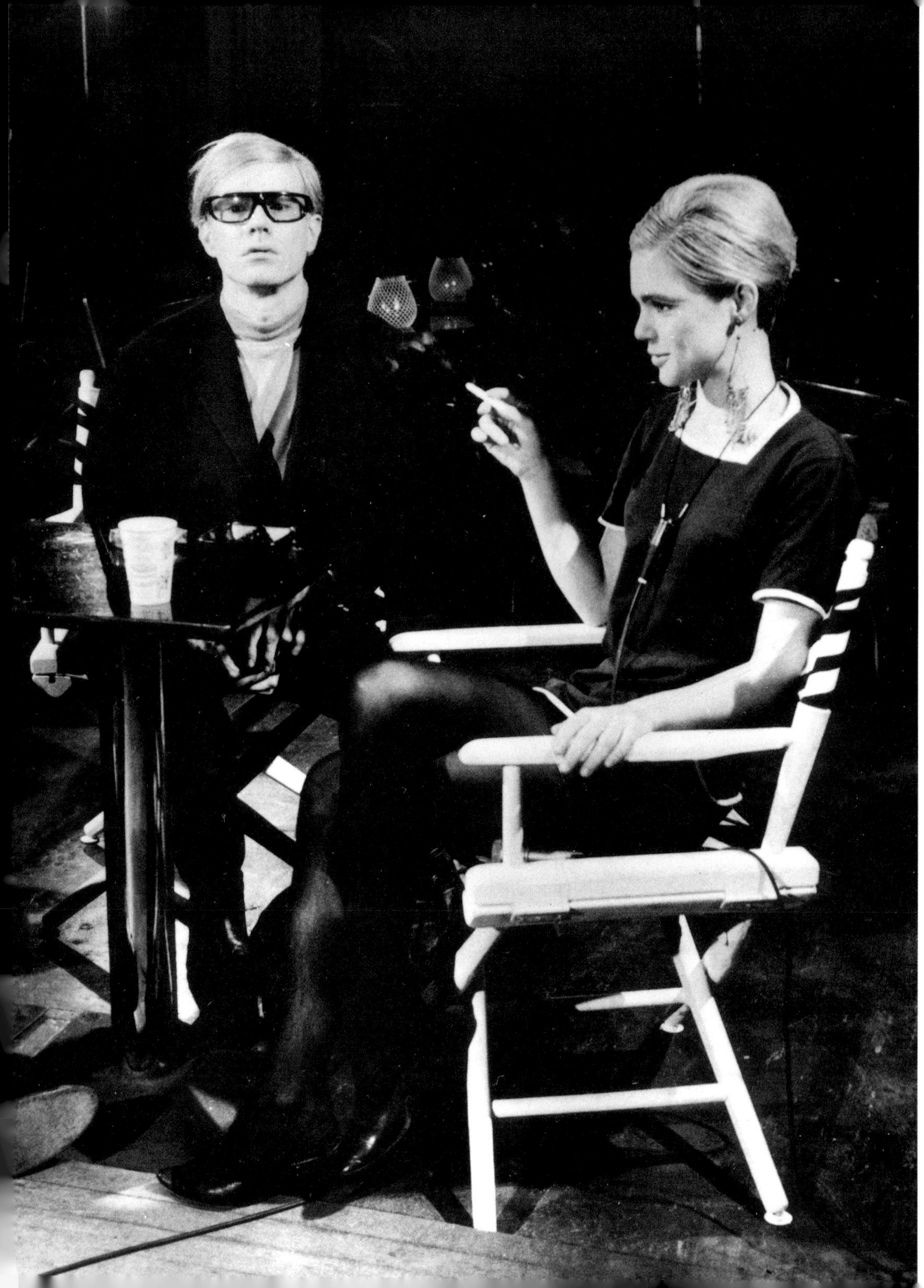

Andy Warhol and Edie
Sedgwick at The Scene,
NYC – 1965.

fullest. Her life imitated art to the extent that it was colourful and ephemeral. She could be very easily moulded. She had the one ingredient essential to being a star – glamour. When you characterize someone as glamorous, you're saying that the person is beautiful. Glamour is not beauty, but it can become that. Glamour is aura. The person who already possesses aura becomes beautiful. Andy was deeply fascinated with glamour on this level. He had an eye for it.

Edie's first starring role in which she talked in a Warhol film was *Poor Little Rich Girl*, shot in her one-room studio. Her close friend Chuck Wein fabricated some notes and coached Edie. The concept of "embracing the mistakes" played an integral part of how the film came to exist in its present form. We shot two reels. When they came back from the lab, we previewed them and, to our horror, found them to be extremely out of focus – not even close to salvageable. After replacing the lens, we re-shot the two long takes a week later, and got it right. We took the first reel, from the first version, and sequenced it with the second reel, from the second version, so the film opens with an out-of-focus thirty-five-minute take. That takes a lot of guts.

As the months progressed, Edie appeared in a number of films, some especially scripted for her, the first of these being *Kitchen*. The films would have an instant audience; reviews would appear in the press; and Edie's career was launched, so to speak, but she wasn't getting paid. She thought Andy was making money with the films, because of all the hoopla, but he wasn't. The sales from his paintings were supporting a highly speculative venture into filmmaking. If anything, the films were a drain on him financially. Nevertheless, Edie wanted to get paid, but Andy never indicated that any payment, however small, would be forthcoming, except to say to her every so often, "Be patient." But Edie's patience had run its course.

Andy assumed, wrongly perhaps, that if he started paying everyone for whatever the work involved, the end result would be of a lesser quality. He was convinced of this. This attitude, ironically, turned on him with the portrait commissions he executed during the '70s.

At around the time Edie was contemplating leaving Andy, an opportunity presented itself. Bob Dylan's *confidant* and roadie, Bobby Neuwirth, acted as liaison in getting Edie to come over to the Dylan camp.

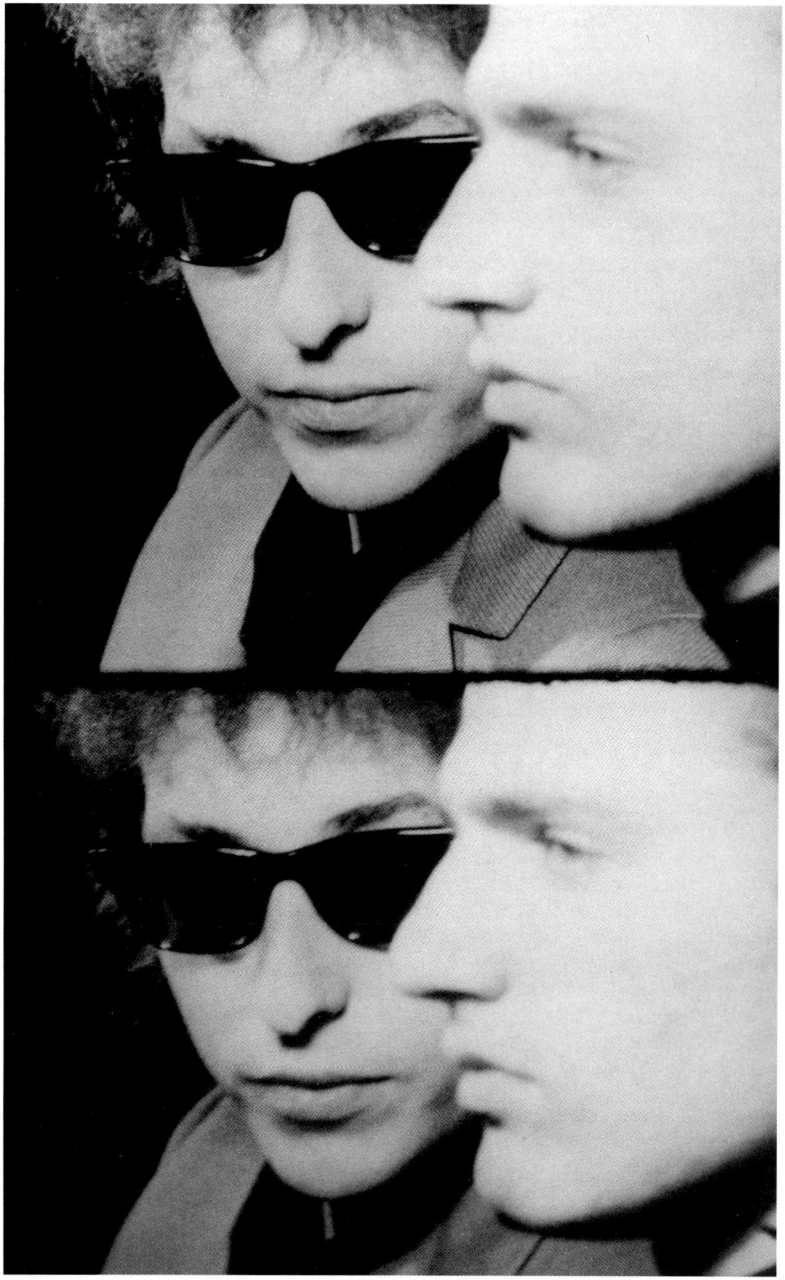

Bob Dylan and Gerard Malanga in a shot from Gerard's *Film Notebooks* (1965).

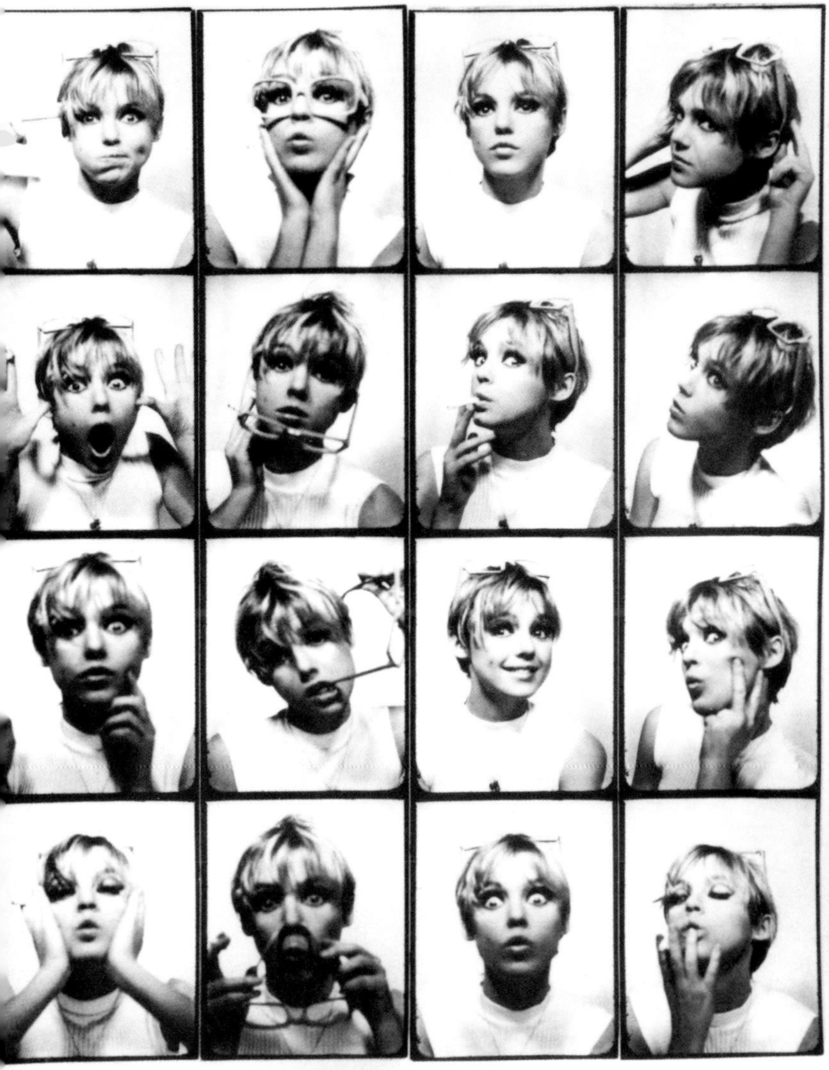

Edie Sedgwick photomaton assemblage by Gerard Malanga, 1966.

The people advising Dylan had this illusion that they could develop Edie into a singer and in turn capitalize on her already-established reputation in the media. So it was easy for Edie to finally leave Andy. By switching allegiance she became part of a heterosexual milieu. Andy represented every bit a homosexual sensibility and the Dylan group was staunchly hetero. Edie had assumed that being promoted as a singer was promised her, but her situation never developed in any viable way because her talent was totally under-developed. She thought she could further her career by being associated with Dylan, but this was merely an optimism based on hope and dreams. She soon learned that he had been secretly married during this time.

There are many different points of view about Andy. Edie somehow came to be a damaging one. A good deal of myth-making was perpetrated about Andy's association with Edie, as chronicled in the Jean Stein/ George Plimpton biography, *Edie*. It was hyped to a certain extent. Andy did not turn Edie on to drugs. She got caught up in the drug scene shortly after leaving Andy. The closest Andy ever came to taking drugs was a prescription for the diet pill Obitrol. At the time, Edie was taking Obitrols to get through the day. Andy was taking them to lose weight. It had much to do with vanity.

What made Andy glamorous was his unique appearance with his silver wig and lack of pigmentation, thus he was instant material for the media. By this, Andy recognized his oddness early on and saw the advantage of using it to gain attention for himself as a public relations ploy. He became his own instant star.

Andy was very simplistic. If he said to me, "Oh, that poem was fabulous, wow!" that was the end of the topic. He didn't get into any in-depth talk about the nuance and function of metaphor. But Andy was more real than his hype because he really was intelligent. He was not an impostor. Reality did cut through on lots of occasions. It wasn't like we got on a bus and took a trip to Des Moines, Iowa, rented a motel room, and conveniently Truman Capote would be there to record all the great remarks. On trips, many a time, we would share the motel room. So that says something about the relationship I had with him. Maybe it wasn't all that verbal, but a sense of trust existed between us in a genuine way. And he was frightfully modest. Not once did I ever see him undressed. Wherever we travelled he always kept a small satchel. Once I took a sneak peek and discovered a roll of Johnson & Johnson adhesive tape, scissors and hair spray – the apparatus for maintaining his silver bonnet. His trust in me was simply that Andy probably never wanted to be alone. He lived with his mother for the greater part of his adult life, up to the time she died in the late '70s.

This fear of being alone was very much a part of his being an extremely shy and private person. I don't think Andy was consciously trying to hide something about himself as much as attempting to maintaining a mystique, as a cover for his own inadequacies. His shyness allowed him to be private. He felt that his sexual preferences were really no-one's business, and therefore he didn't go out of his way to make pronouncements like "Here's my new boyfriend".

Many people seem to agree that the '70s were bad years for Andy, but in the '80s he seemed to have made an extraordinary comeback. The '70s were a less urgent period than the '60s. I call the '70s the "Age of Hibernation", and Andy was simply out of touch with those from whom he truly could have benefited creatively, had it not been for his fascination with the so-called rich and famous. Those people never really had anything to contribute to his art except by way of their vanity. They paid dearly for a forty-inch square canvas of themselves – that speaks of the vacuity of their intellect. The vitality of Andy's creativity diminished to the point where all he was making were these ooh-and-ah celebrity portraits, receiving incredible sums of money for them. Who would want those works today? I don't believe for a second that he had any genuine interest in the people whose portraits he made. Friendships like these are created between agents. But the very thing that Andy had identified in his artwork in the '60s became identifiable icons for the '80s. This complete circle of events gave Andy a new surge of optimism and self-confidence... and then he died.

Andy could have survived 1987. He should not have died when he did. Unfortunately, much deceit and confusion exist now in his wake. Attributions to several artworks are misleading, improvised. And since estate certification is a way to manipulate Andy's auction and resale value, toes inevitably get stepped on.

Andy's fate is sealed. There's no denying that he is part of the history of art in the modern world. But which amplifies what? Andy Warhol the social phenomenon boosting up Andy Warhol the artist, or the other way around? Some people would say that his greatest achievement was the adage, "In the future everyone will be famous for fifteen minutes". That in itself is a frightening thought because the culture seems to be developing in ways that would allow one to be famous merely on charm.

If you were to meet him for the first time, and Andy liked you, he became your instant fan, and this, in turn, would create in you a feeling of self-esteem. It's as if he were collecting people. He had a hypnotic power to create a personality for someone. This is perhaps connected to Andy's adulation of Hollywood movie stars when, as an adolescent, he would draw from the 8 x 10 inch glossies for hours on end. He would be recreating his daydreams on paper. The secret to Andy's success was his own self-effacement.

Gerard, this is Benedetta. Benedetta... Gerard." Leo Castelli completed the triangle and looked at each of us, with generous, fraternal touch of arms outstretched, as if he were bringing us closer together. All else – the swirl of activity at Rauschenberg's loft the night of Saturday, February 6, 1966 –

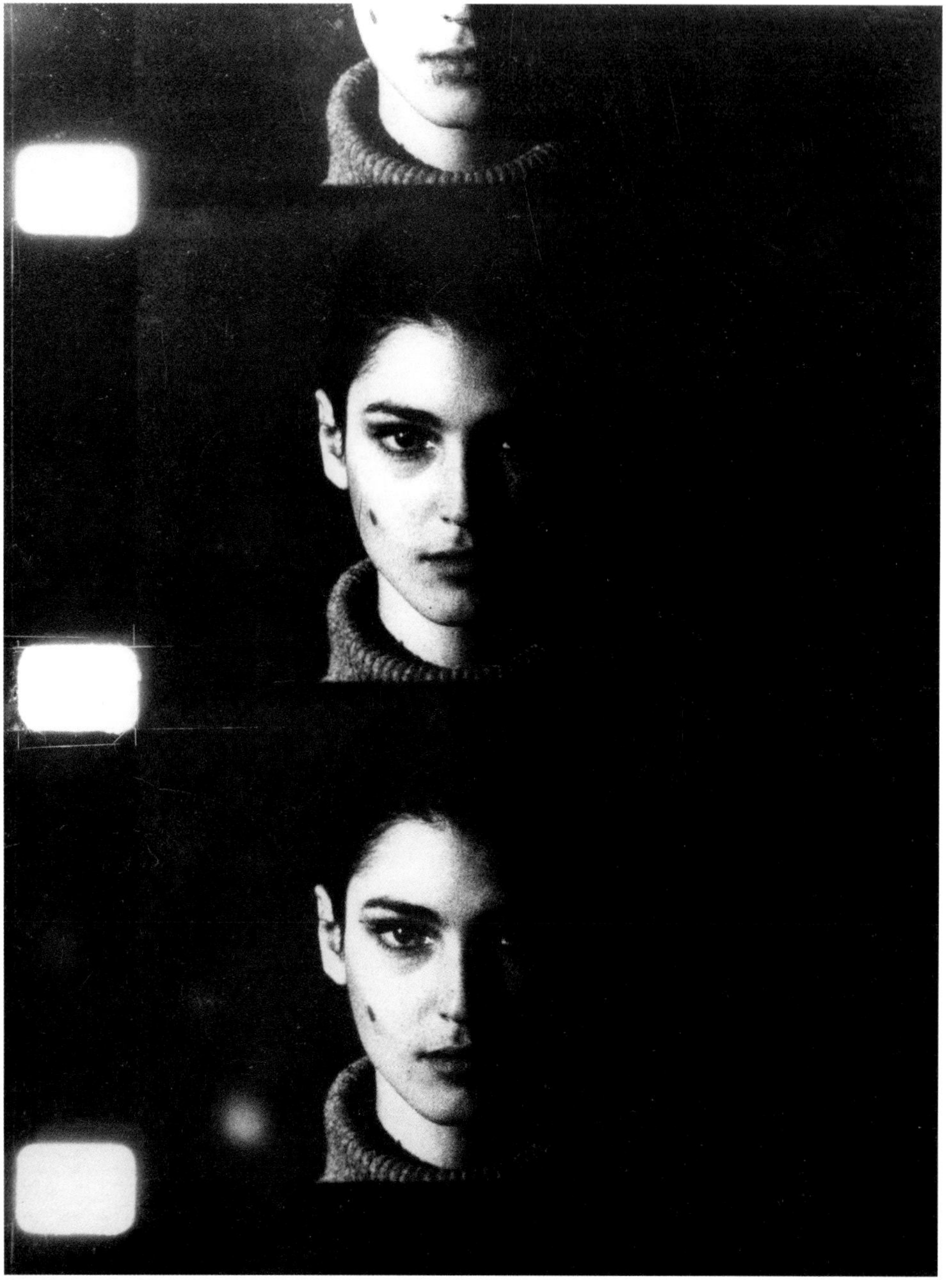

Benedetta Barzini Screen Test, 1966.

seemed to fade in the background.

Of course I'd seen Benedetta before! The beauty mark on her right cheek was her trademark. She was fast becoming one of the most recognizable faces in *Vogue* and *Bazaar*, but here in the flesh she transcended all expectation of being perceived otherwise.

Benedetta was wearing a velvet dress – burgundy hue – embroidered trim. She had an inch over me, standing about five feet, seven-and-a-half inches tall. Her black hair, pulled tight in a bun, accentuated her chiseled features and a delicate, aquiline nose. Her complexion, the colour of pearl – warm, translucent. But it was her eyes, like two emeralds, unflinching and deeply soulful... those wide, startled eyes, that gave total absorption. The lyrical lilt of her voice. Refinement, discretion, understatement, nobility. Her intricate intellect was what magnified her beauty even more.

She was cultivated, smart as a whip, with a no-nonsense approach. She said she grew up in Manhattan, enrolled at Lycée Français, East-Nine-Fifth Street at about the same time I was attending PS 46 in the Fordham section of the Bronx. We joked how we could easily have played together as kids in a Central Park playground. We talked poetry. Her tastes were eclectic – from Dante and the Greek and Latin classics and Apollinaire, to Rilke, Yeats, Pavese, Voznesensky. I was impressed.

Had anyone told me then she was one of the world's great beauties, it would have been a gross understatement and misleading besides. It was as if Benedetta's inner beauty had emptied my consciousness, causing my sight of her to become pure, mirror-like. I was momentarily mesmerized, and though everything from that moment on would no longer be the same for me, the significance of that change would not be felt for quite some time – several months, in fact.

Robert Rauschenberg – as reported in the next week's edition of the *Village Voice*, under a photo by Fred McDarrah – at exactly 12:18 am of a Sunday morning, balanced himself atop a ten-foot ladder, "unscrewed a 500-watt lightbulb, held his arm outstretched momentarily, and descended – thus completing his rarely performed Statue of Liberty happening. Removal of the bulb was the signal for spontaneous dancing of the frug in the dark by such luminaries as Lawrence Alloway, Leo Castellli, Barnett Newman, Dennis Hopper, Larry Poons, Tom Wolfe, Clay Felker, Andy Warhol, and Gerard Malanga." Where was I? I was in a state of reverie, as if hit by a thunderbolt from the gods. I had met a young woman; I was attracted to her; my emotions were moved, my sensitiveness increased, my intellect excited, and that dim state of being which we call the soul purged and cleared. That pretty much summed it up.

Paul Blackburn, poet-impresario, had scheduled a reading for me at St. Mark's Church In-the-Bowery, for March 24, a Thursday. The theme of the reading centred around my father, when – shortly after arriving in New York in the mid-1920s, living alone and barely speaking the language – he'd had a photo of himself made, which formed the centrepieces for my design of the flyer, with the banner "THE GERARD MALANGA STORY". Three hundred flyers were clandestinely run off by Marie Menken at her office at *Time-Life* and mailed out two weeks in advance of the event.

Shortly after, I would encounter Allen Ginsberg at a party in Elaine de Kooning's loft. He was astonished to learn that my reading coincided exactly the same day and hour as Andrei Voznesensky's first public appearance in America at Hunter College. Allen insisted that I cancel my reading and attend Voznesensky's instead. When I told him that the flyers had already gone out, he urged me to print up a cancellation announcement and dictated how the copy should read: "In honor of the Soviet poet Andrei Voznesensky, reading at Hunter College, Thursday, March 24, Gerard Malanga has cancelled his reading at St. Mark's Church." Allen even handed me a twenty-dollar bill to cover postage. Ideally, as he had theoretically surmised, anyone planning to attend my reading might likely want to come hear Voznesensky.

But my reason for cancelling was not entirely altruistic. I remember Benedetta mentioning Voznesensky as one of her favourite poets. I rightly intuited that she would be at his reading. It would be to my advantage to make my presence felt, even if only affording me a glimpse of her at a distance.

On the morning of March 24 I would run into Blackburn on St. Mark's Place. I couldn't ascertain for sure whether he was red in the face from a late-niter at McSorley's, the local pub a few doors from his flat on East Seventh, or just plain ripped at my *fait accompli*. His attitude was abrupt and we went our separate ways. At that moment all else didn't much matter. My sights were elsewhere. Not even my own reading could prevent my being in Benedetta's sphere.

As it happened, Andy and I were only two rows behind from where she was seated with friends, so in exiting we rushed up to each other, hugging and kissing. Mission accomplished. I had a foot in her psyche, so to speak. I was testing my power, but I would not see her again until the coming Fall.

What are the images that I can recall now? I begin about Benedetta in the present tense of our lives with each other as they were then. I'm reading through "The Secret Diaries" – a notebook I maintained during much of this time – from where Benedetta re-emerges as a real presence to the point where a rapport soon develops.

September 27, Benedetta is back in New York after a summer spent at Williamstown Theatre Festival – "I can build sets – run the light board – make costumes – fly in the flats – work the Follow Light and the whole thing was an illuminating experience. I acted – I also sang in *Annie Get Your Gun,* of all things!..."[1] We're to attend the Whitney Museum inaugural.

1. Letter dated September 22, 1966.

I purchase formal slippers and a tuxedo shirt at Brooks Brothers. Marie Menken supplies me with her black tie-jacket and trousers. It's arranged that Benedetta meet me at the Factory so she can change from blue jeans to evening clothes, but Billy Name locks the downstairs door and she spends fifteen minutes in the garage across the way trying to reach me by phone, but Andy's on the line, so she finally heads home and gets through – she'll come by and pick me up by car. Andy is also planning to attend the opening, so – why not – I invite him to join us.

Andy, Benedetta, and I arrive as a trio through the doors of the new Marcel Brauer edifice. Fred McDarrah is positioned inside the lobby and takes our picture. Looking at the photo now, Andy and Benedetta focus their attention on me. Was I the boy of the hour, or did I just crack a joke?

Benedetta without question is the most beautiful woman at the opening. She's wearing a stunning, shocking-pink wool Cardin dress and ruby studs. I introduce her to Stephen Shote, Michael Marsh, and René Ricard who, when I turn my back for an instant, is already all over her conversing in French. Joe Dever asks our names for his column. René is spilling champagne and placing empty glasses on the floor. Charles Moore

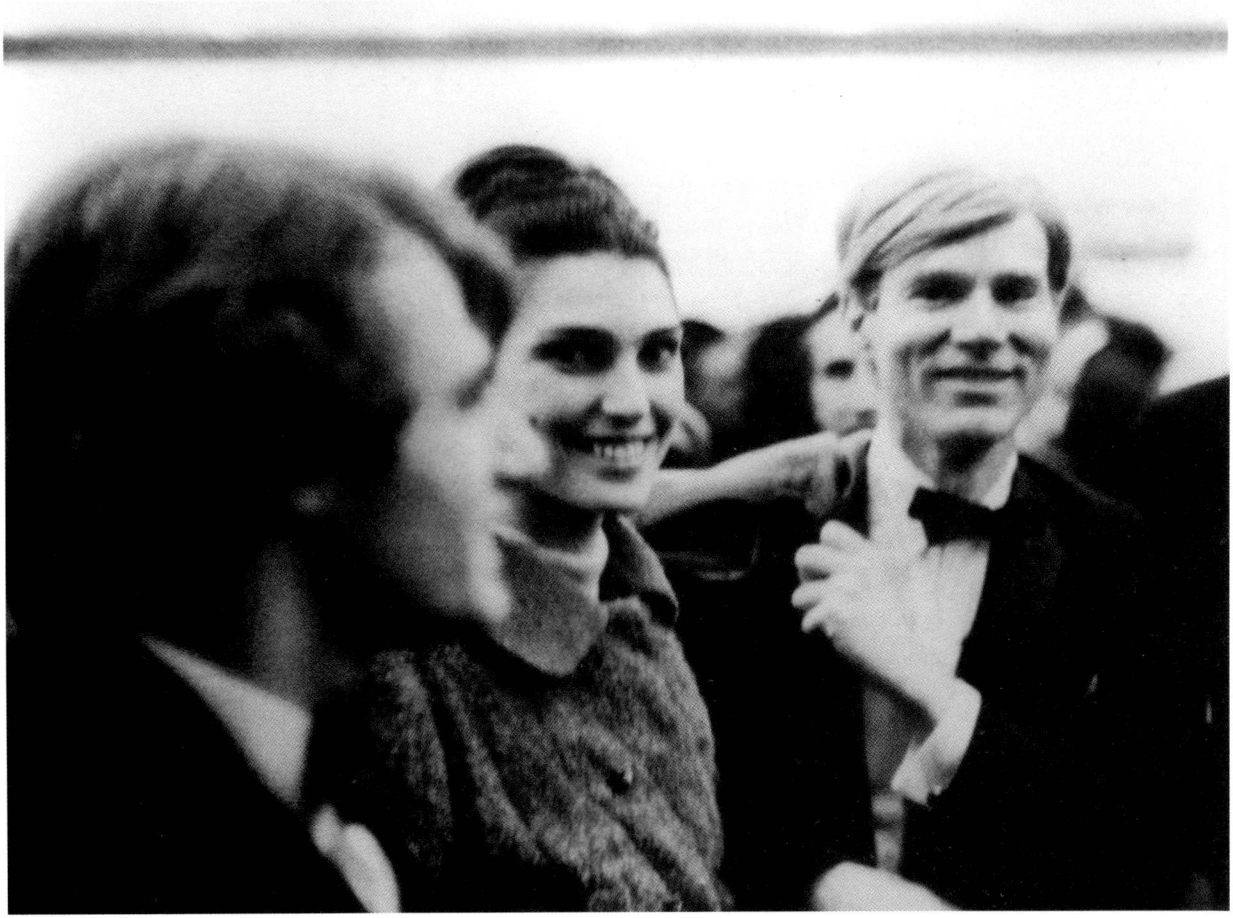

Gerard Malanga, Benedetta Barzini and Andy Warhol attending the inauguration of the Whitney Museum, NYC, September 27th 1966.

asks me to take our picture – Andy, René, Benedetta, and me huddled together in a mock pose.

October 15, according to my notes, I'm reminded that I'd spoken with Allen Ginsberg earlier in the day – he's nervous about the reading he and Peter Orlovsky are to give at Town Hall. He's reserved four comps for me. Benedetta and I were to pick up René and drive uptown, but the plans got turned around. I leave a note for him at the Factory that he should go directly to the box office to pick up his ticket.

Benedetta calls. I tell her to meet me at Max's between 7:00 and 7:30. In honour of Allen I purchase matching white Moroccan robes fashioned with hoods at a shop on St. Mark's Place. Benedetta arrives promptly at 7:30. We have drinks and dinner.

On the way uptown I turn her on to some grade-A j. It takes fifteen minutes to park the car. We put on the robes, walk into the lobby. All eyes are now focused on us. Andy is off to the side. Benedetta walks up behind and kisses him on the back on the head. I introduce Benedetta to Barbara Rubin and Rona Page. The girls get it on. The lights signal that it's time to take our seats. Andy is lost in the crowd. The lights dim. Allen and Peter walk out on stage and take bows and then quickly seat themselves stage center.

The performance opens with two Indian mantras. Peter starts with a Vietnam anti-war poem followed by a series of poems about assholes and vegetables. Allen follows, accompanying himself on the harmonium with a few William Blake songs, some love poems for boys, and concludes the evening with a new poem – a sweeping, panoramic vista called "Wichita Vortex Sutra" with its

...wreathes of naked bodies, thighs and faces,
small hairy bun'd vaginas,
silver cocks, armpits and breasts
moistened by tears....

with its... houseless brown farmland plains
rolling heavenward
in every direction...[2]

2. From Allen Ginsberg's *Collected Poems 1947–1980*, Harper & Row, 1984.

Allen asks, "What if I opened my soul to sing to my absolute self..." The audience goes wild. Benedetta folds her hand inside mine and leans her head on my shoulder. This, as I seem to recall, is the first instance of her initiating physical warmth.

After the reading we all meet up in the lobby – Rona, René, my secretary, Susan Pile – and on the way down to the Balloon Farm the car fills up with marijuana smoke. The Velvet Underground is performing tonight and I'll be dancing on stage with them. Benedetta watches the show from the balcony, near where Andy and Paul are working the projectors. Tonight I'm dancing from my heart. Allen is now in the audience gazing up at me.

Benedetta and I split immediately after the show for Max's to meet up with friends from her summer in Williamstown. Her enormous appetite consumes her. Finishing her meal she starts in on mine. She claims she has a tapeworm. René joins us, making a mockery of everything and everyone around him, turning over ashtrays, and screaming at anyone who dares to walk past our table. Andy walks in, shrewdly avoids René for fear of embarrassment, sits at another table.

I'm looking over my "Diaries" now and I see that on October 17 I visited with Edie Sedgwick. "I've never seen her more beautiful. She pulls on red leotards and a tight, red cotton top. I weed out the seeds and twigs and fill one eighth's full Camel with Acapulco Gold. We're high. She tells me her attempt at withdrawing from the media attention, from Andy, the parties. I mention that I've been seeing Benedetta. Edie is very happy for me, comments that 'Benedetta has a good head on her shoulders'."

I leave Edie falling asleep. Pick up maquettes to be shot for silkscreens. Run into Benedetta on Lexington Avenue, near where she lives up the street from Andy's house. Psychic thought providing physical encounter.

On October 18 – Benedetta is unable to join me at Timothy Leary's concert. "Turn on. Tune in. Drop Out." She's having dinner with her father, who's in town for one week of conferences with CBS. Says she'll call me at Max's. She doesn't call but surprises me – showing up a half-hour after me. I order her second meal of the evening. "Where does it all go?" We start joking around. We scribble notes to each other on matchbook covers, like "I missed you when I didn't hear from you Monday night." She replies, "I don't even dare miss you. XXXXXxx".

After dinner we decide to head out for Ondine, a discotheque on the Upper East Side. We grab an inconspicuous table off in a corner. During a live set of the Doors, we continue to exchange notes on matchbook covers. Benedetta writes: "Shy in your presence ever since I first met you – Am 'afraid' – can't figure out what it is all about (inside). Am fighting something but would like to know about you – the whys and wheres and hows and

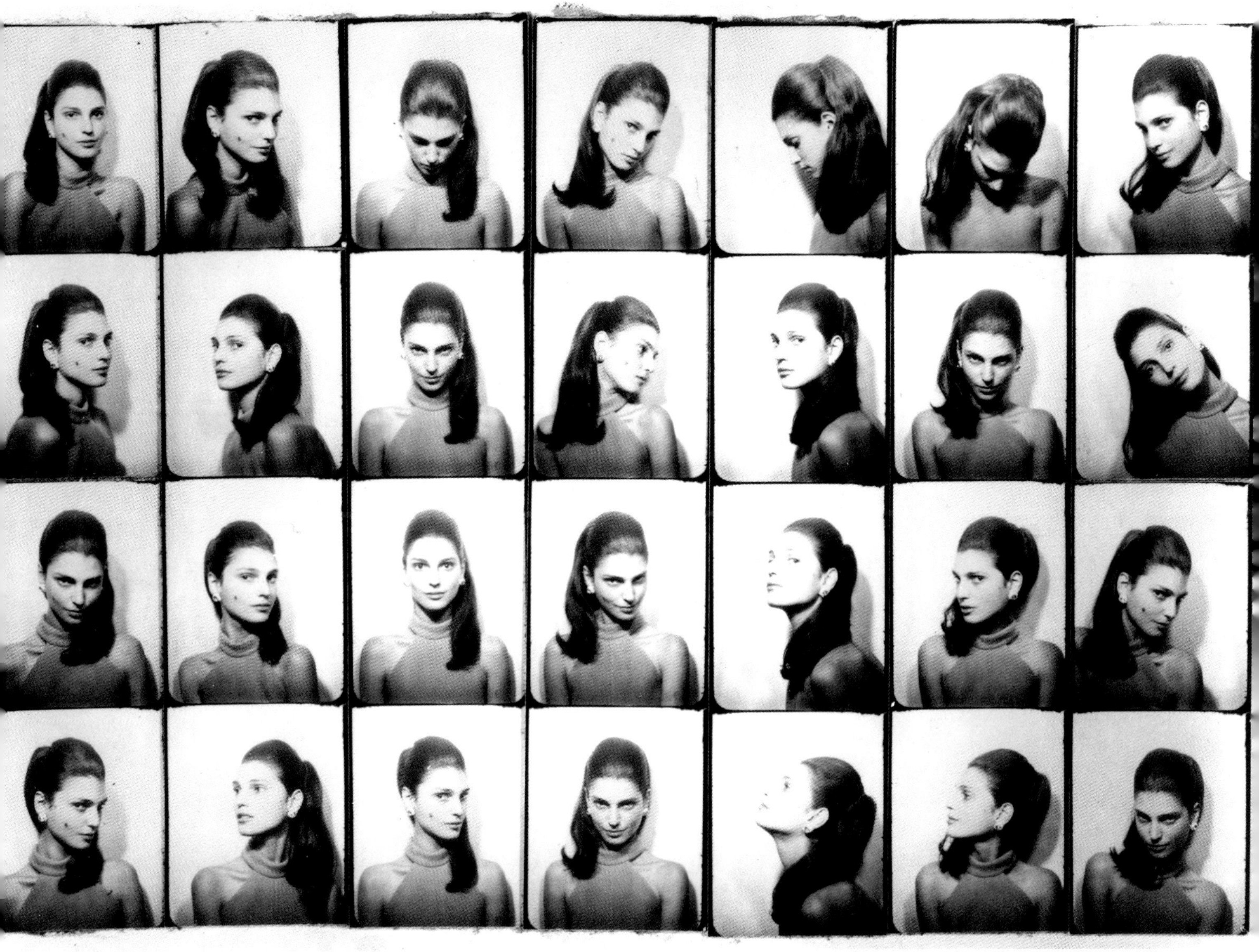

Benedetta Barzini,
photomaton portrait by
Gerard Malanga, 1966.

things. Do you really talk?" I write out, "I am so shy in your presence and always was from the first time I met you. When I am silent I am really thinking of you." Benedetta writes: "I'm a false person." I cross out the word "false".

Benedetta attempts to relate an incident that occurred several years back – at eighteen she'd been living at the estate of a boyfriend's mother not far from Venice for the summer. She'd walk the dogs in the rock garden, curl up with a book in the candle-lit room. Time passed slowly and then at summer's end she realized he was not coming back, the feeling of suddenly being dead inside consumed her. I could picture her words even now. She buries herself among the bed-sheets. The boyfriend not in Venice ends in the dream of her cutting her hair-ends. The footsteps that never reach her... the long, silent walks in the rock garden all afternoon become a dream, but the feeling of injury leaving her empty is not a dream.

The next day I pick up silkscreen transparencies and drop them off for Andy to look at. I visit Edie in Lenox Hill Hospital. Two days earlier, after leaving her asleep, her apartment caught fire.

"Tonight Benedetta said she loved me" is a line in the "Diaries" for October 23. Did she tell me this over the phone or in person? I can't recall now. The entry also states that she is with her father, visiting Philip Johnson in Connecticut at this "house left out in the rain", as René calls it.

On October 24, René and I go shopping for a leather jacket, scarf, one dozen red roses for Benedetta. John Wieners is giving a reading at the Ninety-second Street Y, but for one reason or other Benedetta can't make it, so we arrange that she meet me at the Paradox afterwards, "I take a mescaline trip, but am very tense inside and on the way up to the Y we have the taxi stop at least five times so I can get out and vomit, though my stomach is empty."

After the reading we head down to the Paradox. Rona is with me. Benedetta arrives wearing the same dress I remember her in when we first met at Rauschenberg's loft. "My head is on the table. Benedetta lifts my head up and I hand her the roses. She looks at me with a smile and concern. She hugs me and kisses me on the head, on the lips. I feel so good inside."

We drive over to the reception Bob Wilson has arranged for John in the West Village, at the home of a friend. Benedetta meets John for the first time. As she unwraps the roses to show John, "all the petals fall to the floor like snowflakes".

October 29 was a very fortuitous day. The *Exploding Plastic Inevitable* is scheduled for a light-and-sound performance at the Boston Institute of Contemporary Art to coincide with a show of Andy's art. I suggest the trip to Benedetta and she's excited to come along.

That morning, René and I wait outside Paul's apartment. Benedetta drives up at 10:00 and we head up Third Avenue to Castelli Gallery to pick up a signed Warhol Liz Taylor poster – Benedetta's gift to a friend, a Harvard student.

Leo asks Benedetta if there's room in the car for a French writer from *Réalités* who is doing a story on Andy. Jean Clay would characterize me in his article as a "dishevelled poet". I write poems in the front seat the whole way up.

I have arranged with Gordon Baldwin, a close friend, for Benedetta and I to spend the night, so when we arrive in Cambridge to drop off our bags, he has set aside his own bedroom for us.

We drive over to the ICA. The movies, including *Vinyl*, are being projected and two spotlights are aimed directly on the rotating mirror ball, giving the auditorium a luminous revolving glow.

The movies end. The Velvets walk on stage and begin setting up and tuning their instruments. Fifteen minutes into the first number I step out on stage and slowly work my way into a new dance routine – a crucifixion attitudinal pose. Rona stands behind me with two flashlights, aiming their beams, through my outstretched arms, at the audience.

At the show's end, backstage, I notice Benedetta in an unusually upbeat mood. I stop outside the dressing room for a moment and Rona follows me. She tells me that Benedetta is having "woman problems". Rona, smiling, tells me "how beautiful Benedetta looks at this moment and how much Benedetta loves me".

We head over to Ed Hood's flat where a small party in our honour is underway. She places her hand over my own on the front seat. Within the hour it's become a Buñuelian nightmare – one can barely move any which way. The room fills with cigarette smoke. Time to skidoo.

We make our way out into the open night air and walk a few doors east on Mount Auburn Avenue to Gordon's flat. While Benedetta is taking a shower I turn off all the lights and take a match to a candle and then light up a joint from its flickering, golden flame.

Focus for remembering it all. Now a mental picture: small, damp tendrils of hair over neck and ears. Neck curving gracefully into collarbone. The skin is translucent, the face aglow, the head backlit, as if a halo instantly took form and changed also. Candlelight bouncing off wall. Nightgown lifting past shoulders... flat-bellied. A Lucas Cranach painting in posture and grace. Her eyes wide open in love, I could see in the darkness. She remembered herself bleeding for the first time in five years, suddenly awakened in her passion – that she could feel alive once again. The evaporation of the long wait on the Venetian estate she'd hinted at became the end of a part of her life now beginning with me. Benedetta is smiling at me; her shy, sorrowful, cat-like gaze, her innocence, her guilt and "the last few years of struggling and suffering, from the inside" – as her father once put it in a letter to me – come to an end.

She climbs into bed and we hold onto each other for what seems an eternity. The candlelight flickers... goes out. I kiss her gently behind the ear. I press my lips against her temple, the hollow of her cheek. Benedetta looks into my eyes, stares straight at me, and says, "If I get pregnant, we'll have the child anyway."

Sunday morning in Cambridge, Masssachusetts. Sunlight cast on the blood-stained white sheet. The night never ending...

We pose for Marie Cosinda's large-format Polaroid camera set on tripod in Gordon's kitchen. Marie makes three attempts on getting it right and presents me with the third shot, commemorating this more auspicious occasion of having us pose for her. Marie also made a triple portrait with John Wieners, René, and me.

"No woman is virtuous / who does not give herself to her love / – forthwith" – William Carlos Williams, in Book Five of his long poem, *Paterson*, apropos to what's now realized. It's October 31 now. According to "The Secret Diaries", it's my first night back in New York. I'm staying with John Wieners at the Chelsea. I phone Benedetta at 3:00 am. She tells me she loves me. November 1 – Benedetta calls, tells me she has to meet "someone" at the Plaza and we arrange that I meet her at 10:00 across the way at the Pulitzer Fountain. We walk the entire block circling the fountain, arms around each other's waist, trying to come up with a place to have supper. Head over to Serendiptity III. We have cheese omelettes – Benedetta having more than her share, digging into my plate as well – and finish off with a pineapple frost lime, coffee, and icebox cake. I joke about getting Duchamp to sign his name to a shovel for her as a Christmas gift.

It's November 2 now – my last night in New York before I leave for a tour of Ohio and West Virginia with the Velvets. I arrive at the Tucci apartment and Benedetta introduces me to Mrs. Tucci and we're about to head out. We drive to Chinatown for dinner. Afterwards we head over to the Chelsea to pick up John and René for drinks at Max's. It would be around midnight that we leave Max's and drive up to her place, because I see now that the time is noted in the "Diaries" as 2:00am, about the time I would have departed and headed home.

We sprawl out on her bed looking at each other's family snapshots and talk about what it was like for us growing up, discovering similar interests, similar dreams, goals, aspirations.

Benedetta telling me it has been five years since her last period... Could this be directly linked to her sense of abandonment a few years earlier on the Venetian estate? I don't ask. The fact that she has even brought it up is relevant to her personal history and the way in which she places trust in me indicates as much – that what we are feeling for each other is not illusion.

I ask Benedetta if she has ever thought about marriage. She asks me to repeat what I just said. "She tells me she loves me" I have typed here, followed by, "I ask her to marry me". She says, "Yes". Looking at her long enough I understand what she has been seeing in my face for some time now.

We take a vow not to call long-distance, not to break the self-imposed silence we've promised each other during the four days that I'll be away. Time will be suspended for us. We will continue as if a break hasn't occurred. I remember what she wrote in one of those matchbooks I've saved – "I don't even dare miss you".

Next day – November 3 – before I would meet up with Paul, Nico and the Velvets at the Factory – Andy would not be coming on this trip – "I phoned my mother", according to the "Diaries", "to tell her the happy news about my marriage with Benedetta". My mother says, "When you come home in a few days the wedding bands will be here waiting as my gift to

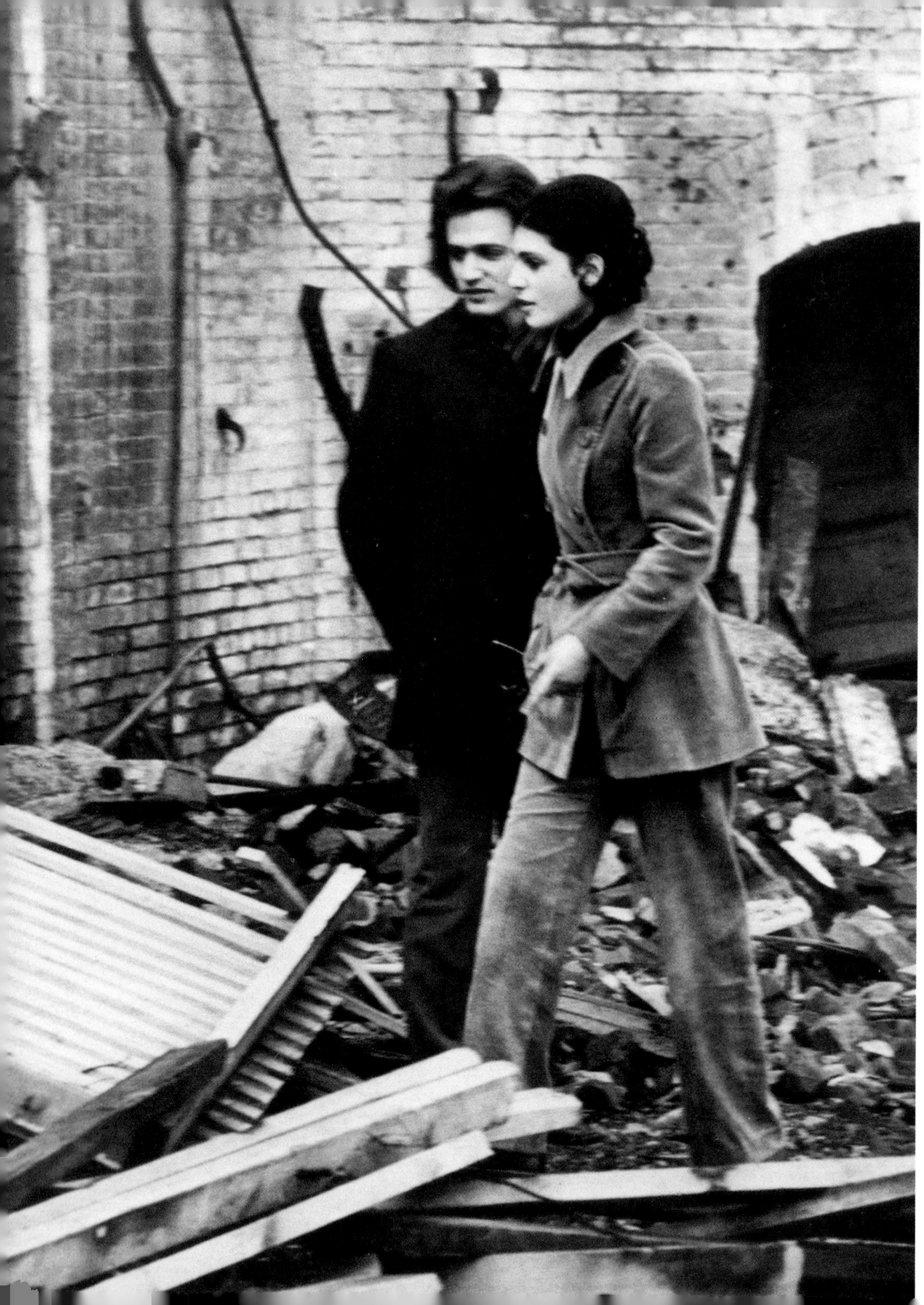

Gerard Malanga and
Benedetta Barzini, NYC
1967.

you and Benedetta."

(It's August now, the second to be exact, 1992. I call my mother long-distance. I want to hear her words about this personal history, these private moments, of someone she's never met. After all, she's eighty-seven and she had a direct part in this too. She says, "No, I don't know who even she is [*sic*]." Just as I thought.)

Benedetta, at the last minute, thinks to meet up with me in Morgantown, West Virginia – the last stop on the tour – where as plan would have it "we would stop here and there on the way back to New York". For some unknown reason, now that I look back at what I've written, I discourage this plan, simply feeling that to undertake such a trip seems a bit impractical, as we have work waiting for us the start of the week. I foolishly don't consider the romantic implications involved.

On November 3, after arriving in Cincinnati, in what would be the first show of the tour, I send a telegram: "The most beautiful question receives the most beautiful answer. I love you, Gerard." When we reach Columbus – November 5 – I wire her flowers.

On November 5, upon arriving at the University of West Virginia – the last leg of the tour – I note that I will be sending Benedetta a wire to reserve a double at the Chelsea. I still maintain our vow with regard, calling her directly.

It's November 7 – "the last leg of my journey home – United Flight #146 to Newark. I draw B's on the starless night sky window. I keep thinking she should have received the news of my arrival on such-and-such time".

It's nearly 1:30am when we arrive in Newark. Close-ups of an empty airport conjure images in an Antonioni movie of the mind. "A few people. Silence. Loudspeaker occasionally announcing an arrival/departure to nowhere. The newsstand bathed in a ghostly blue hue. Faces staring out from magazine covers." I call. No answer. The phone rings four or five times. I ask at the check-in counter, but no message has been left in my name. No use standing around waiting for the probable/improbable. I hitch a ride with Paul, Lou, and Nico. It's 3:00am when we reach Paul's flat. I try once again. This time Benedetta picks up. She tells me "the four days we were apart from each other felt like one hundred years had passed. I'll phone you tomorrow at 6:00 at the Factory. Goodnight. Ciao."

The entry for the night of November 7 is a bit confusing. It's noted that although I missed Benedetta's call, I told Paul Katz that she'd be meeting me at the Paradox after 10:30. So, to kill time, I attend a poetry reading: Louise Bogan and W.S. Merwin at the Ninety-second Street Y, just up the street from where Benedetta lives. It's 9:30 now – the reading over. I head south along Lexington and as I pass the building where Benedetta lives I notice her Dodge Dark parked out front. "I stop. Go back. Walk up the stairs. Meet her in hallway." Long moments of silence as we walk to the car. A few words here and there. I give her the lead. We drive to a small bar on Seventy-third Street, Third Avenue. Wine is brought to the table. "She explains that she cannot love me. I am speechless and in a state of shock" is what I have typed here. It's very cut-and-dried. It all sounds rehearsed, as if she spent double time seeing her analyst. It's as if a bomb went off at the table and I no longer exist, or I'm just plain dreamin', unable to get back through to the other side, as if observing all this at a short distance. My pride prevents me from making an attempt to be persuasive or argumentative. I've lost all sense of speech, but more than that I've lost my magic and power. In a matter of a few minutes the happiest man on earth is reduced to unfathomable unhappiness.

She drives me to Anne Waldman's flat on St. Mark's Place. As I'm stepping out of the car, she leans over and says, "Don't do anything foolish." The Dodge pulls away, turns the corner, and is gone. All else – traffic and honking sounds, cabs whooshing by, crowds of pedestrians, shop-window lights – dissolves slowly into white.

Henri Cartier-Bresson writes that "We photographers deal in things which are continually vanishing, and when they have vanished, there is no contrivance on earth which can make them come back again. We cannot develop and print a memory". Perhaps it was my perception of Bresson's theory that finally led to the creation of what I am doing in my own picture taking. The works that were made over the past twenty-five years emerge from my commitment to an essentially private vision: the desire to look and to make a record of that looking.

As an ardent admirer of Duchamp, who believed that aesthetic boundaries exist to be breached, I remain open to all possibilities and alternatives in the creative process. I embrace the mistakes.

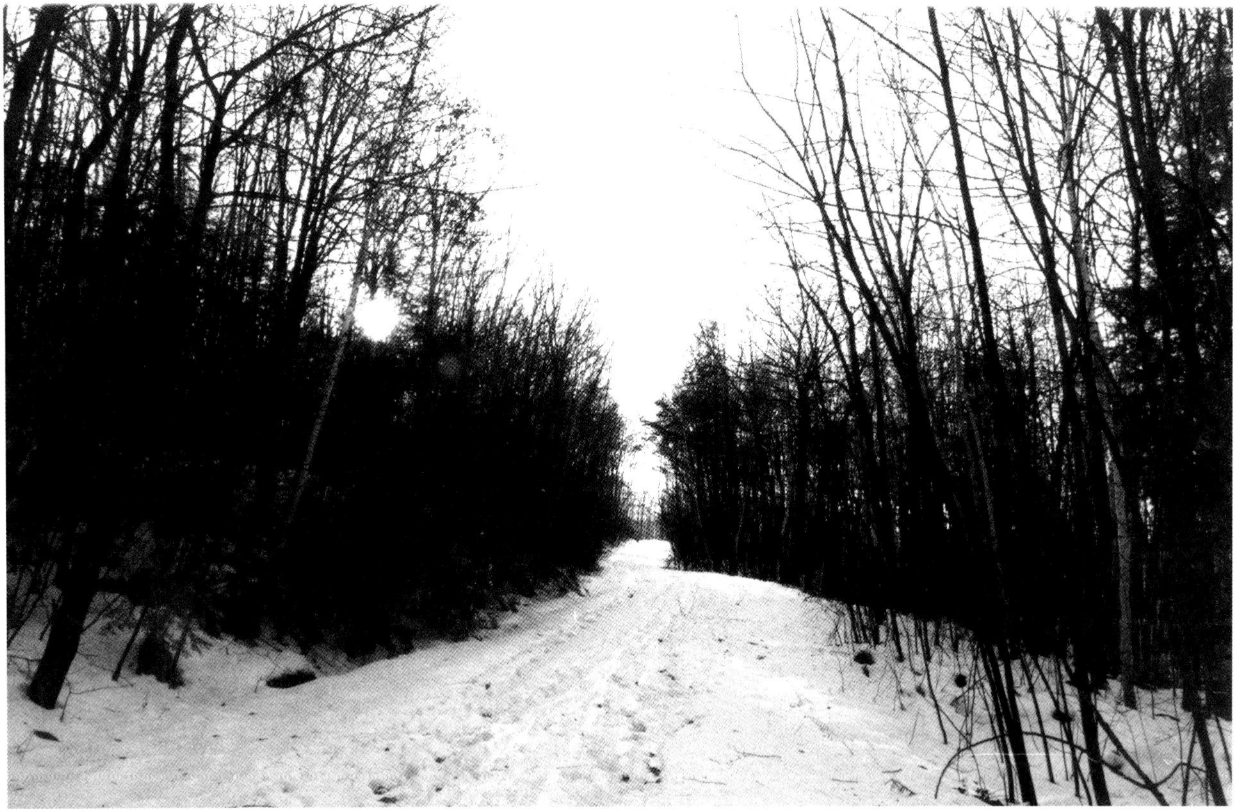

The Appalachian Trail, Warner Mountain, Gt. Barrington, MA.

"In the city time becomes visible. In the country time is invisible." Lewis Mumford said that. The present tense: where I now live affords me the opportunity of a retreat in order to look inside myself. When I create a new work – whether it be a poem or photograph – I do not begin with a concept or an image, but rather allow the experience to dictate the direction and focus of the piece. Each experience has its own essence and reality.

Moving to the Berkshires was not an escape but a release. In my capacity to be alone I'm constantly discovering myself. I'm my own best company. The art of learning has always been an adventure.

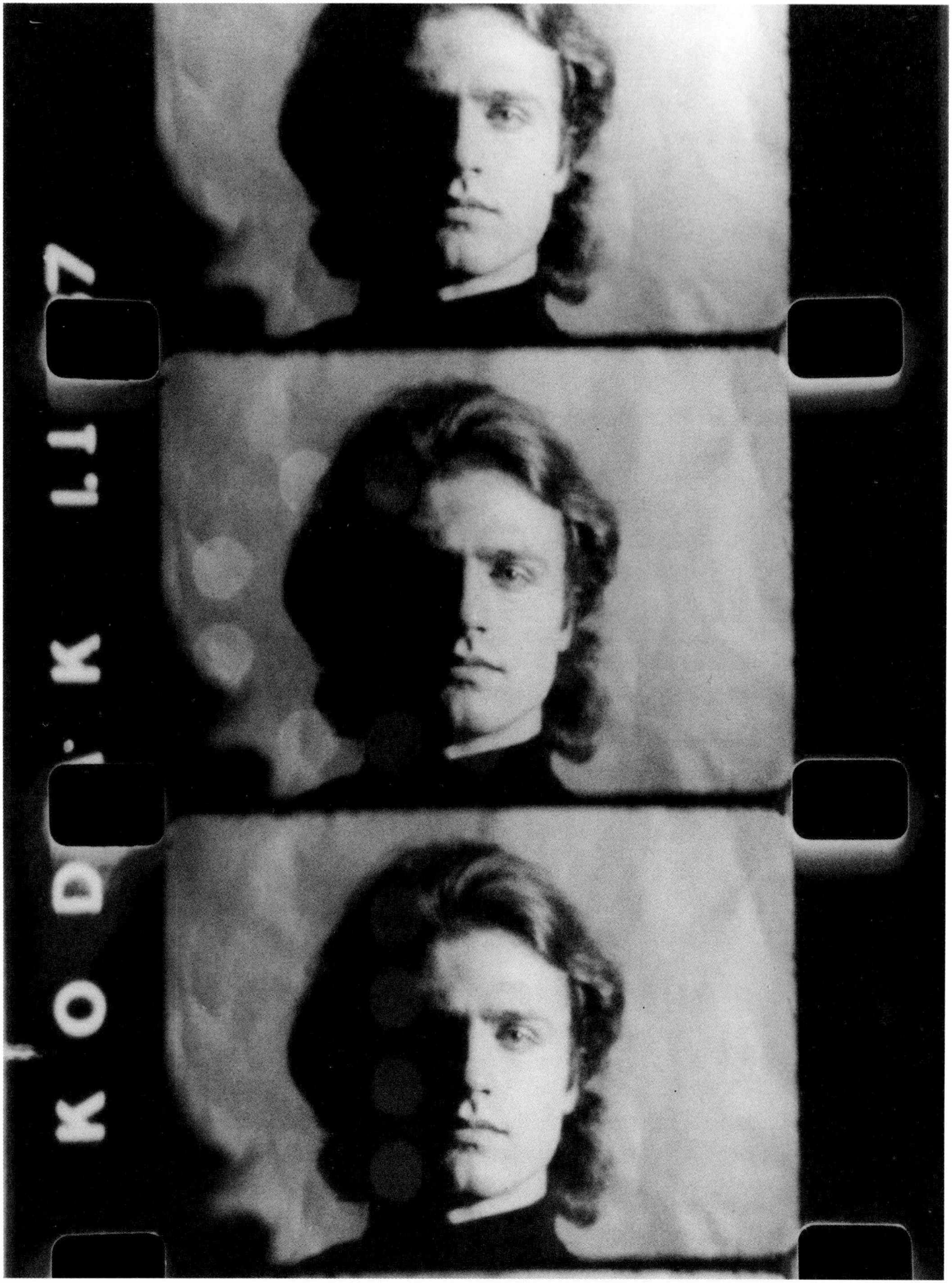

three
the first screen test

Sometime in December 1963, a couple of months before our move to the 47th Street Factory, I asked Andy to shoot a roll of movie film framed as a "headshot" composition that I could then replicate as a publicity headshot.

The double or multiple-frame reproduction, sprockets and all, was nothing new, but had its origins with Stan Brakhage's *Anticipation Of The Night* (1958) and *Window Water Baby Moving* (1959), conveying a cinematic quality in reproduction and not meant as an artistic device at all.

After studying the 8 x 10 inch photoprint, which I had chosen from the original footage, Andy and I thought this would be a quick way to continue as a series. The title just came to us, *Screen Tests*, a homage to a bygone Hollywood era.

Andy toyed with the idea of using this material for a series of silkscreen paintings which he did not pursue, opting for the photobooth pictures instead, which to his mind were both expedient and less costly. This, too, was abandoned, yet we continued the movie film portraits, which took on a momentum all their own.

So, in a sense, the *Screen Test* portraits happened quite by accident, and were not initially a conscious effort on our part. Many of these portraits were also compiled into other emerging series by Andy, most notably *13 Most Beautiful Boys*, *12 Most Beautiful Women* and *50 Fantastics*.

There was no formal discussion involved, set budget, or what final direction this series would take. We went ahead, buoyed by our enthusiasm in seeing what we could do and what the final result would be. In the end, it was purely a social vehicle, a form of entertainment.

For the next two-and-a-half years, either separately or together, we

Opposite: Gerard Malanga Screen Test, 1965.

filmed approximately 400 individuals, though the exact number has never really been determined. The series coincidentally came to an end in January 1967 when we began selecting portraits for the book, aptly named *Screen Tests / A Diary*, for which I also furnished a run-on text of prose poems.

The film portraits, taken as a whole, provide an intimate and informed picture of the 1960s during the most creative period of our association. It should be noted that neither Andy nor I were photographers at the time. Thus, by virtue of our collaboration with the motion picture medium, in creating what amounted to post-photographs, we became photographers.

3-Minutes B&W Silent

is all that remains.
Some biographical data is still missing, like who was born when or died when, or if it's still early autumn.

Decades ago now seem non-existent.

A fiction takes place.

Film degrades restlessly over time.

The background is black mostly.

Truth is no longer 24 frames per second nor 16 and no-one remembers.

The face slowly flickers and fades.

Coded numbers appear as white circles moving, then nothing.

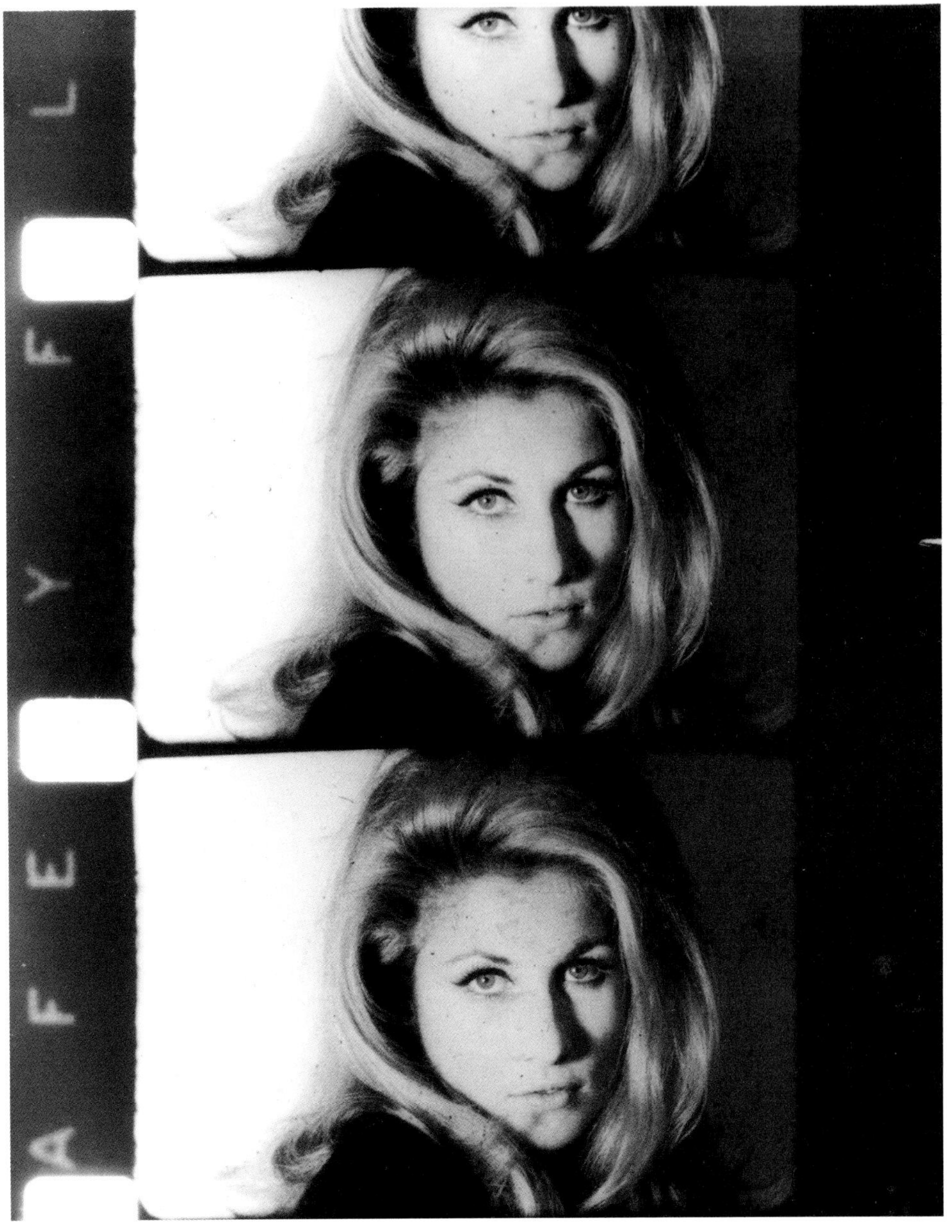

Baby Jane Holzer
Screen Test, 1964

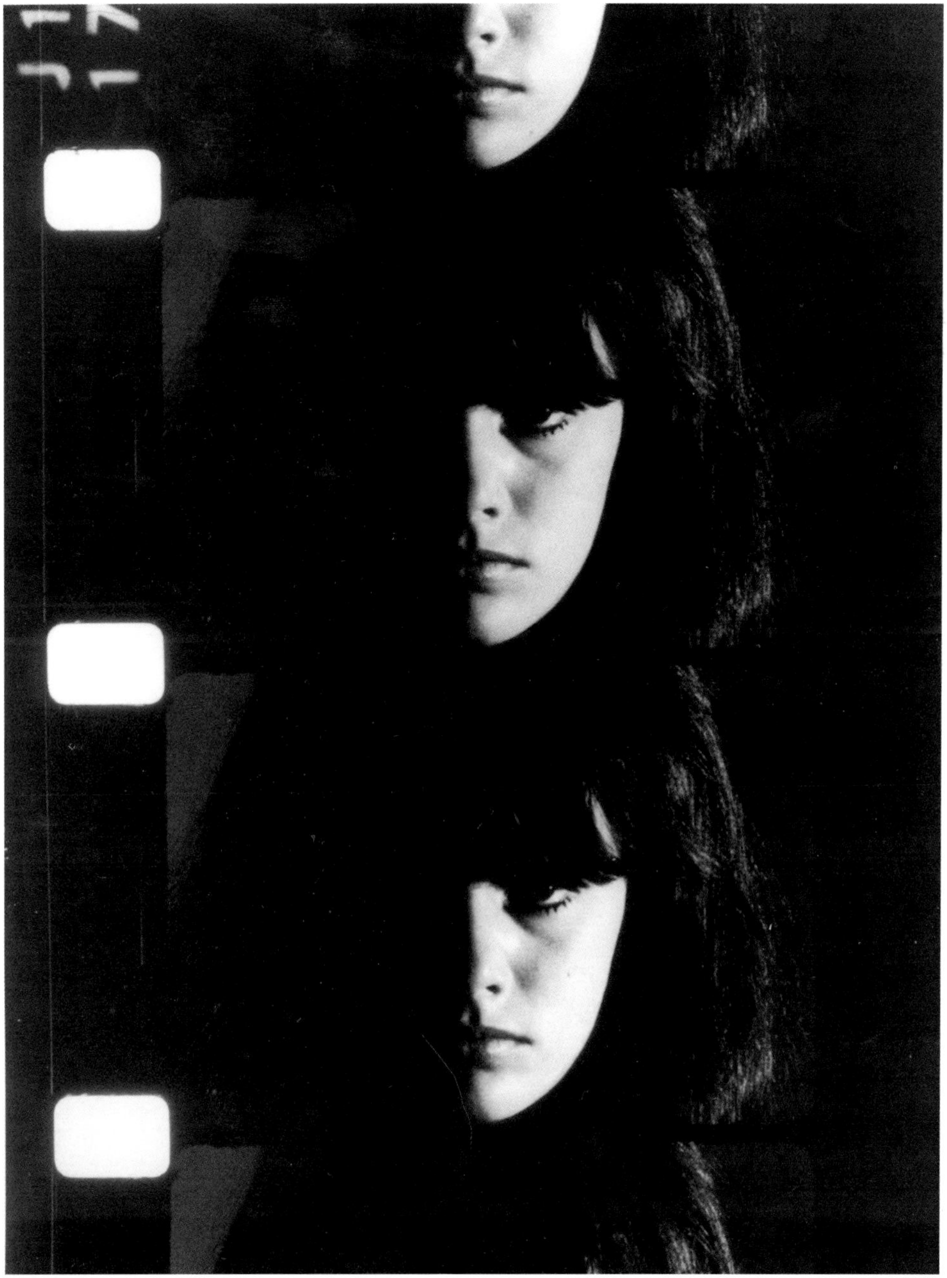

International Velvet
Screen Test, 1966

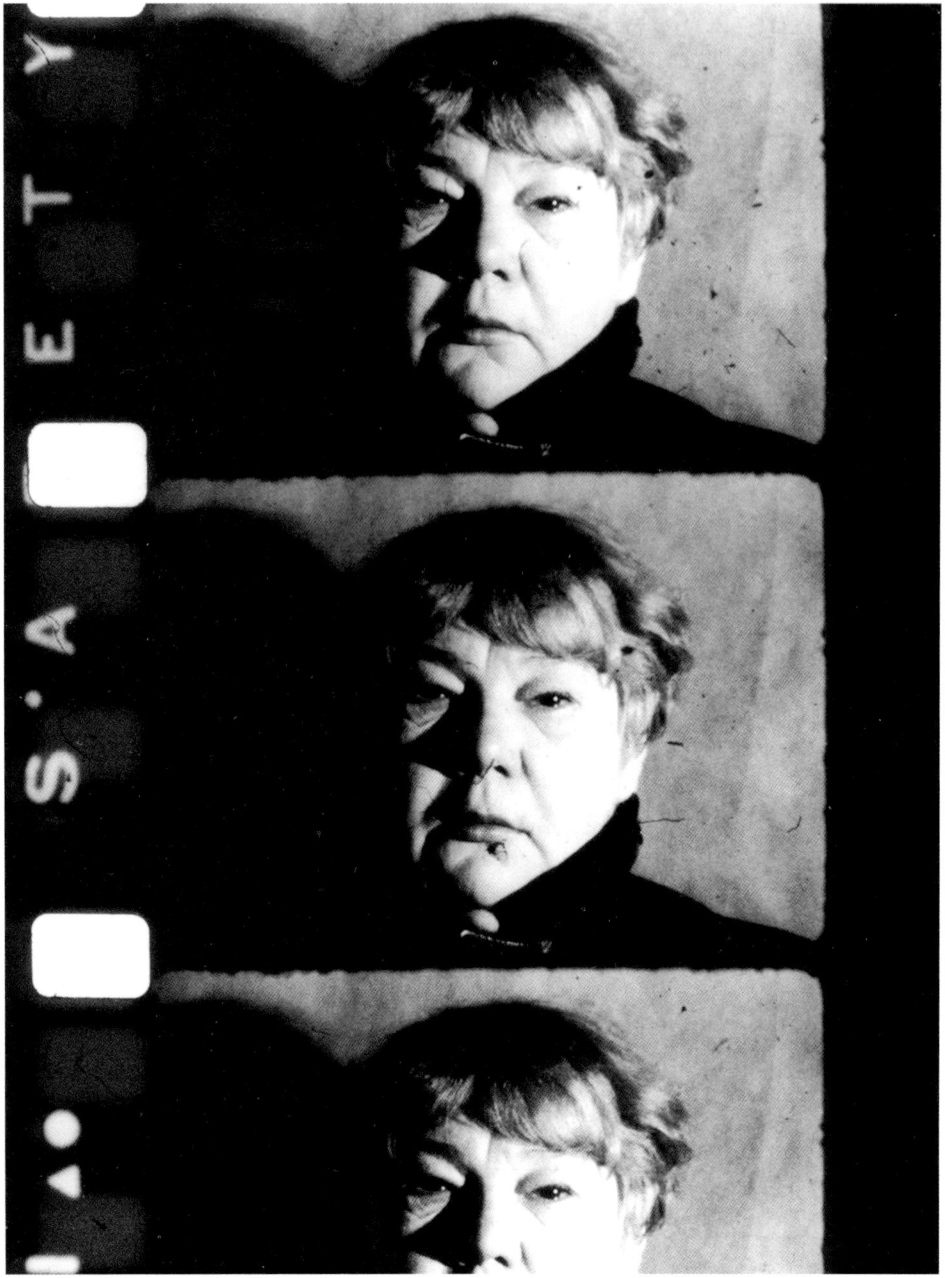

Marie Menken Screen Test, 1966

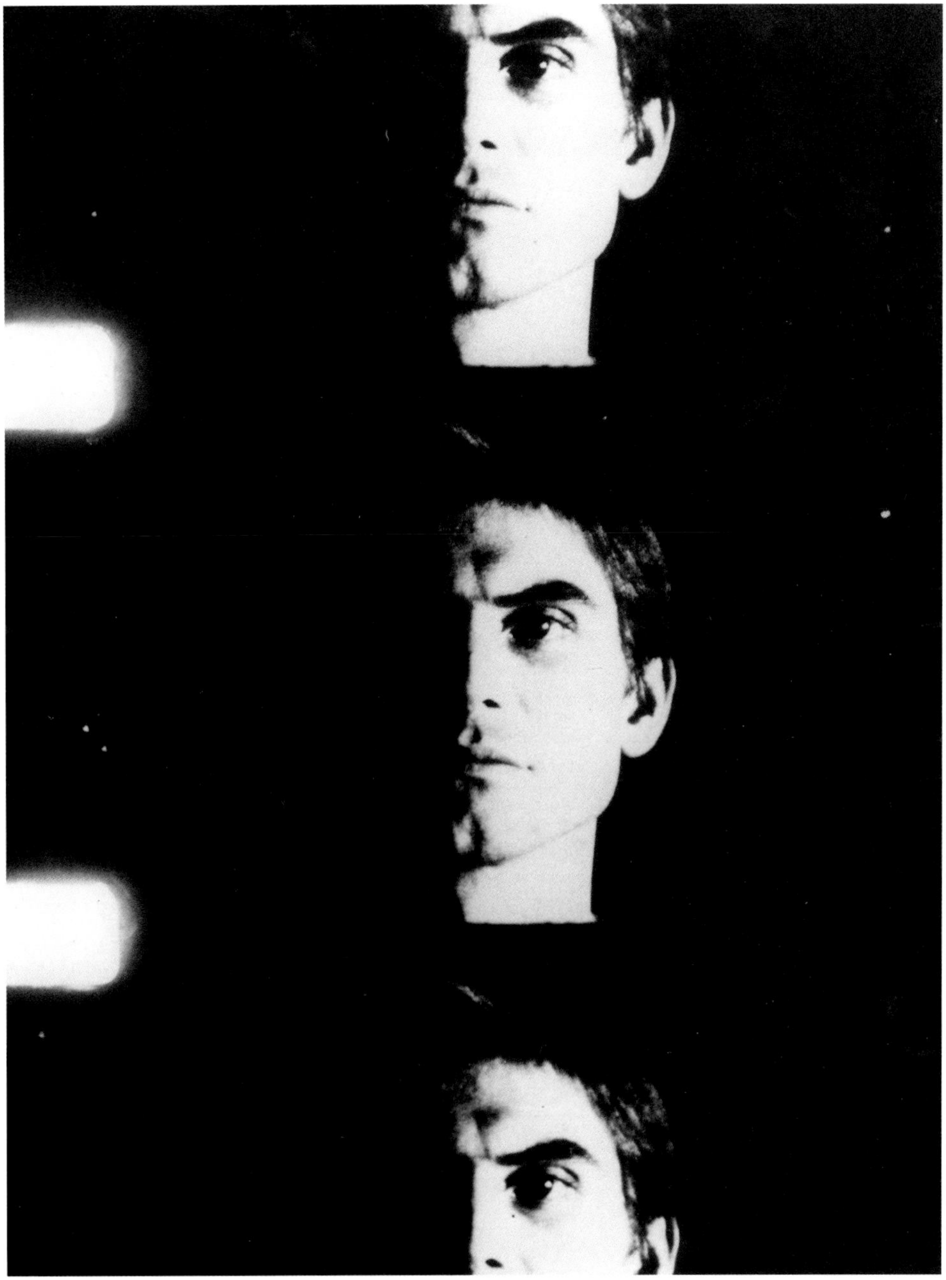

Allen Midgette Screen
Test, 1966

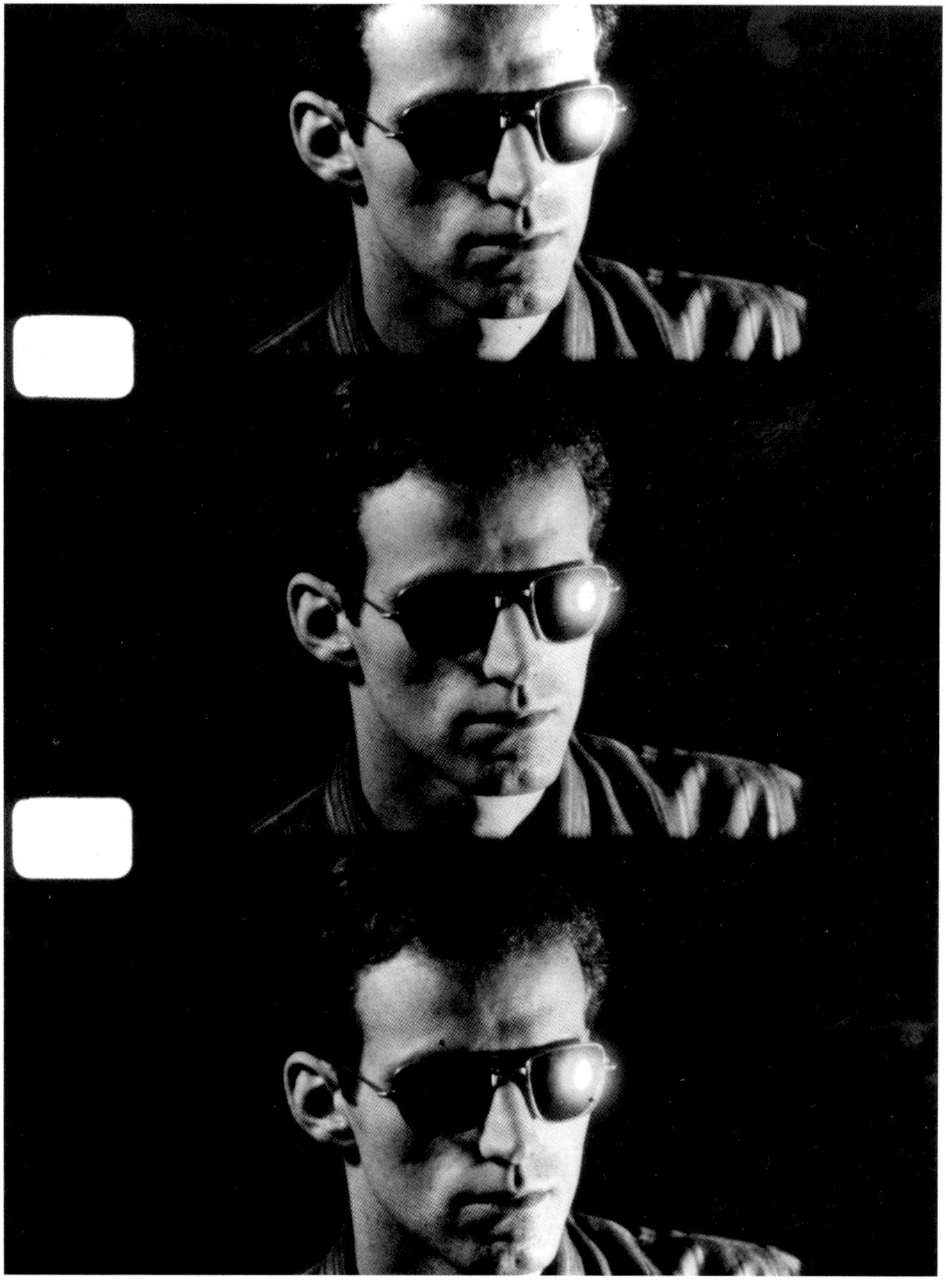

Billy Name Screen Test,
1966

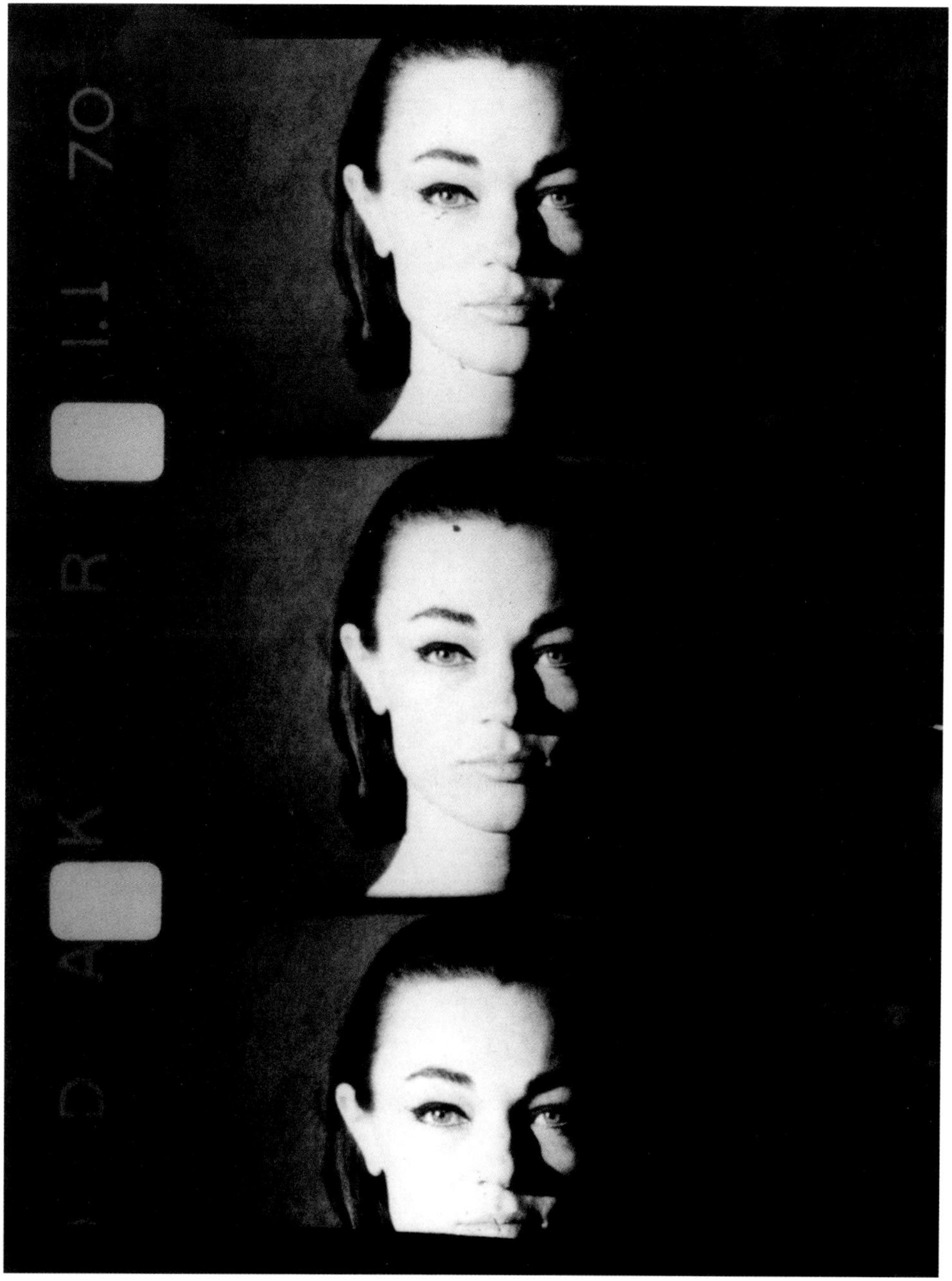

Ivy Nicholson Screen Test, 1965

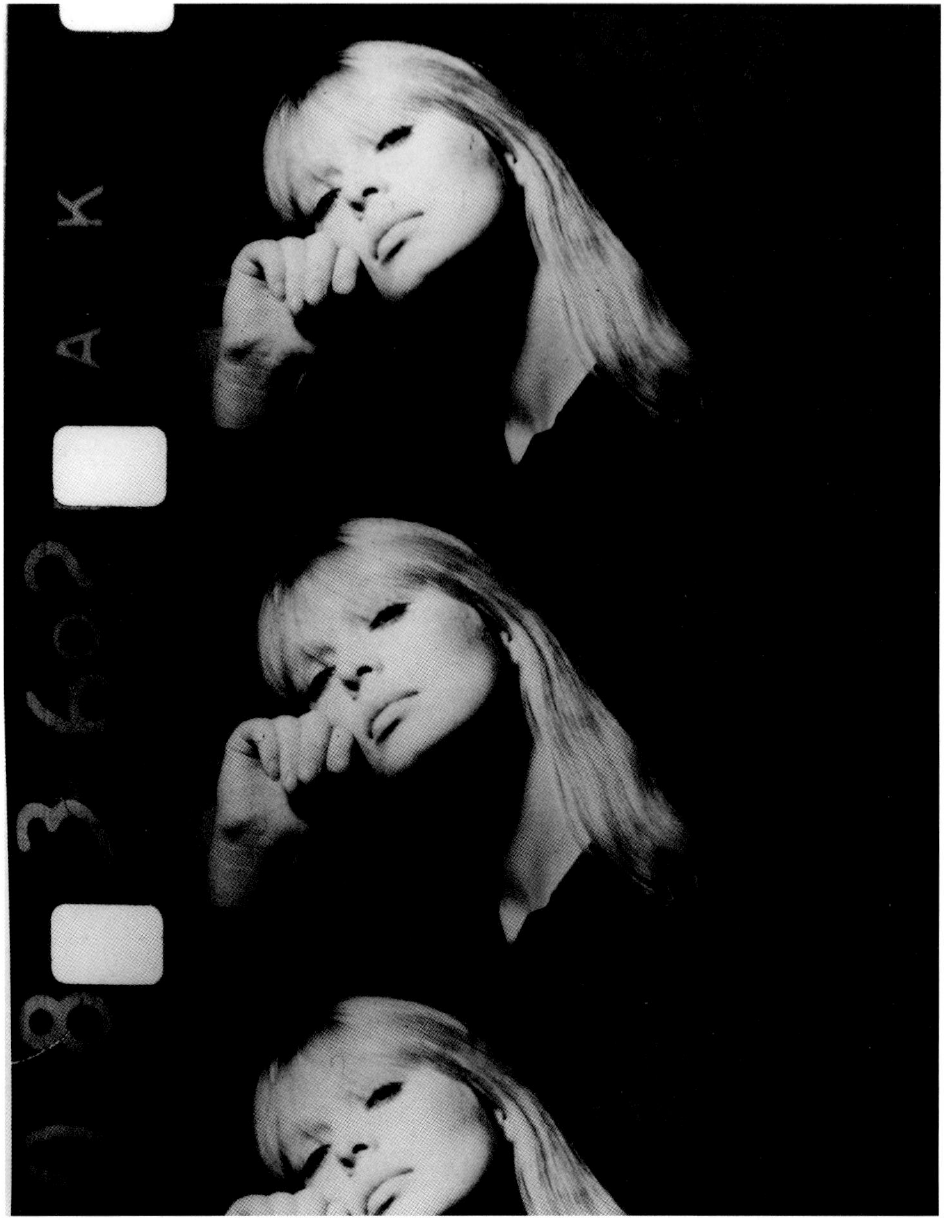

Nico Screen Test, 1966

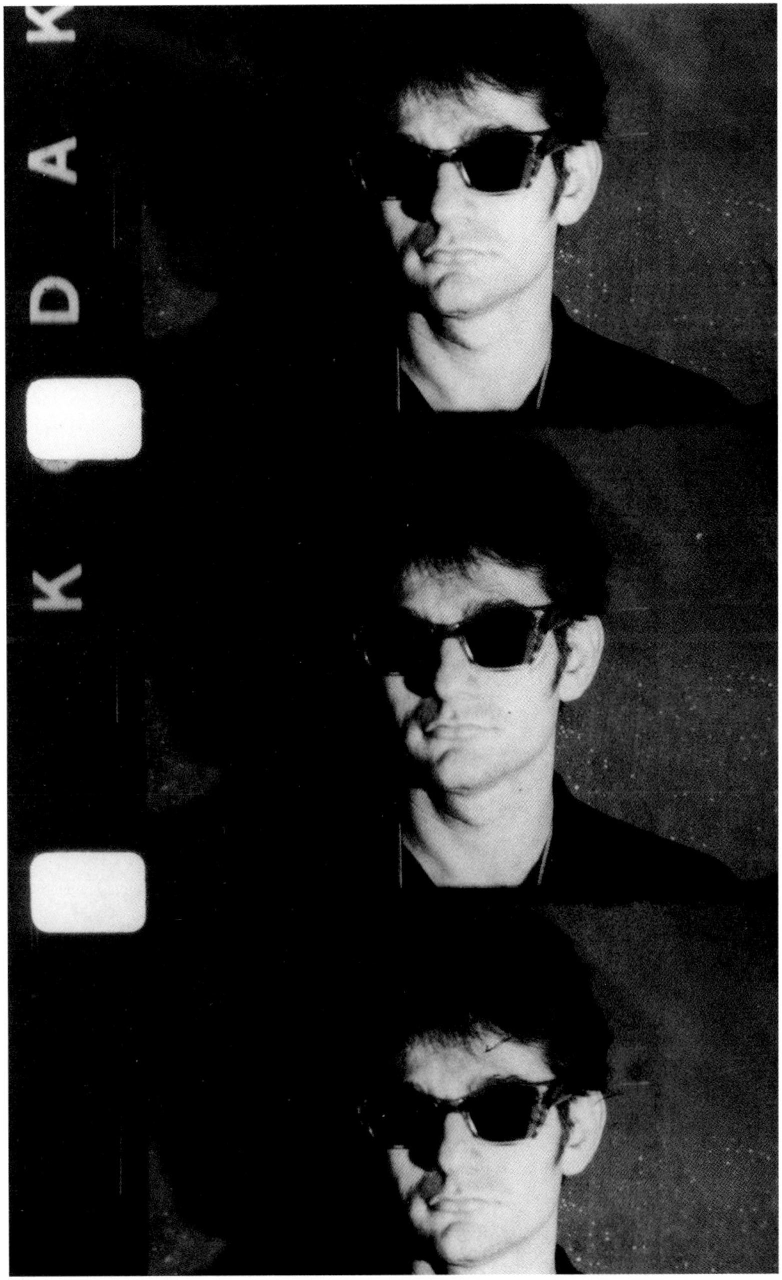

Ondine Screen Test, 1966

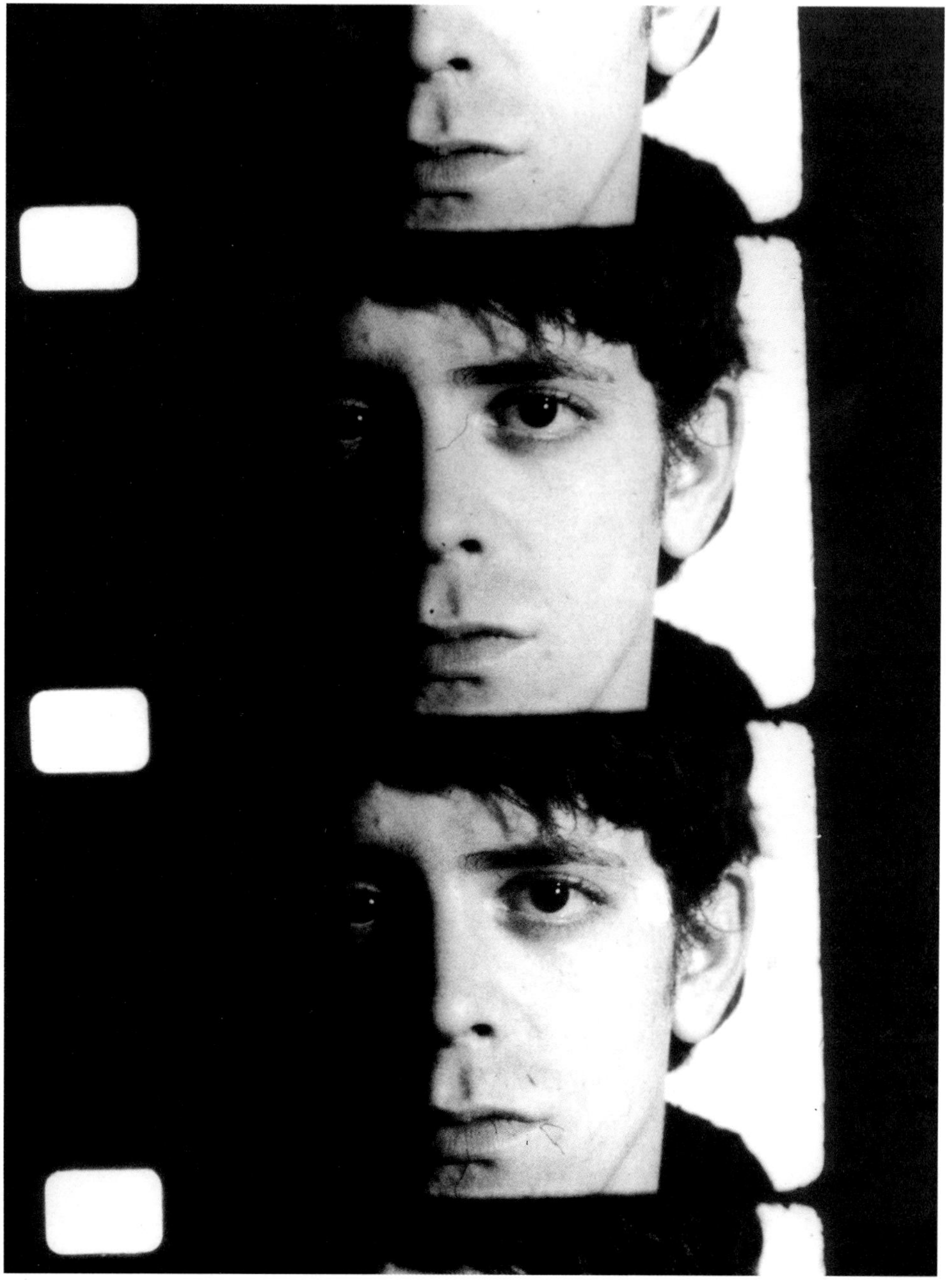

Lou Reed Screen Test,
1966

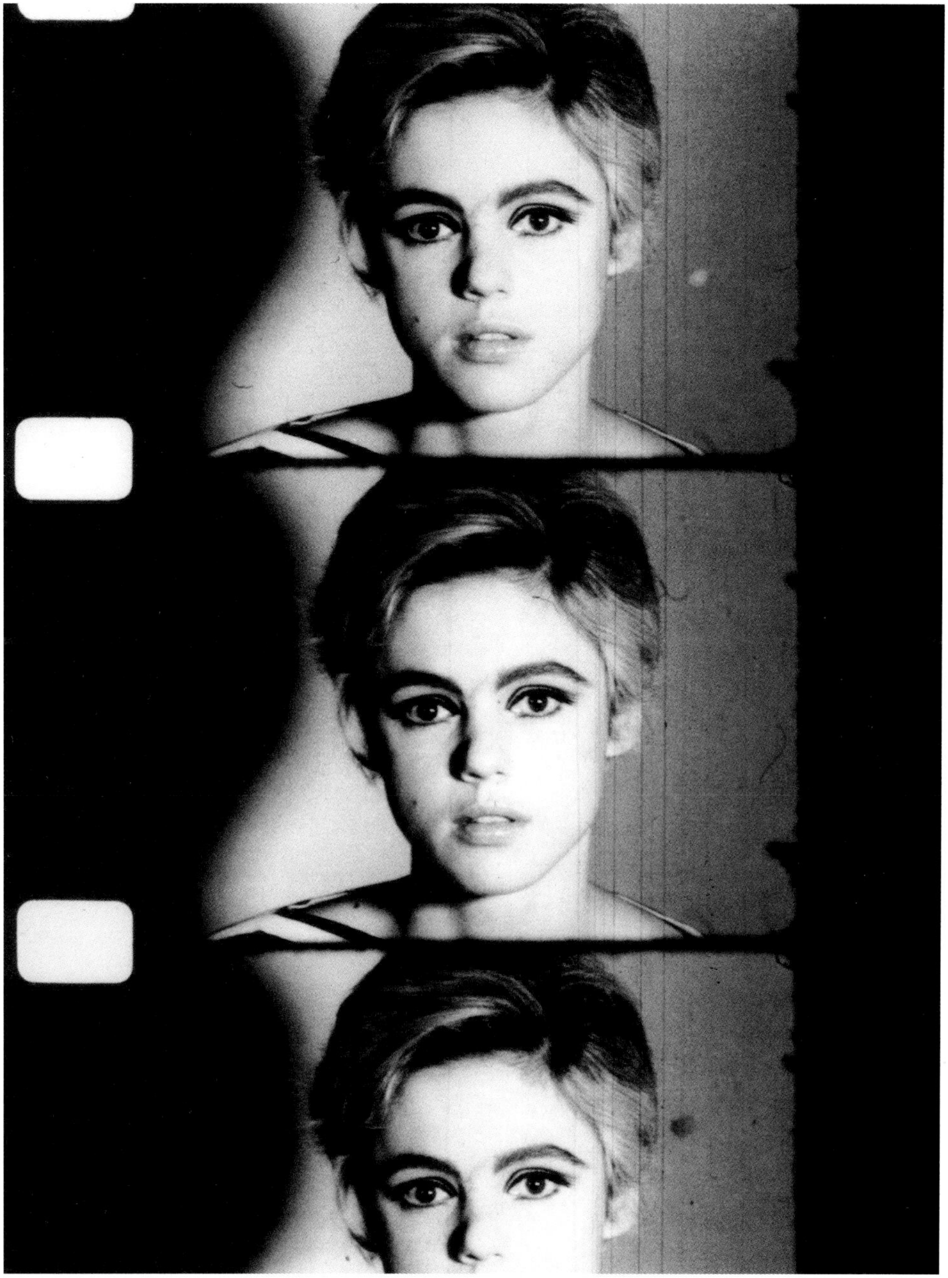

Edie Sedgwick Screen Test, 1965

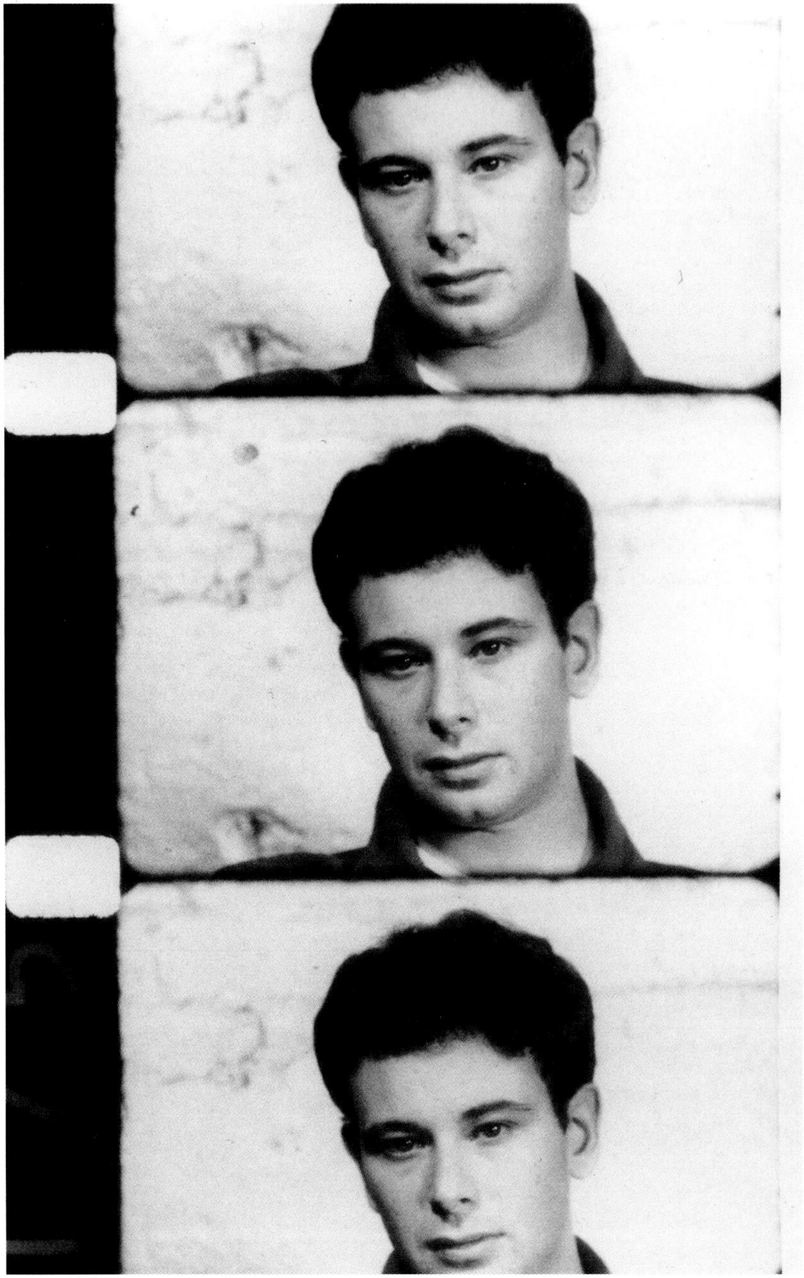

Ronald Tavel Screen Test,
1965

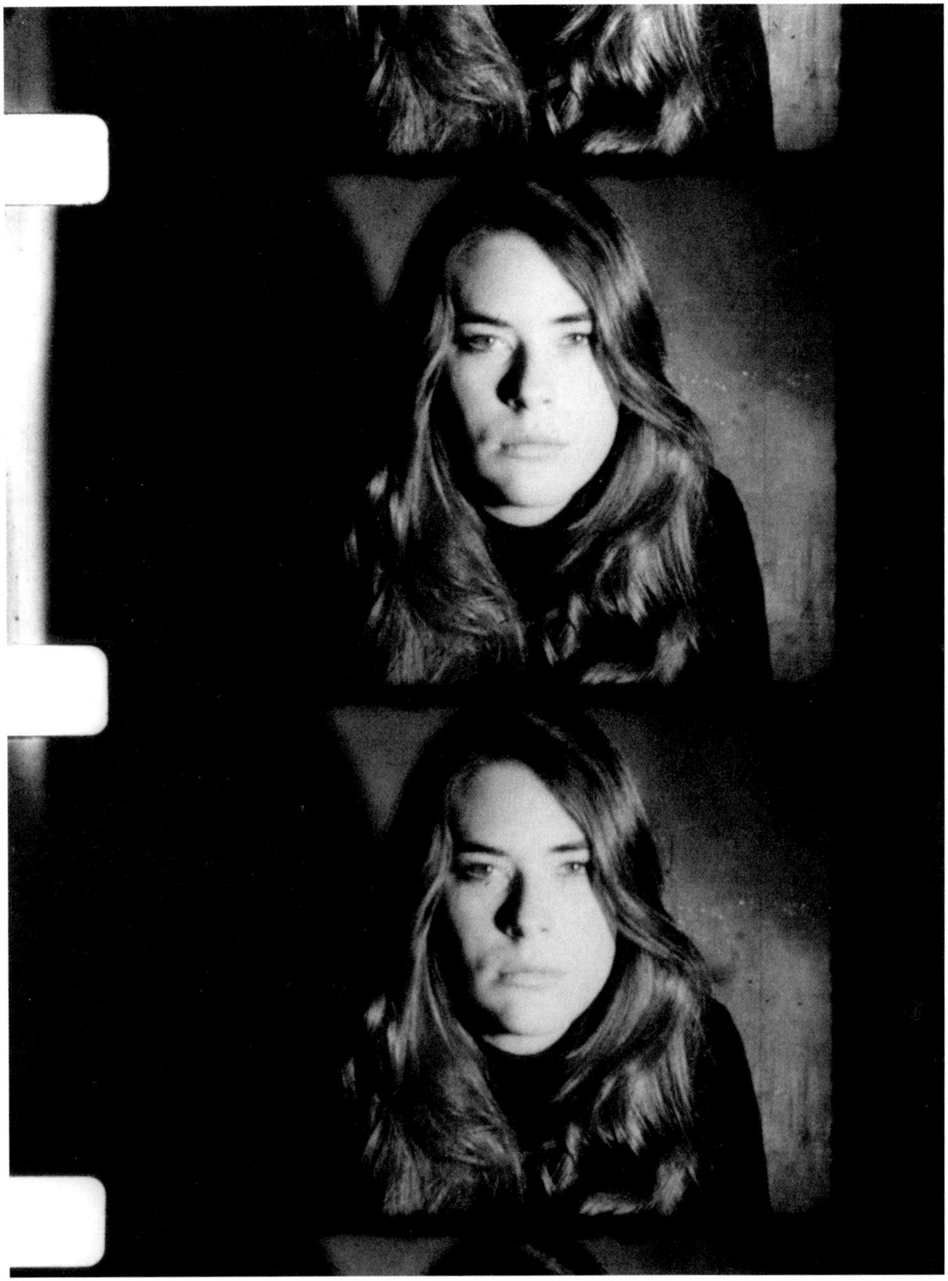

Mary Woronov Screen Test, 1965

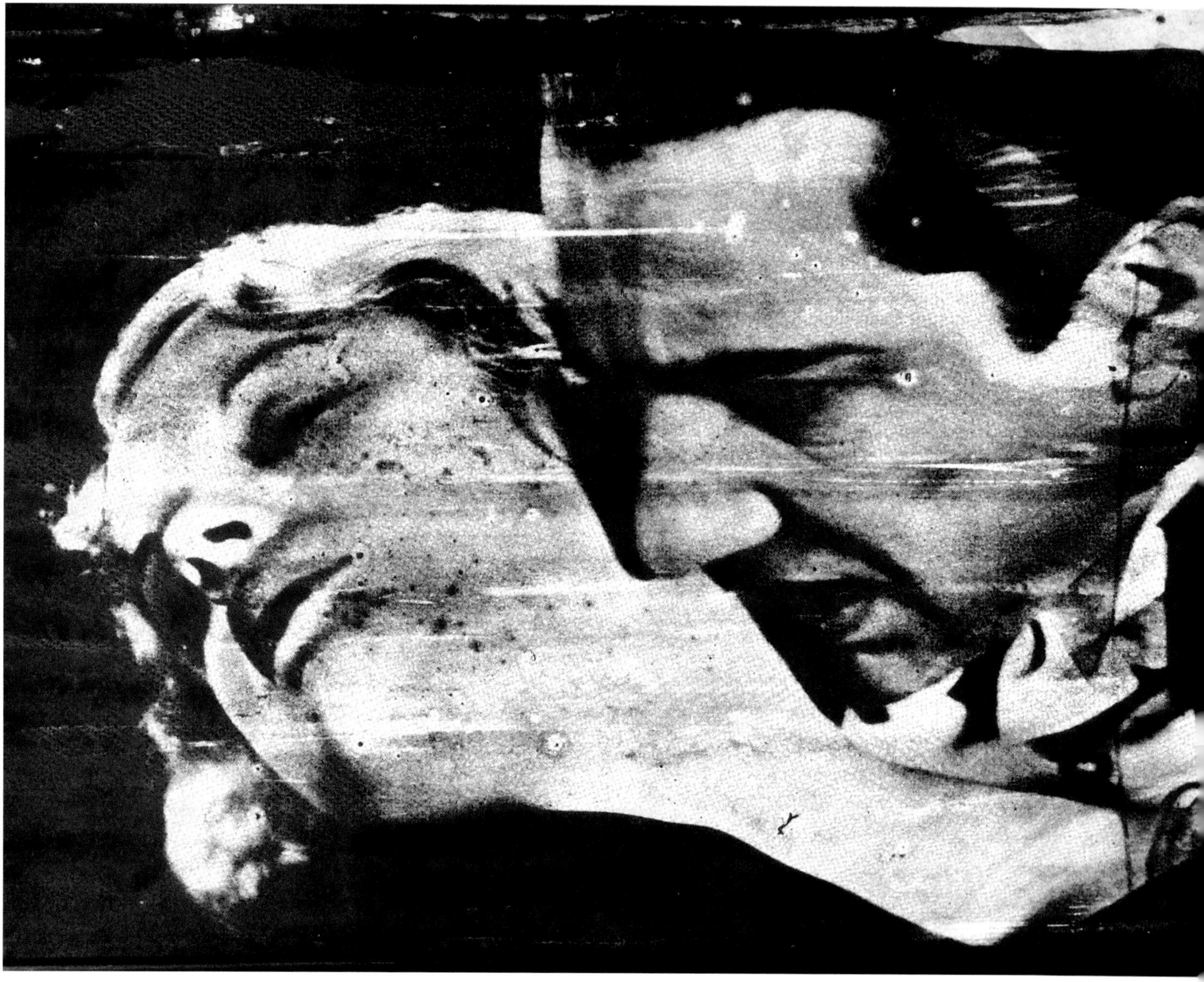

four
the kiss

When Pablo Picasso last visited with Henri Matisse back in 1954, Matisse said from his bedside, "When one of us dies, there will be some things the other will never be able to talk of with anyone else." [1] Silence is deadly.

1. Francoise Gilot & Carlton Lake, *Life With Picasso*, McGraw-Hill, New York, 1964.

Yet Matisse's remark would mirror and resonate through the legacy I've inherited from my friendship and working relationship with Andy... Andy Warhol.

In the early afternoon of November 22, 1963, Andy and I are walking through Grand Central Station – for whatever reason, I cannot recall – when President Kennedy's assassination breaks out over the airwaves. When we reach the exit facing Lexington & 43rd, Andy turns to me and says, "Let's go to work."

We hop the Woodlawn Express to 86th Street, head straightway to the "Firehouse", as we called the ramshackle building with a facade of chipped paint, once home to "Hook & Ladder 13", where we silkscreened the paintings. And it's here, as the afternoon light filters through the dusty-second-floor windows, we silkscreen what would come to be known as *The Kiss*, the now infamous image of Bela Lugosi, taken from a film-still from *Dracula* (1931), biting into the neck of a rapturous sleeping blonde, Helen Chandler, his co-star.

What's the significance of how this day unfolded? Perhaps none. But the nation's leader had just met death and disaster at the hands of an assassin somewhere in Texas, and here we are on our hands and knees, pushing the squeegee across an ordinary sheet of white paper upon which an image of ghoulish violence emerges from an earlier time.

Opposite: *The Kiss (Bela Lugosi)*, 1963. Silkscreen ink on paper, 30" X 40".

Though seemingly unrelated, the two events are, I believe connected by gesture. The hand has a hand in it, and eyes, too. Two pairs of hands, in fact.

Could this day at the Firehouse been Andy's ironic way of separating himself from the immediate reality of a violent event with an equally violent yet fictive cinematic *tableau vivant* framed as a publicity shot? Was he dispelling any notion of actually creating an artwork, one that had the potential to deeply affect him? Was this yet another instance of his apparent indifference – "When you see a gruesome picture over and over again, it doesn't really have any effect"? We had no way of knowing.

At another time, Andy remarked upon several news photos I had researched on car crashes, "Are the victims still alive?" Was he playing dumb or just being his usual, amoral, deadpan self? He rarely let on how he felt.

If we look more closely at *The Kiss*, we see motion where there's stillness. It's apparently night; the young woman's bedroom. The physicality of all these human mistakes is nearly tactile, rough in places. We'd invariably miss a spot, here or there. Whenever we set out to silkscreen an image, we had no idea how the final print would turn out. Magic takes over. The kind follows. What might've been prose is now poetry.

In one of his most detached, yet equally revealing and self-deprecating remarks, Andy was quoted as saying, *I wish I were a machine. I don' t want to be hurt. I don' t want human emotions. I' ve never been touched by a painting. I don' t want to think. The world would be easier to live in if we were all machines. It' s nothing in the end anyway. It doesn' t matter what anyone does.*[2]

Did he really believe this?

The Kiss looks quite different today. Its aura of sexual violence has been returned to the original context of celluloid make-believe, though the gesture of its re-creation, as I mentioned a moment ago, still remains visibly intact in those spontaneous, dried-out streaks, as if in that one frozen moment a flash of lightning lit up the violence from a window nearby.

Now, only the silence remains, only the give-and-take rapport let loose in the New York air, an image we lived through for a day, some things I could never be able to talk of with anyone else.

2. John Hellpern, "The Fantasy World Of Warhol", *The Observer* Magazine, London, June 12, 1966.

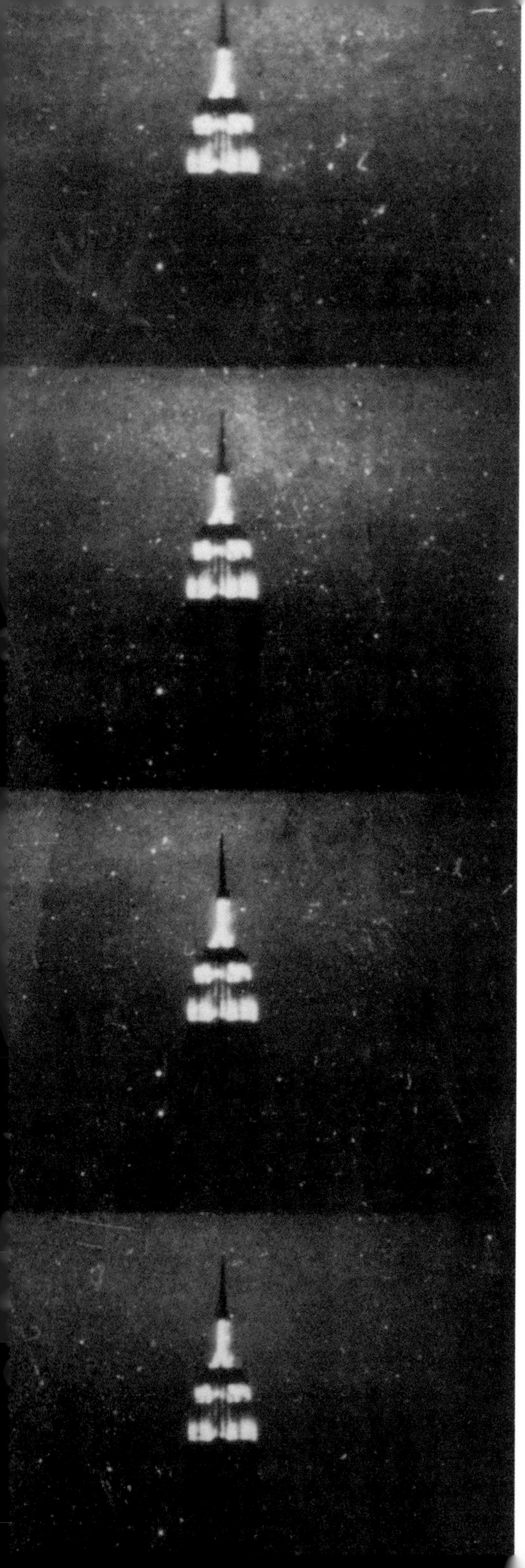

five

the empire state building is a star!

On a somewhat hazy afternoon – Saturday, to be exact, 25 July 1964 – a group – Andy Warhol, Gerard Malanga, Jonas Mekas, Marie Desert, and John Palmer – enter the Time-Life Building, corner of 50th/Avenue of the Americas, with bags and boxes of camera equipment in tow, and ascend to the 44th floor headquarters of the Rockefeller Foundation, to be met at the front door by Henry Romney, a Vice-president of the foundation.

Henry ushers us into his office, which offers an unobstructed view of the Empire State Building, 16 blocks to the southeast. After a few minutes of schmoozing, we begin breaking out the equipment, separating cables, film-loading bags, tripod, and boxes of Eastman Kodak raw stock, and with meticulous care, fix the Auricon camera onto the tripod's metal plate. This is the first time Andy would make use of this highly professional, though antiquated piece of equipment.

It was John's eye that established the compositional frame that would remain fixed for the next seven hours. John and Jonas took turns loading and threading the film every 35 minutes. Henry, Marie, Andy and I looked on in wonder, absorbed at times by the slightest change in cloud movement or of airplane lights flickering across the night sky – gradually, as the night wore on, becoming overcast. For the most part, Andy looked bored, as he pored his way through pictures in magazines. He had a habit of speed-reading this way. To break the monotony I decided to notate a few minutes worth of conversation verbatim.

John Palmer: Why is nothing happening. I don't understand.

Henry Romney: What would you like to happen?

Opposite: Frame enlargement from *Empire* (1964).

John:	I don't know. Is the Foundation going to know that you did this?
Henry:	I have a feeling that all we're filming is the red light.
Andy Warhol:	Oh, Henry! Jonas, it's your turn to say something – you're being written down.
John:	Jonas is changing the films just like me.
Henry:	Andy, now is the time to pan.
John:	Definitely not!
Henry:	The film is a whole new bag when the lights go off.
John:	You have to go to where the action is.
Andy:	Henry, what is the meaning of action?
Henry:	Action is the absence of inaction.
Andy:	Let's say things intelligent.
Gerard Malanga:	Listen, we don't want to deceive the public, dear.
John:	We're hitting a new milestone.
Andy:	Henry, say Nietzsche.
Henry:	Another aphorism?
John:	B movies are better than A movies.
Andy:	Jack Smith in every garage.

Marie Desert: Someday we're all going to live underground and this movie will be a smash.

John: The lack of action in the last three 1200-foot rolls is alarming.

Henry: You have to mark these rolls very carefully so as not to get them mixed up.

John: Why, are we getting sloppy?

Marie: I read somewhere that art is created in fun.

Jonas Mekas: Did you know the Empire State Building sways?

John: This is the strangest shooting session I've ever been in.

Gerard: We should set up windowpanes for the audience to look through.

Andy: The Empire State Building is a star!

John: Has anything happened at all?

Marie: No.

John: Good.

Henry: The script calls for a "pan" right at this point. I don't see why my artistic advice is being constantly rejected.

Henry to Andy: The bad children are smoking pot again.

Andy: It's like Flash Gordon riding into space.

John: I don't think anything has happened in the last hundred feet.

Gerard: Jonas, how long is this interview supposed to be?

Jonas: As much as you have.

Andy: An 8 hour hard-on!

Gerard: We have to maintain our cool at all times.

John: We have to have this film licensed. I wonder if Ivy will look at this movie?

Gerard: I thought you said "I wonder if Ivy will look this good".

John: That's your hang-up.

Andy: You're supposed to be writing things down.

John: Nothing has happened in the last half hour. The audience viewing *Empire* will be convinced after seeing the film that they viewed it from the 44th floor of the Time-Life Building and that's a whole bag in itself.

Jonas: I don't think the last reel was a waste.

Henry to John: I think it's too playful.

John Palmer, a young filmmaker, should rightly be credited with the concept for the film, *Empire*. It was John's ingenuity and proficiency that most impressed Warhol to go ahead and rent the movie camera needed to see this project through. John was considered something of a *wunderkind* among the underground filmmakers, like Ron Rice, Jack Smith, and Harry Smith.

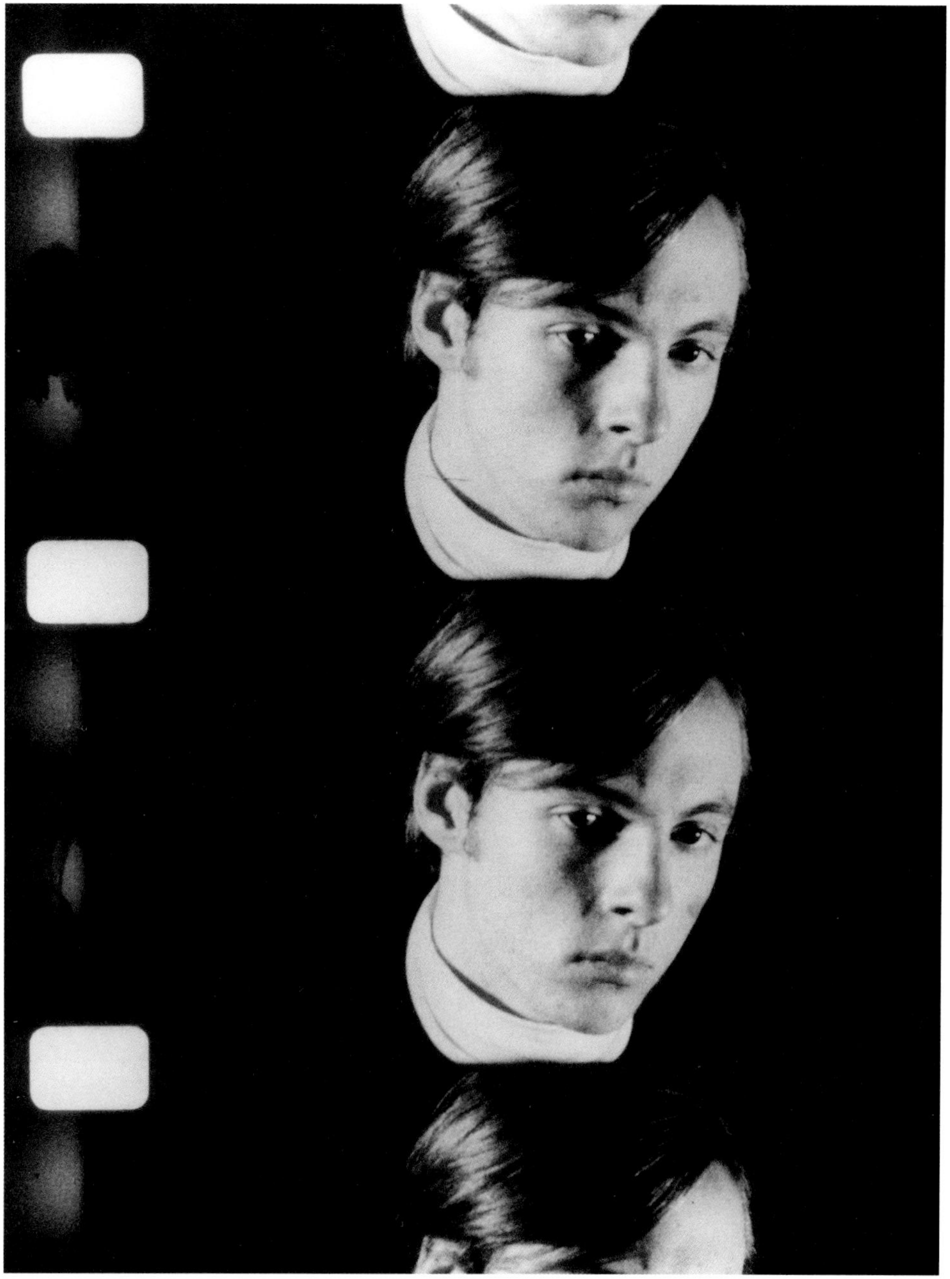

John Palmer Screen Test, 1964.

The Auricon, a 16mm single-system sound camera, had the distinct advantage of accommodating a 1200-foot magazine, allowing for a 35-minute take at the flick of a switch. Ironically, the camera was chosen not for its sound capacity, but in cutting time while reels were being changed, to assimilate the nearly exact ratio of reel time to real time, as first theorized by John – "1 to 1" – adhering to a Warholian principle already established to an initial degree with the film, *Sleep*, a year earlier.

It was also through John's acquaintance with Henry Romney, that we would secure Henry's office for the making of the movie. John had met Henry through Frederick Eberstadt, a society photographer he assisted shortly after arriving in New York from Hartford, fresh out of high school.

It was through Andy's bank-rolling the film that John was to realize his dream, though he never once assumed to want credit for his ideas – and John's mind possessed an abundance of concepts. This enthusiasm translated into an activity in the name of art.

John arranged for the rental of the Auricon through F & B Ceco, a film equipment outlet over on West 43rd Street. At John's instructions I placed an order with Eastman Kodak, which maintained facilities on 72nd Street and York Avenue (now occupied by Sotheby's, ironically) for fourteen 1200-foot rolls of black & white Tri-X stock, which totalled 8 hours/10-minutes unedited running-time, though we had no way of knowing that we'd end up with two unexposed rolls. *Empire* consists of 12 reels (at about 35-minutes apiece), totalling 7 hours of unedited 1-to-1 ratio footage. "The Long Take", as Pier Paolo Pasolini, the Italian filmmaker, once characterized it in another context.

The camera's rental would cover for the weekend only, so Andy decided to use up the remaining two rolls on Henry Geldzahler smoking a cigar for 70 minutes at the Factory while sitting in one position on the infamous couch of *Couch* fame. This film would be aptly titled, *Henry Geldzahler*.

In one weekend Andy was able to add two films to his already burgeoning list of titles. He would manage to create more films in one year than any of his contemporaries could claim in a lifetime. Jonas Mekas spearheaded him on. In four months Andy would graduate to sound. His Bolex would be a thing of the past.

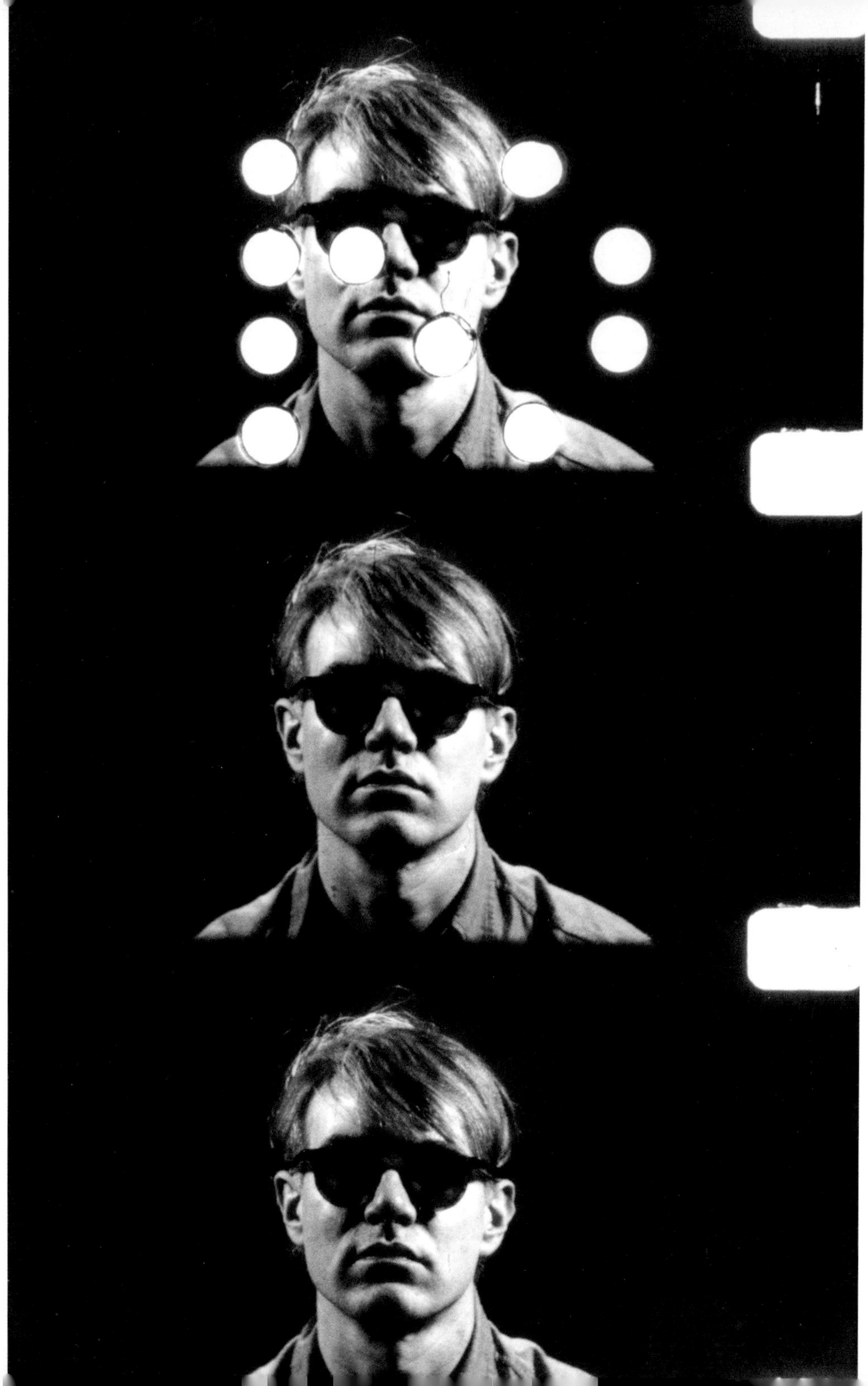

six

andy warhol on: people places food art

PEOPLE

We're pop people. We're formed by television. I think people are becoming plastic. I love plastic. I want to be plastic. A pop person is like a vacuum that eats up everything. He's made up from what he's seen. Television has done it. You don't have to read anymore. Books will be out, television will stay. Movies will go out, television will stay. And that's why people who can give things back are considered very talented. We took a tour of Universal Studios in Los Angeles and inside or outside the place, it was very difficult to tell what was real. They're not-real people trying to say something. And we're real people not trying to say anything.

PLACES

California will be the first state to go nude. I think it's wonderful. The people are so gorgeous. The people are cleaner and more gorgeous here than in New York. All the new fads start here. Everything's so gorgeous here. In New York there's everything to do. In Los Angeles there's nothing to do. And San Francisco is in between, a lot of things happening and kind of compressed together. The City is glamorous. Like Paris. I didn't think I'd like Paris, but I did. I think Paris knows more about everything.

But you see things like in Hollywood. Los Angeles is a dream city, it's the first American city. I love the look of it, it's so American. It's really gorgeous.

I don't make quality judgements. Things just are. You know, wow!

Opposite: From *Andy Warhol: Portraits Of The Artist As A Young Man*, a film by Gerard Malanga, 1964–65.

FOOD

I don't eat very much. I just like to have food as decoration, just to look at.

ART

I don't paint things anymore. I still make movies. I don't believe in editing my movies, they're all just cut in the camera. Now I'm making a film that will be 31 days long. It's the story of Christ. I quit painting because people said they were getting bored with what I was doing. Now we're doing what before I was just painting. Now what we do is a totality – music, sound, lights, patterns, everything. This is total. If you're bored with one thing, you can do something else. If you don't like the music, you can look at the films. It's pop Hollywood. It's what Hollywood is all about. It's like going to Disneyland and deciding what trip you want to take. The show is so simple there's nothing to explain or understand.

–ca. 1966.

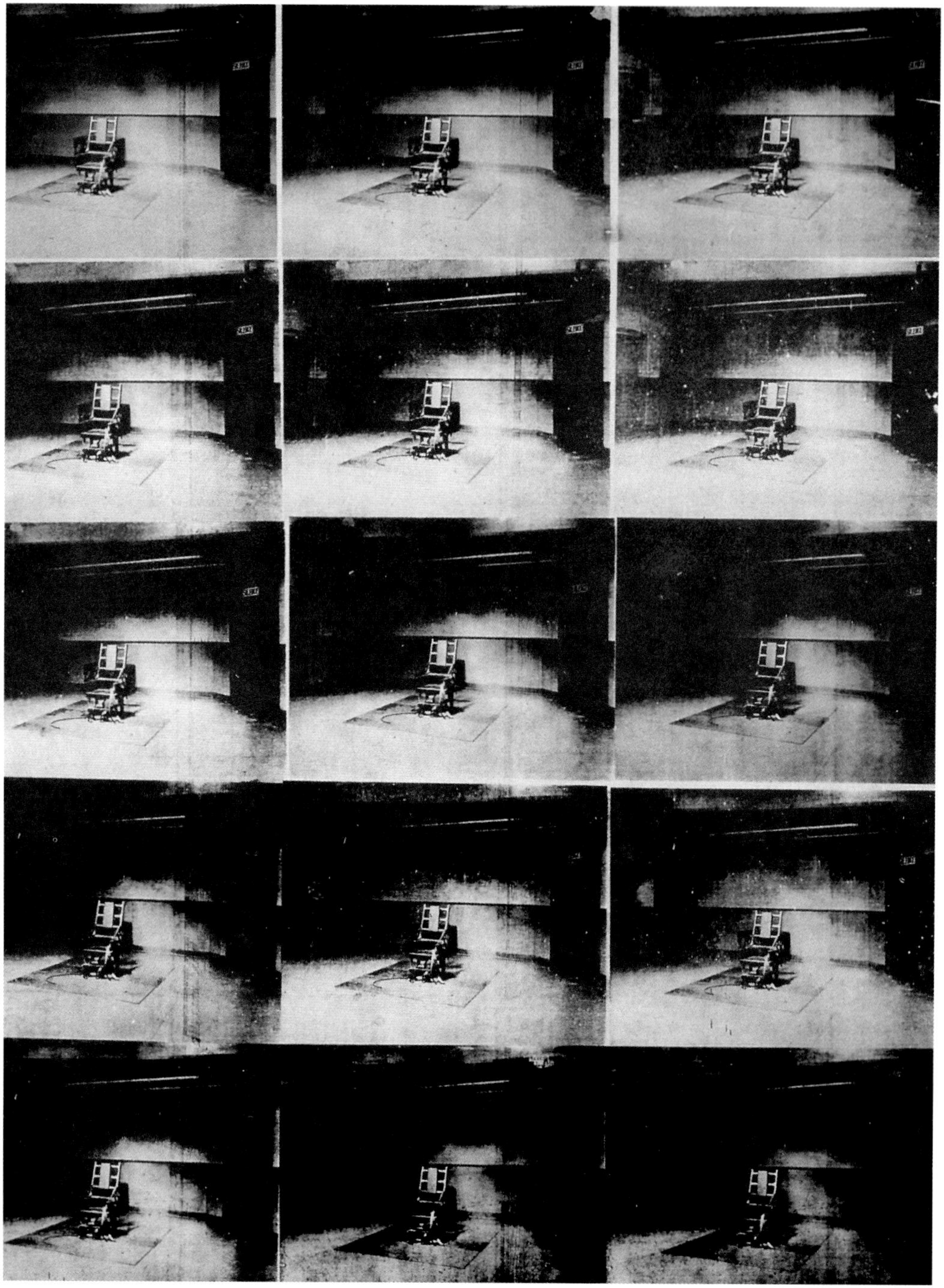

seven

electric chairs on display in toronto for first time!

I don't remember rightly who came up with the idea that we take a train from New York to Toronto. Was this Andy's way of secretly experiencing "real time" at the moment it's happening? I think we were both intrigued with the idea of extended train travel. I was certain I'd get some work done. We didn't anticipate how long that journey would be. Andy's *Electric Chair* paintings would be on exhibit for the first time as a group at the Jerrold Morris International Gallery, and that's what this trip was all about.

On March 18th 1965, Andy and I embarked on the New York Central departing Grand Central Terminal around 4:00pm. We sat across the aisle from each other immersed in *Vogue* and *Bazaar* and *The New York Times*, killing time as it were. I brought along John Ashbery's *The Tennis Court Oath*, which I'd already read, figuring I might write something epic along the way. Occasionally we'd share enthusiasms for some fashion pictures. A bit of gossip here or there. Neither of us had ever been to Toronto before, so we didn't know what to expect, simply not knowing anyone there who could show us around.

The train came with a dining-car, which proved a respite from what was becoming a very tedious trip. There were even artificial flowers in a vase. We both ordered the meat loaf. Andy opted for economy coach, so we slept in our seats, rolled up in our coats.

Early the following morning, soon after the train pulled out of Buffalo we were awakened by the conductor announcing that passengers would be required to present their passports upon reaching the Canadian checkpoint. It would be fully an hour or more before the train would reach Toronto in a blustering rain.

Opposite: Detail from *Blue Electric Chair* (1963). Silkscreen ink on synthetic polymer paint on canvas; two panels, each 8′ 9″ X 6′ 8.25″.

Will Toronto remember us? It could be we never arrived as our brief stay still remains a fleeting memory. Or it could be that Toronto, for those couple of days, ceased to exist, and we merely had gone somewhere and come back with our lives snatched from memory, or vice versa.

I can't remember how it was coming into the station. I'm certain no-one was there to greet us. We hailed a taxi. I looked out at the streets everywhere. The city was consumed in a light rain. The sky was a large gray haze. It seemed there were few people.

The hotel room was modern and bland and with twin beds. The big bay window looked out over much of the skyline and beyond a shiny gray sky. The sun was trying to break through. It would take another decade before Toronto would discover the skyscraper.

Imagine, the première of Andy's *Electric Chair* paintings in Toronto! *Electric Chair*s assembled four up and six across, or am I just making this up? It could be an entirely different installation altogether. Each painting seemed identical, yet no two were really alike. Every color imaginable. I remembered, then, while slowly looking at them, Andy's remark how adding pretty colors to a picture as gruesome as this would change people's perceptions of acceptance. Suddenly the space of the room cancels everything else out. The chair is no longer a weapon and it's not the chair anymore.

The opening for the most part was uneventful, uninspiring. Hardly anyone showed up. Star-seekers were elsewhere or perhaps non-existent. Even the press was a no-show, as I recall. I kept thinking to myself, "Where are we?" Somehow I felt we were meant to be elsewhere. I even lacked any impression of the restaurant we'd been taken to afterwards. For all I know we may have eaten alone.

Toronto was a sleepy city in 1965. Nothing about it seemed up to the moment – more hermetic as if waiting for us to discover its secrets. It was like a *film noir* experience transposed into a dusty metropolitan light. Next day we had less than a day to search and explore. Our time was not entirely our own. Much to do. One or two meetings had already been arranged with the press, and then we'd be on the same train back to New York.

As much as Andy professed an attraction to chance, he was not much into walking the streets. We did little wandering. Discovering a bookshop was like an oasis for me. Andy meandered around the news counter and I made a bee-line for the poetry shelves where I'd discover all these books by this poet unknown to me, Leonard Cohen.

I regret not having the time to explore Toronto's streets, to search out their mysteries. The train took us back to New York.

The return trip seemed even longer, imprisoned by time. I was glad to be back. We took the subway up to his house and Julia, his mom, made us lunch. Later, I headed down to the Factory, sorted through papers, did some prep work. I was mentally and physically exhausted. I think by the next day we started setting up for a huge painting of an atomic bomb blast. We never spoke of that trip again.

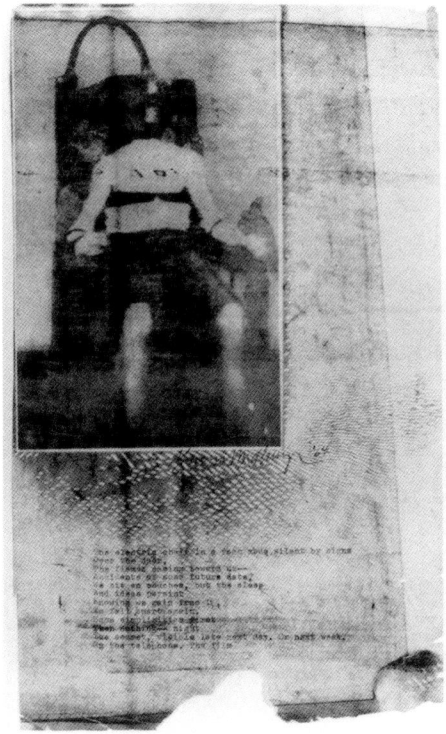

Untitled (The electric chair in the room made silent by signs); Gerard Malanga/ Andy Warhol, from the Thermofax Series, ca. 1964.

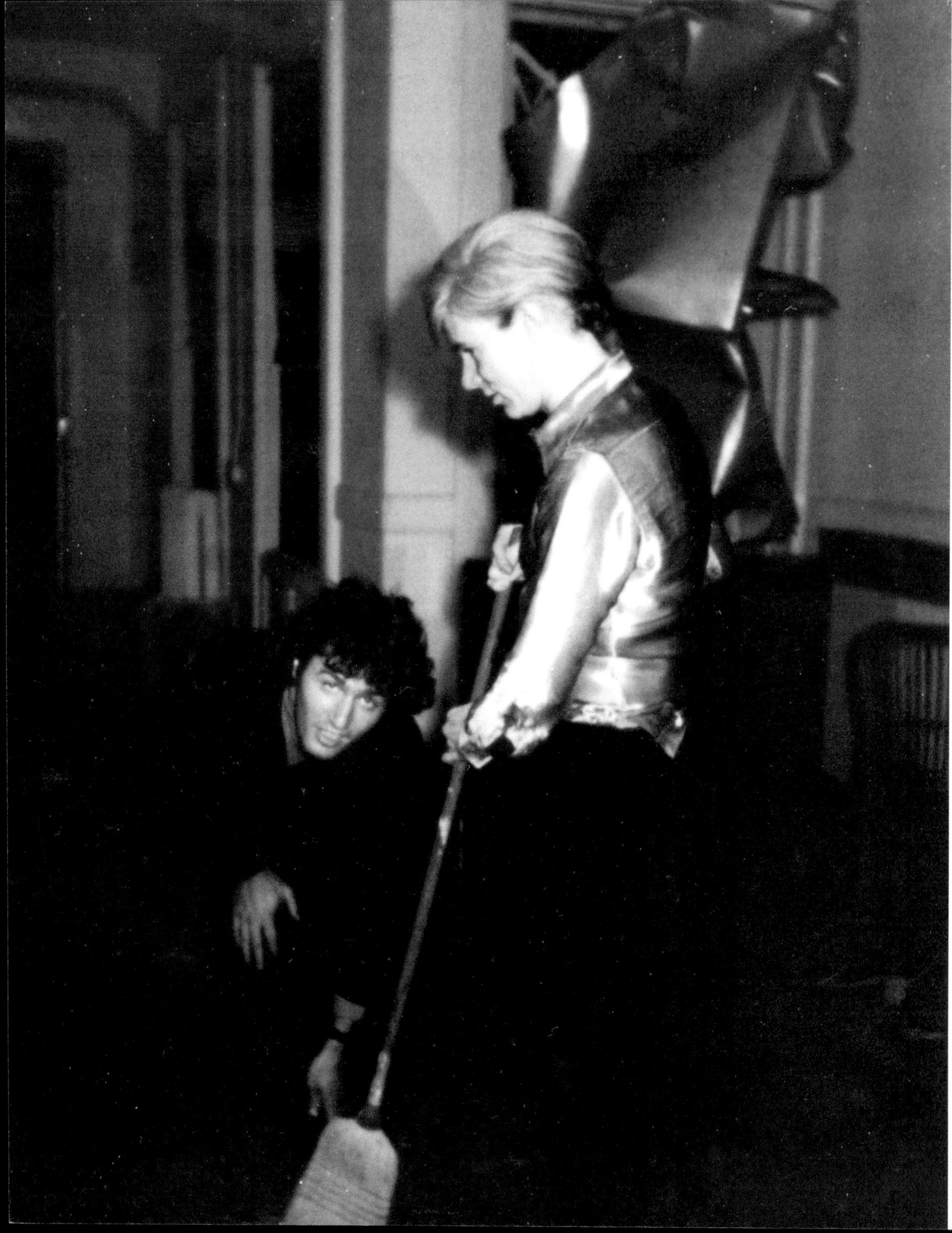

eight
the warhol / yale lecture

Delivered at Yale University under the auspices of Dr. Rainer Crone and the Department of Art History. November 10, 1976, New Haven, CT

The poet Charles Olson has said: ONE PERCEPTION MUST IMMEDIATELY AND DIRECTLY LEAD TO A FURTHER PERCEPTION. He did not intend that one perception leading to a further perception be linear; for what he emphatically states is exactly what it says, is the matter of, at *all* points in the topic to be discussed. In other words, my thinking, my perceptions are an instance of all the complexity of a way of remembering and thus re-creating my life from where I am now *physically* in time. Likewise, and perhaps more to the point is what Robert Creeley maintains: "If you say one thing it always will lead to more than you had thought to say." Everything in effect is or will be falling into place as I begin to work my way through the past and the terms of this talk which, in effect, is meant to give form to time.

At sixteen I wrote a high school term paper on the French poet, Lautréamont – precursor to the Surrealists. I had already read nearly all the works of the French Symbolists, dadaists and Surrealists, including important criticism written about them by Anna Balakiah and Wallace Fowlie; the WPA poets of the '30s; the "War Poets" of the '40s; the poets centered around Black Mountain College; the poets of the San Francisco Renaissance; the poets comprising the New York School during the period of Abstract Expressionism. By the time I was eighteen I was a well-seasoned poet, like they say.

Opposite: Andy Warhol and Gerard Malanga sweeping up the Factory floor, 33 Union Square West, 1969.

I was studying poetry with Daisy Aldan who was my highschool English teacher. She was my guiding spirit through the world of poetry and poets. She made me aware of my feeling for language. She guided me in such a way that I willed myself into becoming a poet, to assume an identity – the identity of being a poet.

It is by fixing the mind on the possibilities of combining words to create an image that a man becomes a poet. The poet is merely the outcome of his accumulating by will power mental concepts called poems, becoming that to which his mind has moved towards in making new language.

FLASHBACK

I was introduced to Andy Warhol by the poet, Charles Henri Ford, on June 9th 1963 at a courtyard poetry reading sponsored by the New School for Social Research. Charles was already aware of my skill as a silkscreen technician and knew that Andy, whom I did not know or had even heard of, was in need of someone who would assist him in silkscreening paintings. Andy asked me to come to work for him.

"How much would you want to be paid?" he asked.

"How about a dollar twenty-five an hour?" I said.

"Can you begin tomorrow?"

"How about Tuesday?"

"Okay," he said.

He gave me his address and I told him that I would arrive around 11am. It was settled.

Tuesday. I had no idea what to expect – what would be waiting for me. The address Andy gave me was, to my surprise, an abandoned red-brick firehouse on East 87th Street between Third and Lexington avenues. The door was ajar. I stepped in. I called out to him. From the second floor a voice – "I'm up here."

I climbed the rickety stair. Andy was turning a canvas around on the floor while two people looked on – a photographer, Ed Wallowitch and a young woman, Barbara Rose.

"This is my new assistant, Gerard. He's a poet!" he announced in an almost boyish enthusiasm. A few photos were taken – photos that have since become famous, freezing a moment in historical time – a commemoration of the first day on the job that would last seven years. We take a break – lunch at one of the super de luxe luncheonettes at 86th and

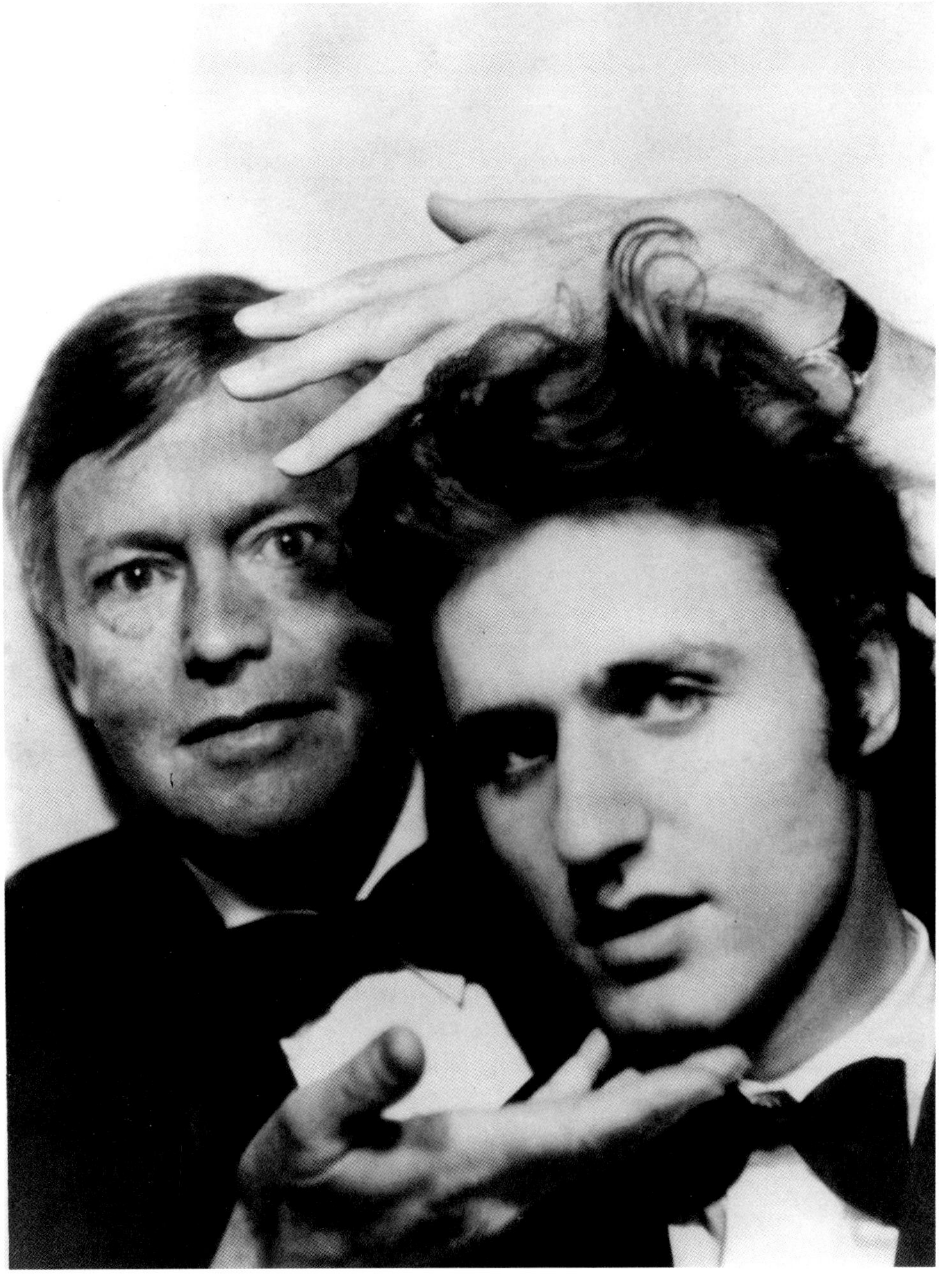

Charles Henri Ford and Gerard Malanga in the photomaton, 1968.

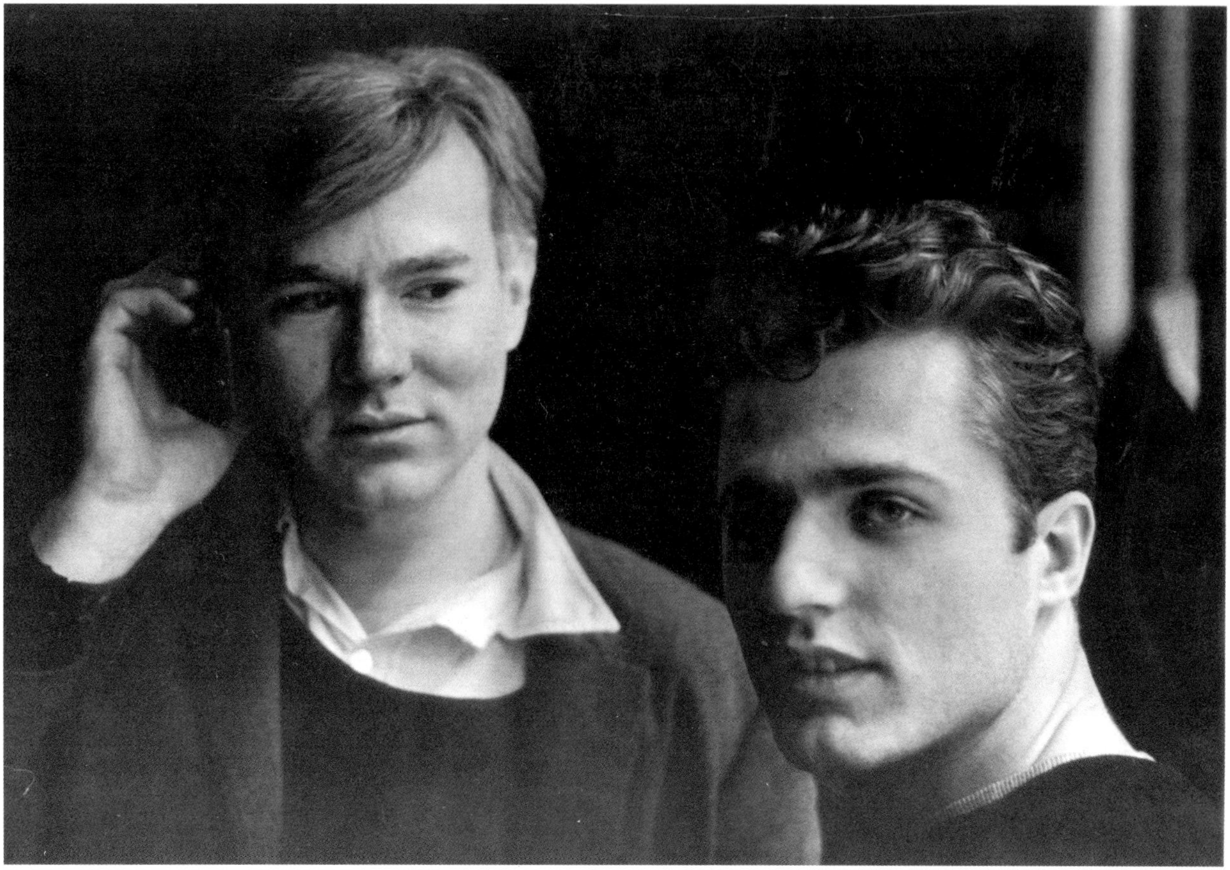

Gerard Malanga with Andy Warhol the first day on the job at the Firehouse, NYC, June 11th, 1963.

Lexington. I sit beside Barbara, inquire about her work. She tells me she's been writing art criticism for *Art News* – "went to school at Smith," etc.

Barbara and Ed part. Andy and I return to the firehouse. He familiarizes me with how he's been working with silkscreens. A simple method, less complicated then when I was screening 30 yards of fabric for a textile firm four summers back. The image – a portrait of Elizabeth Taylor, pink face, red lips, green eyeshadow, painted in by hand with liquitex over a hand-painted silver background. The silkscreen is applied, laid down over the abstract color shapes that Andy remarks look like Alex Katz paintings. Black silkscreen paint squeegeed across the entire screen in one motion and then pulled back again. The paint seeps through the tiny openings in the screen. The complete image is registered at last. A painting, simply titled *Liz, 1963* (40 x 40 inches), the first of hundreds of paintings we were to silkscreen together.

Now the difficult part – cleaning the screen. Varnolene and rolls of paper-towels are used. Newspaper laid out on the floor. I remove excess paint from the screen. I pour the Varnolene, making sure that all parts of the screen are thoroughly soaked. I wash the screen with paper towels in a circular motion. When all paint is removed I dampen the screen with more Varnolene and wipe dry. The painting is finished. The screen cleaned.

"Would you like to come back to my place for some tea? I live just a couple of blocks from here." I become inwardly tense at the suggestion but don't look obvious. I accept the invitation, all the while thinking he wants to put the make on me. It's not so much the invite that makes me tense but something about the way he looks I can't quite make out. He has an almost ghostly appearance, as if the pigment in his skin were sandpapered, transparent. I learn later that he did at one time have his skin sandpapered. And at eight years of age suffered from a nervous condition called St. Vitus Dance.

Andy lives in a three-storey building near the corner of 89th on Lexington. The facade painted an almost shocking flamingo pink. He shows me to the living-room, or what once was a living-room, now cluttered. Everywhere I look – piles of newspapers, UPI photos of car accidents, antiques of Americana vintage, and paintings of Campbell Soup Cans. His paintings! *Why, of course!* I tell myself. Now I know where I've seen his paintings before. He's the one I'd read about in *Show* magazine. He's one of these pop artists. The soup can paintings were reproduced with the article.

"Would you like a 7Up? I'm just going to see how my mother is doing. I'll be right back."

"Okay."

Before he leaves he turns on the stereo: "Sally Goes Round The Roses" over and over again.

Moments later: "My mother made us some hamburgers... and here's the 7Up."

He checks in with his answering-service. He makes a couple of phone-calls. "Sally Goes Round the Roses" in the background. "That's my favourite pop song," he says. "At one time I was going to be part of this rock-group, along with Patti Oldenburg and La Monte Young. It never got off the ground."

Andy was interested in movies. We'd take in three or four, sometimes five, movies a week after work, either on East 86th Street or in the Times Square area. We went to see *The Carpetbaggers* five times in one week. He was impressed that I had a knowledge of film. He was aware of my involvement working with Willard Maas and Marie Menken, husband/wife avant-garde filmmakers. He wanted to make films himself, but didn't know how – didn't know where to begin. Charles Henri Ford was also aware of Andy's interest in films. In fact, he was interested in making films himself. He already had a knowledge of film having worked with photography some years back. Charles and I took Andy to Peerless Camera, a huge retail outlet at 43rd and Lexington, and helped him select an easy but semi-professional camera – a Bolex 16 with zoom lens and automatic motordrive attachment.

Andy was left to his own devices. He thought it would be glamorous to make a film of a movie star sleeping for eight hours. In his mind he cast his favourite movie star, Brigitte Bardot; but he knew that was an unfulfilled fantasy. So, instead he asked a friend, poet John Giorno, if he could make a film of him sleeping and John agreed. Andy spent a few nights filming John sleeping, an hour or two at a time. John had given Andy a key to the apartment, certain he would already be asleep when Andy arrived.

The motorized Bolex set up, loaded with a 100-ft. roll of black & white film. Shooting consisted simply of turning on a small spotlight, starting the camera and letting the magazine run out to the end. There was never a camera-movement and only an occasional zoom. Editing consisted of splicing together each 100-foot take with clear leader, invariably leaving intact the slowly fading light-leaks and the perforated tags that the are beginning and end of each roll. It was Andy's way of not editing or leaving anything out. Everything was useful to his aesthetic purpose and thus took on a meaning where no meaning existed previously. Not every three-minute sequence was shot from the same position however. With each group of, let's say, four or five rolls, Andy would choose a new angle: a close-up of the breathing abdomen, a long lateral shot angled from the knee, thus creating a foreshortening that resembled in part a painting by Mantegna; a close-up of the face, or the body turned on its side away from the camera. A sectioning-off of a torso mostly. What resulted was about six hours of footage; but six hours wasn't eight hours, and Andy had intended the film to be as long in real-time as was average for any sleeping person. So, Andy and I assembled and constructed the film by printing about two-hours of duplicate shots and spliced these shots within the film's continuity to match up with the original footage, thus stretching six hours into eight hours running-and-real-time. When the first reversal print was made the duplicate prints that had been printed from the original footage and reinserted, turned out grainy because they were second generation prints.

Sleep was Andy's first film-experiment and was made about a month after I began working with him. *Sleep* is a fascinating experience to see; first because you sit through it. You don't leave. And, oddly enough, the people who do leave, leave during the first ten minutes of the film. It can almost be guaranteed that people who sit through the first hour will stay to the end. By "sit" I really mean "remain" because people will stand up for awhile, go out for a few minutes to the restroom or have a drink of water or a sandwich, but they come back.

This is an entirely different experience-portrayal than sleep usually receives in a film. We do not see the man in pyjamas taking off his slippers while sitting on the edge of the bed. We do not see the yawn. We do not see the hand turn off the light on the bedside table. We do not see the head settling down on the pillow, the closing of the eyes, and the slight nod and smile. Nor do we see the unmoving shadow of Venetian blinds cast by an unmoving moon. In short, none of the conventions that were used in the past to say "sleep" have been used.

Instead, we see a man sleeping. We see him twitch, move slightly, roll over. There grows up an impression of reality that owes much to this time element. We begin to have a feeling of expectancy. Is he going to wake up? Will he roll over? Will he expose himself before us? What we are seeing is not a statement such as one might read: "John slept last night". Nor is it an episode that shows passage of time. We are approaching the seeing and experiencing and understanding of "sleep" rather than a picture of sleep. The reality is heightened to an astonishing degree. It has some of the feeling of enlightenment that comes from the meditations or contemplations of a mystic.

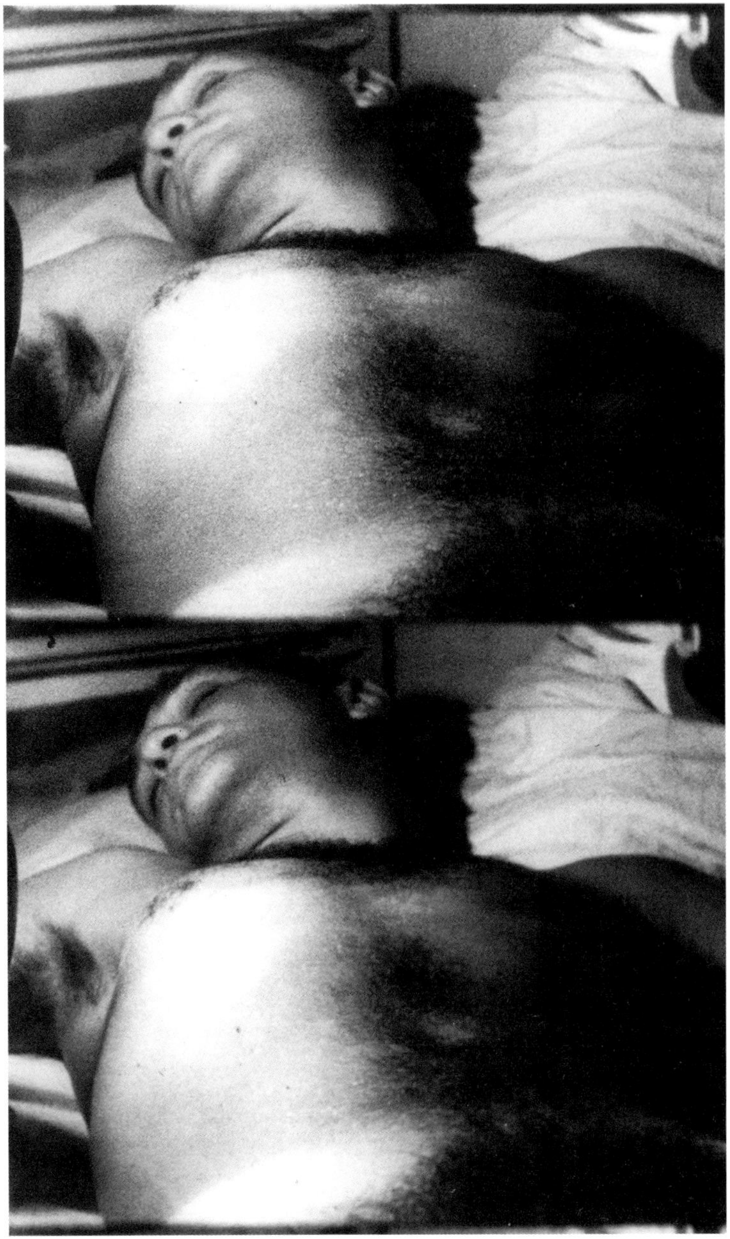

Andy Warhol,'s first
movie, *Sleep* (1963).

In assaying the cost of an early Warhol film there are these factors to bear in mind. The work was done with a 16mm camera. The camera never moved but remained stationary on a tripod. Sets in a literal sense were either non-existent or in a few of the later films improvised, though most were actual rooms in someone's house or apartment. Talent was amateur or in most cases people were used who had little or nothing to do with the desire to "act" in a movie of any kind. I believe Andy played on people's vanity at times. We were all friends, so to speak. The costs, then, were solely comprised of film stock and processing. No editing other than splicing 3-minute rolls of film in the sequences in which they were shot or in the case of the early sound films, comprising two unedited 35-minute reels.

The silent films in most instances never told a story. They were not showing episodes. They were merely trying to present an idea in a compelling way. Whether the sheer graphic simplicity of our work had an impact on the mind of the viewer that had rarely been achieved or whether it would pass by unheeded was a challenge that I think was Andy's and my commitment to resolve; especially when the expenditure was so slight.

The role of setting the pace, of being first, by definition, meant doing things that had not been done before or that had failed in the past. It necessitated a vicious disregard for tradition and common sense. And a vicious disregard for success. For the worship of success and the fear of failure, sometimes force an artist, even more strongly than lack of talent or ability, into the great, grey, dull world of the commonplace and the mediocre. I don't think success or failure were our concerns at that time but merely a way of expressing ourselves.

Working with Andy was a time of growth for us. It was a collaboration within the creative process. At the beginning I had no perspective into the creative process that was feeding back between us – this creative and re-creative day-to-day encounter. I introduced ways of moving the silkscreen off-register from one image in making the same image slightly superimposed over itself in order to re-create the same image on the same canvas. Cecil Beaton introduced this multiple effect with some of his photos, circa 1963. The Elvis Presley portraits are the first example of this method. I conceived of the multiple silkscreen to avoid spending hours painting in areas by hand that could easily be accomplished in one minute. Once these areas were dry we would screen the tones and shades, thus completing the image as it would finally look to the eye. But Andy was fond of repetition. He conceived of art as an absolute. For me this was not growth; it weighed me down.

I realized I needed to rediscover myself; perhaps to repossess the secret of what it meant to be a poet. In order to follow my nature was the literal fact of my eventual parting of ways with the Factory. I needed to find a place in the world; but the place always tended to be where I was not – places abandoned during my travels because they did not possess the secret. Perhaps these places had possessed the secret after all. But it never occurred to me that there *was* no secret, or rather the secret was with me all along.

There is an old tale from Tingri Folk in which it is said that a crow although already in possession of a pond, flies off elsewhere to quench its thirst, and finding no other drinking place returns to the one pond. Similarly, Castenada's don Juan states that "if one starts talking about doing, one always ends up talking about something else. It is better just to act."

The sense I had of myself was being used up – my reality was being used up. Who I was as a poet was not the same person behind the poems because I was slowly being transformed into a myth. The public person who was Gerard Malanga was not the private person and I suppose people would think many things except what and who I was.

Have you ever seen a fox in a cage in a zoo constantly pacing back and forth? The fox moves back and forth because he has no burrow in which to hide. He's in constant exposure to spectators. If a fox isn't given a burrow it becomes a ruined animal, completely destroyed psychically. I am in sympathy with that fox. I needed a burrow of my own also – a place where I could go to be alone.

CAST OF CHARACTERS

Towards the end of September 1963 Andy was notified by the New York City Dept. of Real Estate that he would shortly have to vacate the firehouse because it was being put on the auction-block. Andy by this time wasn't very much interested in purchasing the property because of the lack of heat and safety regulations and perhaps, too, wasn't ready to become a

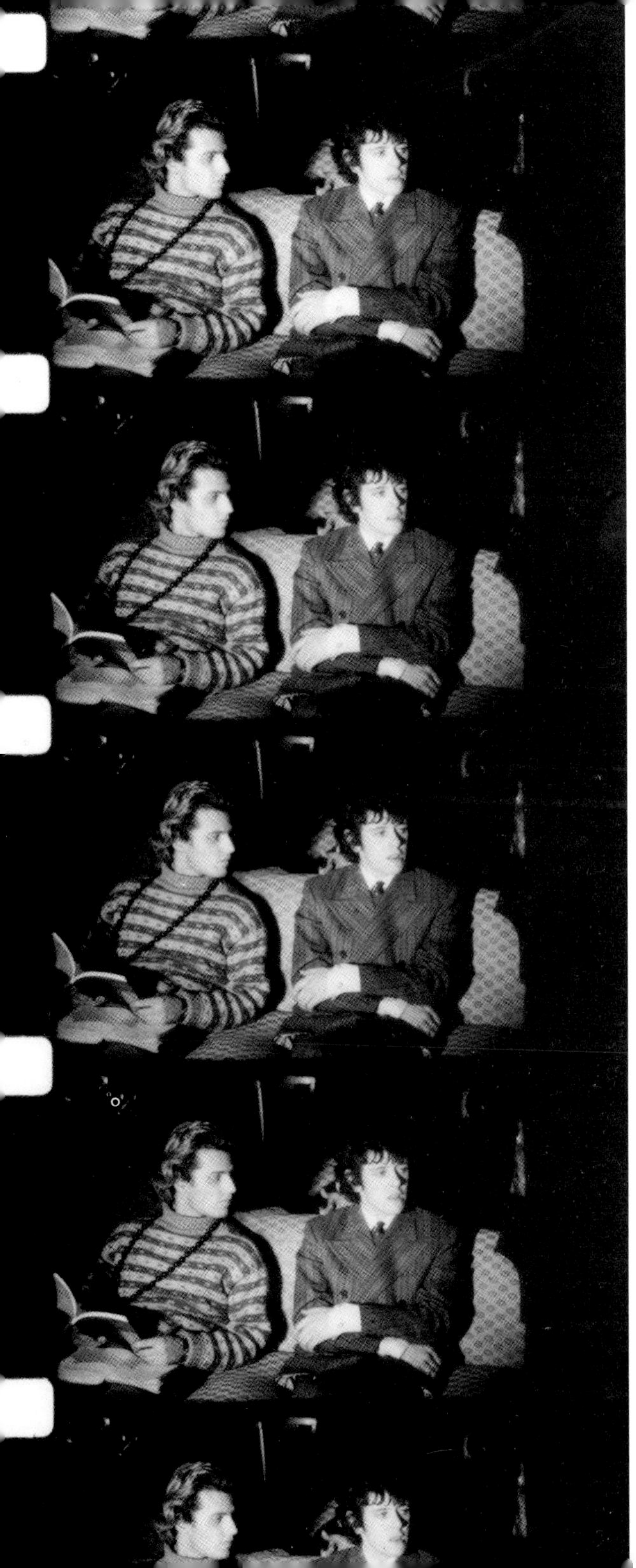

property-owner all over again.

We went loft-hunting. Found an adequate space on East 47th Street that was once a factory of sorts. Andy signs the lease. We move in. Billy Linich tin-foils the ceiling and sprays the walls and floor silver and almost every other object – the telephone, the john, the Coca-cola machine. Then changes his name to Billy Name. The Factory, as it came to be known, became a center of activity even when we weren't making art. It was the gathering place for the jet-set artist contingent – Salvador Dali, Tennessee Williams, Judy Garland, Montgomery Clift, Margaret and Tony, Brian Jones, Bob Dylan, Michelangelo Antonioni – all had paid a visit at one time or other; some regularly. It was also from time to time an oasis for hustlers, transvestites, pretenders who infiltrated New York's art world. It was at the Factory that the paintings were screened and the movies shot. It was the center of Andy's world.

Billy Name was Andy's Factory caretaker. He was also its resident barber, giving free haircuts when needed, which, in turn, inspired Andy's film, *Haircut*. Billy was the foreman and *confidant* for aspiring actresses and amphetamine-heads.

Danny Williams was the light-man and sound-man for the *Exploding Plastic Inevitable*. He handled the work-crew for the multi-media show and was generally in charge of the non-visual end of film production. In 1967 he disappeared mysteriously off the coast on Cape Cod, leaving his clothes by the side of his car. His body was never recovered. Presumably a suicide.

Paul Morrissey looked like a New England whaling captain – tall, spare, aesthetic, reddish-blond, shades of freckles, Irish Catholic, and up-tight conservative. He became Andy's business advisor

Gerard Malanga and Donovan Leitch at the Factory (1965).

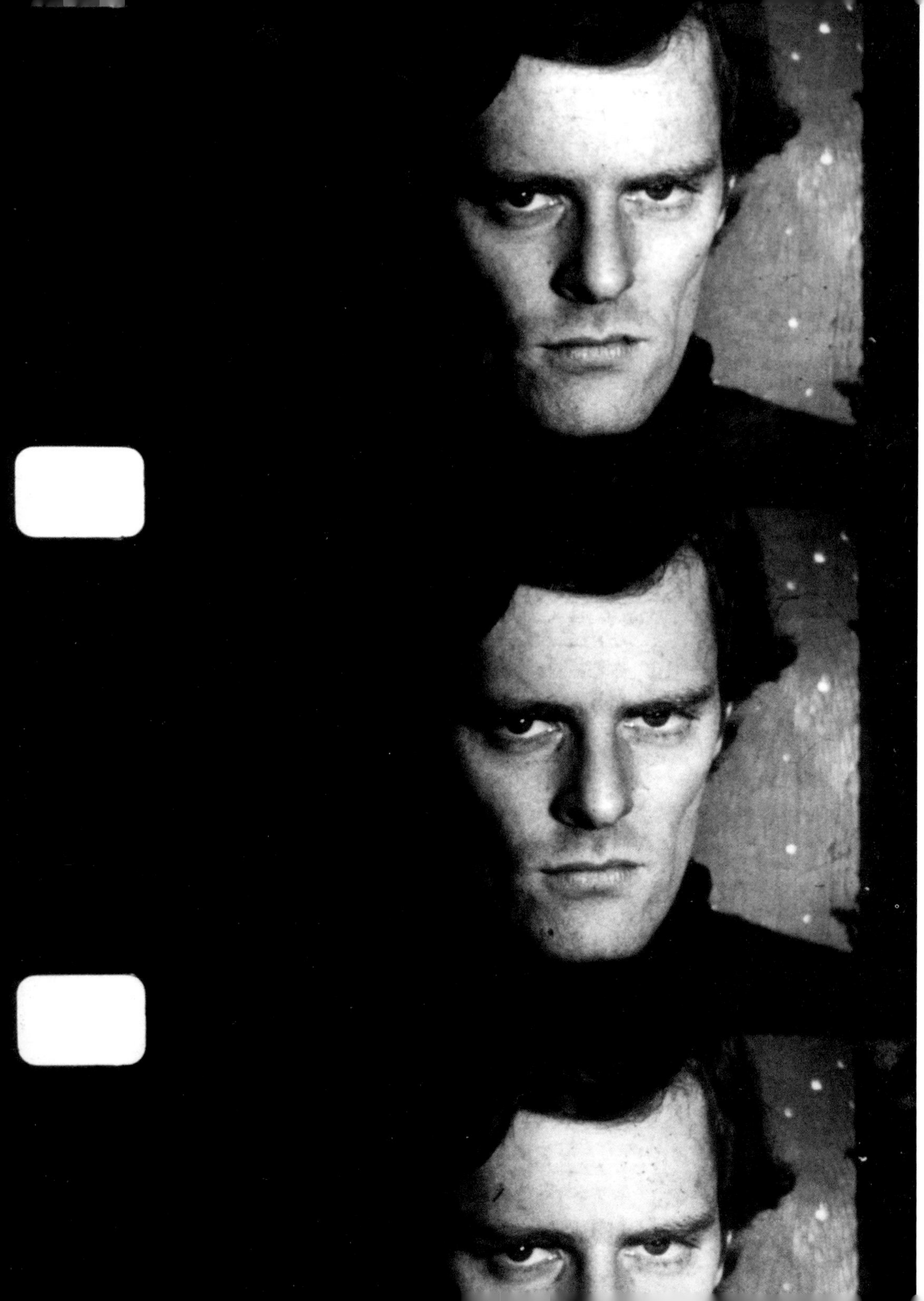

Paul Morrissey Screen
Test, 1966

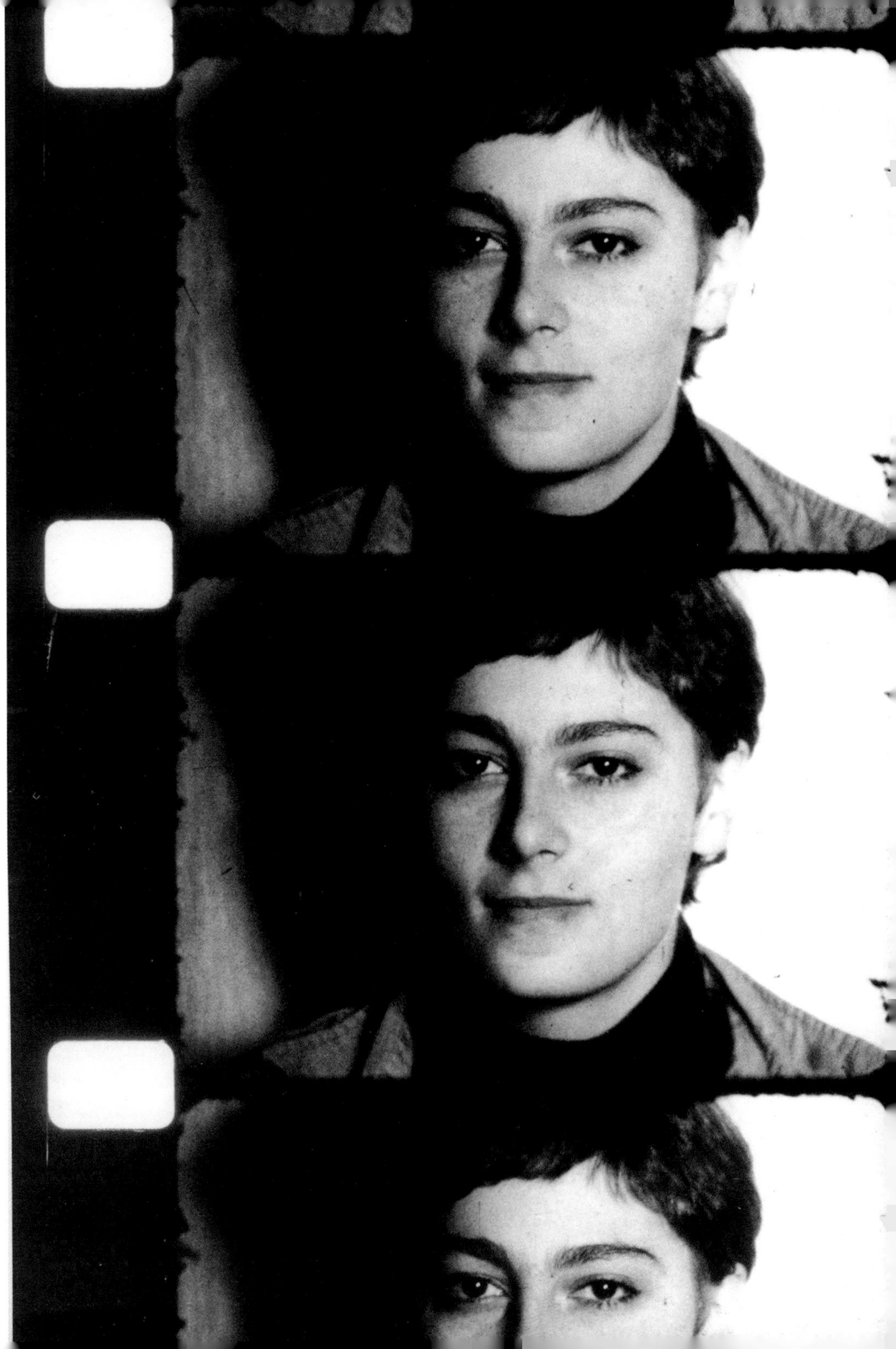

Barbara Rubin Screen
Test, 1964

and later v.p. of Factory operations and its conscience. He balanced Andy's more irrational tendencies.

Barbara Rubin: although she looked eighteen, was actually twenty-one at the time, 1965. An intimate of Allen Ginsberg, Gregory Corso, William Burroughs, Bob Dylan, and Andrei Voznesensky. Barbara acted as the little sister and gadfly of the Velvet Underground. She helped co-ordinate the projection of the films for the *Exploding Plastic Inevitable* and was in fact the originator of Andy's shortlived *Up-tight* series – uptight in the sense of hip-talk for annoyed language. The method was this: Barbara would enter a gathering of people, purposely annoy them and when they were considerably uptight, would shoot movie film of her victims. She and Paul were always at odds with each other – conflicts of interest. Finally, Barbara picked up one day and split the scene.

ENTER, EDIE SEDGWICK

Edie's lineage is Boston Brahmin. Her grand-uncle was William Ellery Sedgwick, writer and teacher and editor of the *Atlantic Monthly* back in the mid-Twenties. She was born April 20, 1943 in Los Olivos, California and grew up on the family ranch not far from Santa Barbara. A strict Catholic upbringing. Sheltered for the greater part of her childhood. Her parents hired tutors to come to the ranch to see after Edie's education.

Edie characterizes something which is all too rare in a human being: Edie had class. She was the personification of *Town & Country* good looks come to life. Her features slight and symmetrical with no outstanding facial bone-structure was, nonetheless, brightened by the vivid and penetrating eyes full of small timidities which recorded perhaps the shocks that too great an honesty expects from life. Her complexion pale and scintillating; a compulsive smoker – a characteristic of Taurus, the sign she was born under. Her mouth animating – perhaps due to the prescription of diet-pills. Epicene figure, brown hair, later calico-color, cropped close to the scalp which she later dyed silver to match Andy's; scar between the brows received from an auto accident which, rather than take pains to hide, she merely accentuated with mascara pencil.

Edie was a lyrical type; she inclined to the spiritual things of life, with a keen conception of the beautiful. She liked to wear large ear-rings. She applied a great deal of make-up before going out. Most of her wardrobe consisted of shirts with tails hanging out and leotards, coordinated what little she had with style. She was the personification of the "poor little rich girl". When she spoke she made sense. She could not be the fool or made to look foolish.

Andy believed Edie had money and so was taken by her. She had none to speak of, except for a modest monthly allowance from her parents, which was quickly spent on lavish dinners, usually at her favourite restaurant L'Ventura, or if it was very late we would take in Rubin's for Steak Tartare. Both restaurants have since vanished from the New York scene – are mere reminders of the decade of the Sixties I refer to as the Age of Beauty. Edie would act as chauffeur with her old beat-up Mercedes sedan. There was always a gang of us. It was not out of character for her to pick up the tab, which usually ran to at least $100 a night by signing for the check or simply paying cash. A night out on the town. Almost every night! It was life imitating art – the kind of activity depicted in books by Fitzgerald, or biographies on the life of Gerald and Sara Murphy or Harry Crosby. One would never dream it could still be made to happen. Edie made it happen. She added something to the ambience of every public place or private home she entered. She was an archetype. She had style.

With Andy we made films, flew to Paris, London, Madrid, Tangier. Attended first-nighters. It was an occasion not more than a year after becoming the darling of New York Society, February 1966, at a crowded table at Maxwell Plum (present were Andy, Paul Morrissey, Donald Lyons, Ingrid Superstar, Barbara Rubin, Nico, Chuck Wein, Lou Reed and John Cale) that Edie confronted Andy about money. She was not footing the bill to this banquet; it was Andy's customary tax write-off. She couldn't. She was not amiable; she had cause not to be. Her parents had long since cut her off from the $500 monthly allowance, because they didn't approve of her activities in New York – her activities with Andy, to be precise. And Andy wasn't paying her for the films she'd appeared in; but, then, Andy had troubles of his own. He wasn't making any real money from the films because they weren't paying for themselves. He was subsidizing the films with income earned from the sale of his paintings and he wasn't about to have his artwork subsidize more than that. Edie was beginning to feel the financial squeeze which was cramping her lifestyle. "But, Edie! I'm not making any money from the films," he retorted in his boyish whine. "You've

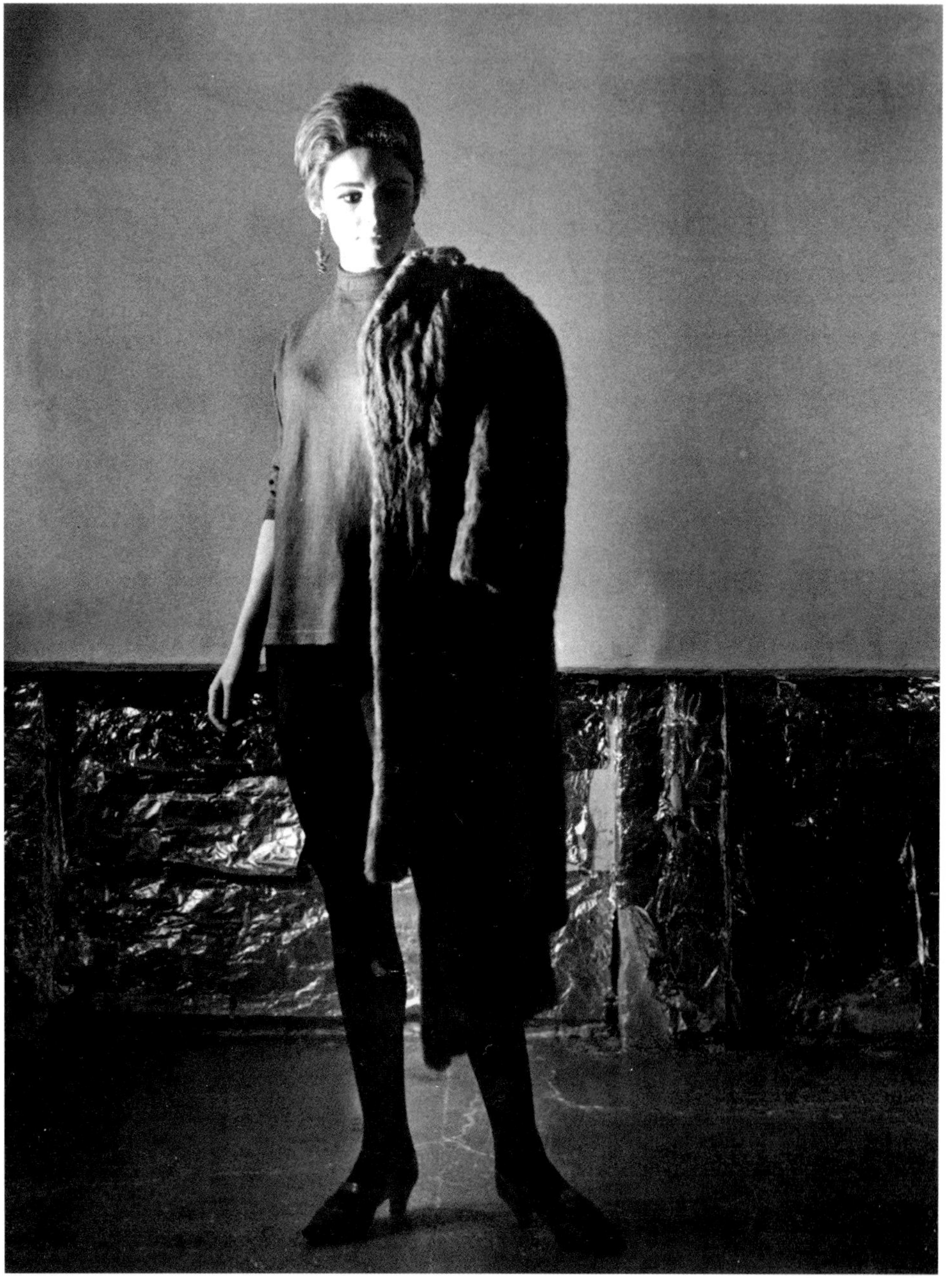

Last-minute portrait of Edie Sedgwick at the Factory, just moments before her departure for Europe.

got to be patient." But Edie's patience was running out.

Andy was fast becoming for her a *cul-de-sac* and she had no time to waste. Andy's interests were also beginning to drift. He started, at about this time, seriously catering to the Velvet Underground and to Nico, recently arrived on the scene from London, as potential money-makers. There was talk of a college tour in the form of a multi-media show which would include Andy's films projected without sound behind the Velvets' live music; there was also an LP in the works which Andy would later produce under the new MGM/Verve label. While he was trying to figure a way of fitting Edie into the scheme of things, she perceived that in no way could she contribute actively in this collaboration that left little for her to do, much less lose the spotlight. Besides, there was no guarantee of money coming in from such a speculative venture. She had other options in the works. Bob Dylan's manager at the time, Al Grossman, had taken an interest in her, or so it seemed. He convinced her, according to Edie, to cut a demo (I discovered later that it never materialized). She began having fantasies of actually having a singing voice and was considering voice lessons. Edie, as talented as she was, had no voice. It was husky, at times. It had character.

At some point during dinner she left the table to make a phone-call, possibly to Dylan himself; returned a short while later, making official her break with Andy, picked up and went out the door. Andy accepted the situation with a sort of philosophical calm. He was red in the face.

I didn't see Edie for several months after that and then didn't know what she was really into, except she and Bobby Neuwirth, Dylan's roadie and sidekick, were hanging out together. Rumours filtered back that she was on hard drugs but one had no way of really knowing.

The image that the media had built up around Edie has begun to tarnish. There was rarely, if at all, any mention of her in the press. Other names had begun to replace hers in connection with Andy but without the glamour involved: Nico, Mary Woronov, Ingrid Superstar, and the untamed Susan Bottomly whom I'd christened International Velvet.

Then suddenly late one night, while sipping an egg-cream at the Gem Spa on St. Mark's Place I recognized Edie standing at the street corner. From the party lights of Park Avenue to the harsh street lights of the lower East Side. A throwback to *Blonde Venus* with Marlene Dietrich. I caught up to her. She shivered and half-fell against me, catching my arm. Her natural

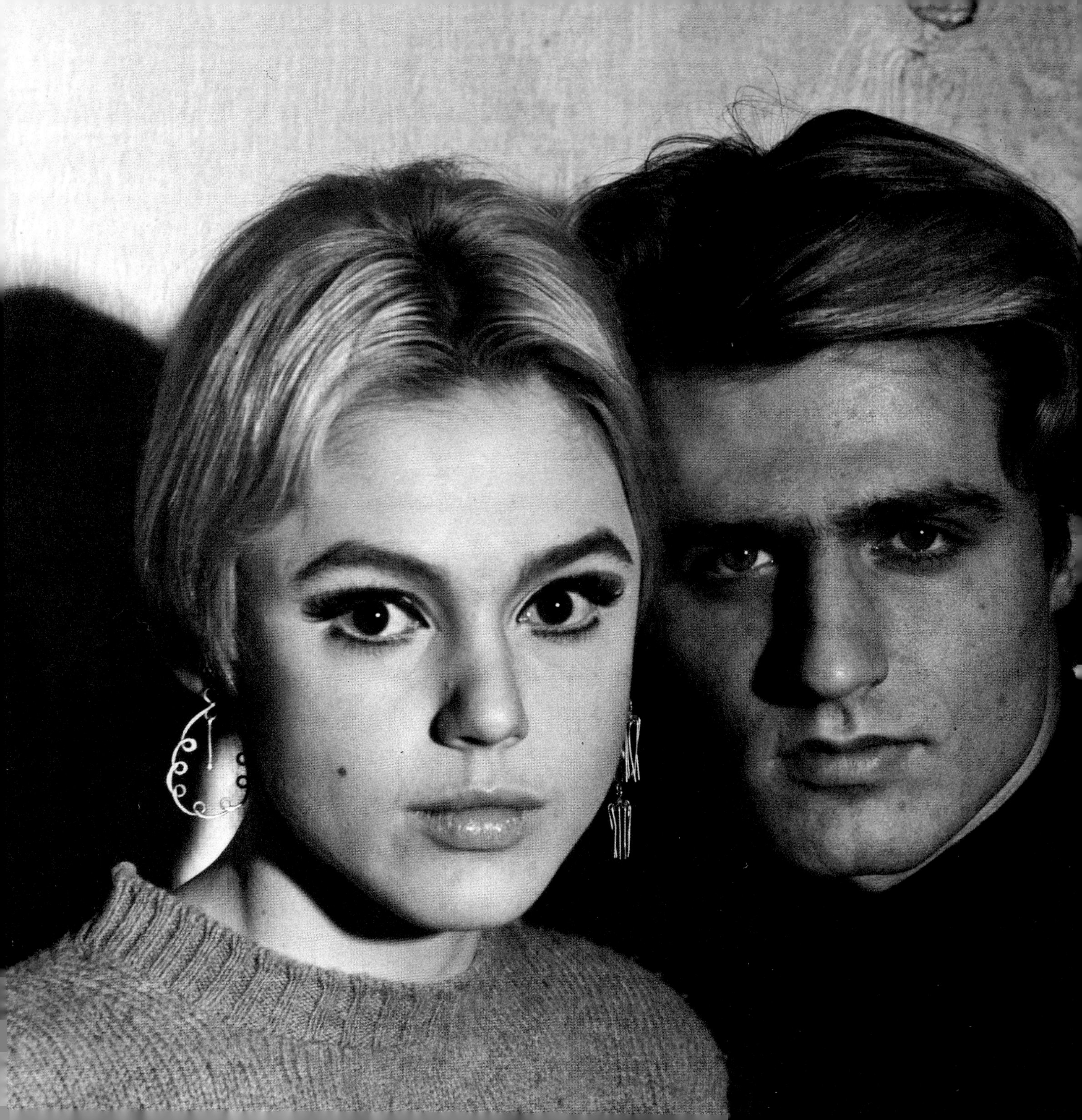

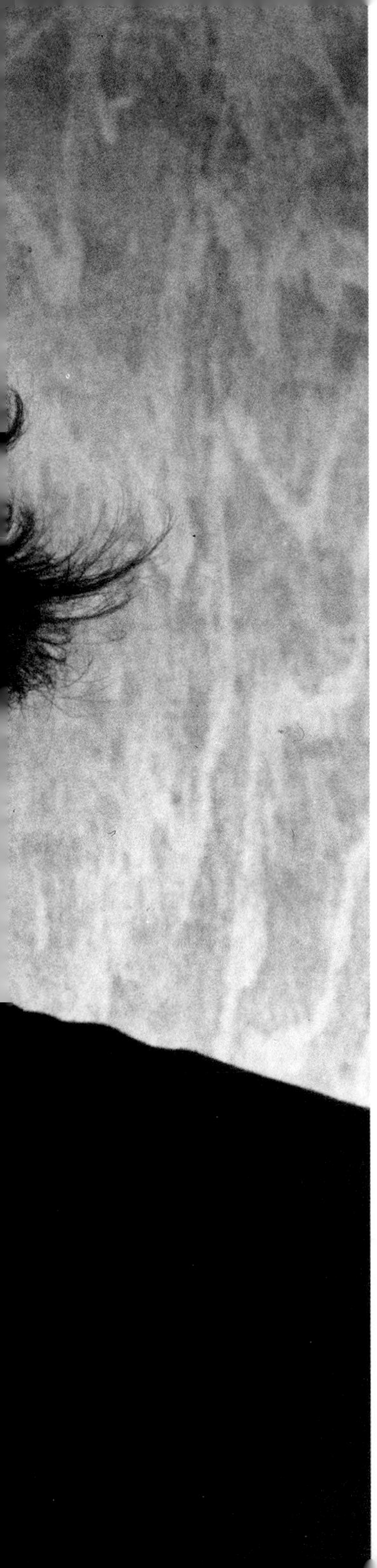

hair-color was growing in at the roots. Her powerful presence had waned a little at the edges, but those restless and brilliant eyes were still glowing. When she spoke, her sentences became disjuncted, cracking, almost lacking coherence. The self-confidence had given way to a helplessness. She seemed a bit unsteady on her feet. Edie was on the dope by this time with the deliberate affirmation which can come only from the fore-knowledge and presence of one's own death. She was forced to move out of her upper East Side flat which was gutted after she fell asleep one afternoon with a lit cigarette. She moved into the Chelsea Hotel.

We saw a lot of each other. Several months later I decided to take a breather from Andy and made plans to visit with friends living in Rome. Edie was thinking about heading out to the West Coast. We parted. I never saw her again. She died three years later from a drug overdose – barbiturates mixed with alcohol. When the *New York Post* reported Edie's death, Andy's response was, "Oh, I thought she died two years ago".

It is significant that there had always been about Edie, notwithstanding all her experiences, something untouched and apart, that stamps those marked for early death. Edie was Andy's first glamour girl and she was his last in the truest sense. She was his ticket to the "Beautiful People". She was the fallen angel. But in a very real way she still had class.

There is still so much we do not know about Edie, and presumably never will, no matter what future books might tell us about her. One just had to be there in the experience of her presence – living history, as it were. I would have to go back very far into the past to understand it all.

What would Edie be today were she alive, I can't quite comprehend. I don't think she could have coped with the past rushing up to her like a smack in the face. She was too sensitive for all the nonsense-play chasing after nostalgia. But feeling captured by the gravitational field of New York she would have been caught up in the experience both of a sense of familiarity and one of alienation with an attempt to measure stability against change, past against present. The seeds of future events are carried within us. They are implicit in us and unfold according to the laws of their own nature. The real obstacle is always oneself.

Edie Sedgwick and Gerard Malanga at the Factory, ca. 1966.

1976

I have been trying to know what it is to be specifically myself in this point of age and have not the answer that would satisfy me entirely; nor do I care to wait around for it, but to keep active so that at times there are experiences that move me to the extent that re-creating their essence with words is, finally, a way of being on the edge of creation – expressing my nature in ways that my life is thereby given meaning in whatever I set out to do.

So on the day I was seventeen I was ready to create an identity for myself and set down to show what I could do, putting into my poetry all that I knew about poetry and what I had absorbed from reading at that time.

I took Yeats's words as a guideline in that "we should write out of our thoughts in as nearly as possible the language we thought them in, as though in a letter to an intimate friend." I tried from that time on to write out of my feelings exactly as they came to me in life, not changing them to make them more beautiful and to have these poems be true to my nature and to my particular time, place and circumstance. Creeley defines this as "how to be in what life makes that time where, when, what is supposed to happen, is waited for so patiently". Poems I was truly given to write were there to be written, and one curiously never does know just when or how or why or in what guise they will manifest themselves as experiences to be re-created as imagery.

There was always a time when I sensed my writing wasn't growing at all. I found myself becoming restricted, by my own writing style. I realized I had to allow for change in my life if I were going to allow for change in my work. I came to recognize that no one can experience anything and still remain the same. Experience changes you. Things change you. Encounters change you.

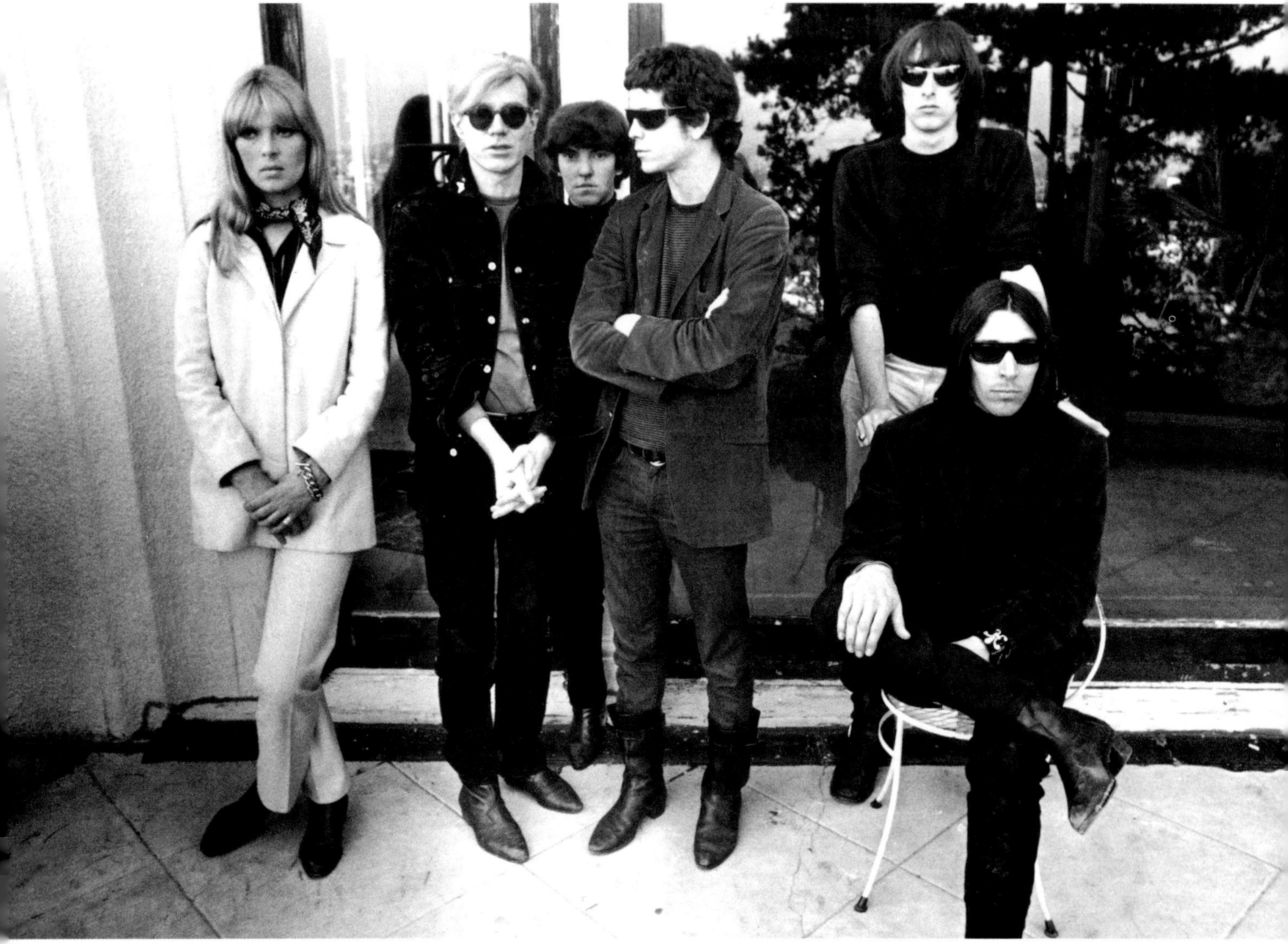

nine

in reply to a request for a statement on the velvet underground

The *American Heritage Dictionary* defines a precursor to be, and I quote: "one that precedes and indicates or announces someone or something to come; forerunner; harbinger". In that sense, then, the rock group known as The Velvet Underground was precursory of an entire generation of music to follow. In itself the group did not endure into the Seventies, but rather its members were dispersed, going their separate ways. Today Lou Reed continues to make music as a soloist, but to an entirely new and much more appreciative generation of troopers; Sterling Morrison teaches English at the University of Texas in Austin. John Cale is a freelance record producer as well as occasionally performing his own music. Maureen Tucker's whereabouts are unknown. Angus MacLise, the group's little-known but original percussionist/spiritual spearhead (this was way before the release of the first Velvets LP with MGM/Verve), died in Kathmandu, Nepal, in Spring of 1979, age 41, in what mutual friend Ira Cohen describes to me in a letter, dated August 13th, as "circumstances of Angus's death were, I suppose, closing walls of karma, consumption & intestinal malady intensified or brought on by junk. He is said to have ripped out the feeding tubes from nose & arm in last days..."

We forget sometimes that no matter what the changes we are the same in our intimacies and with our pasts. The measure. Who shall reap the harvest? To whom shall the praise be given? The Velvet Underground was a very important part of the cultural explosion of the 1960s. They were a group beneath whose force the melody soared – a certainty of music, a unison and dance joined.

The Velvets were, at the same time, besides being the product of a new kind of music, children of a new era in the world, the era which was to

Opposite: Andy Warhol and The Velvet Underground in Hollywood, 1966.

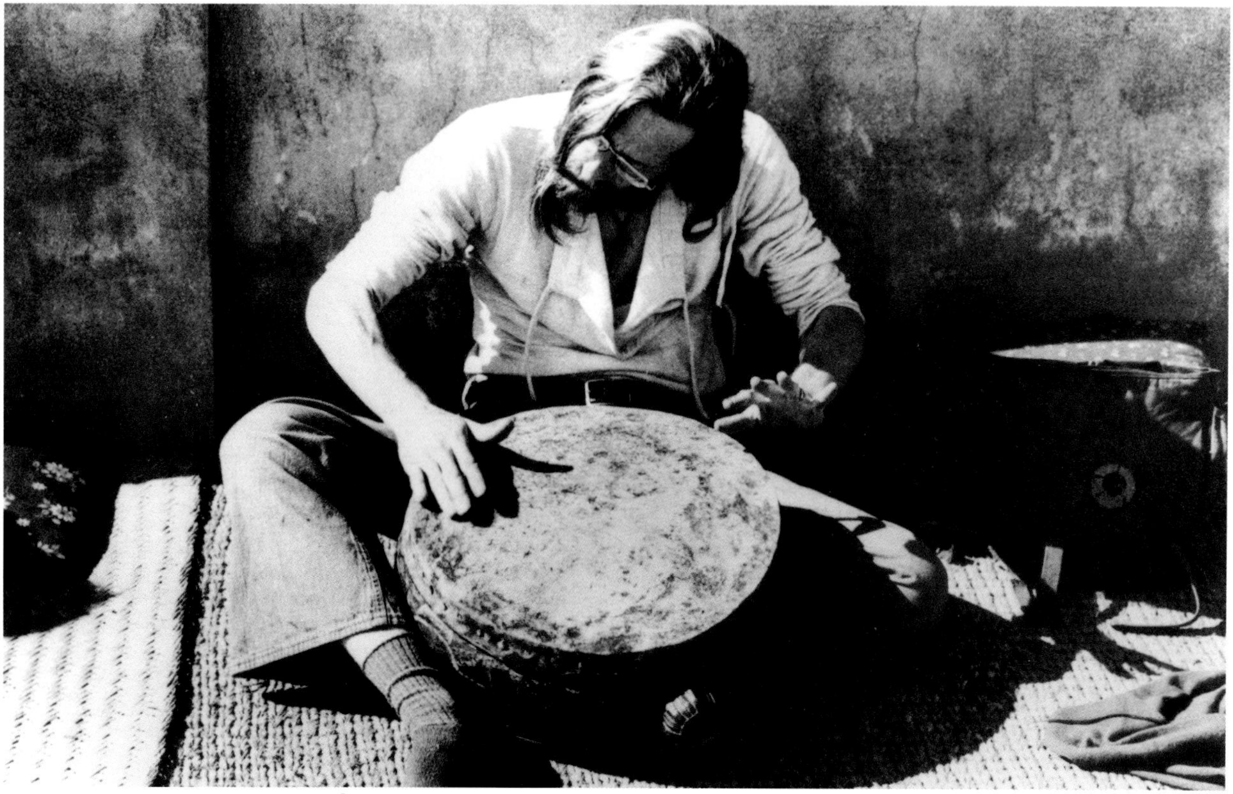

Angus MacLise with drum. Kathmandu, Nepal ca. 1978.

discover among other things the relativity of all knowledge. The generation of the ’80s are the inheritors of an artistic legacy the likes of which perhaps will not occur again – what tradition is all about finally.

The Velvets’ music now thrives through an ever-continuing emergence of new music groups. The seeds have been planted and the new music has added its wonder. Their influence continues to astound.

The Velvet Underground is the break-up and the beginning. There it is and we’d better acknowledge it and write it down. It cannot be otherwise.

—26:viii:79 nyc

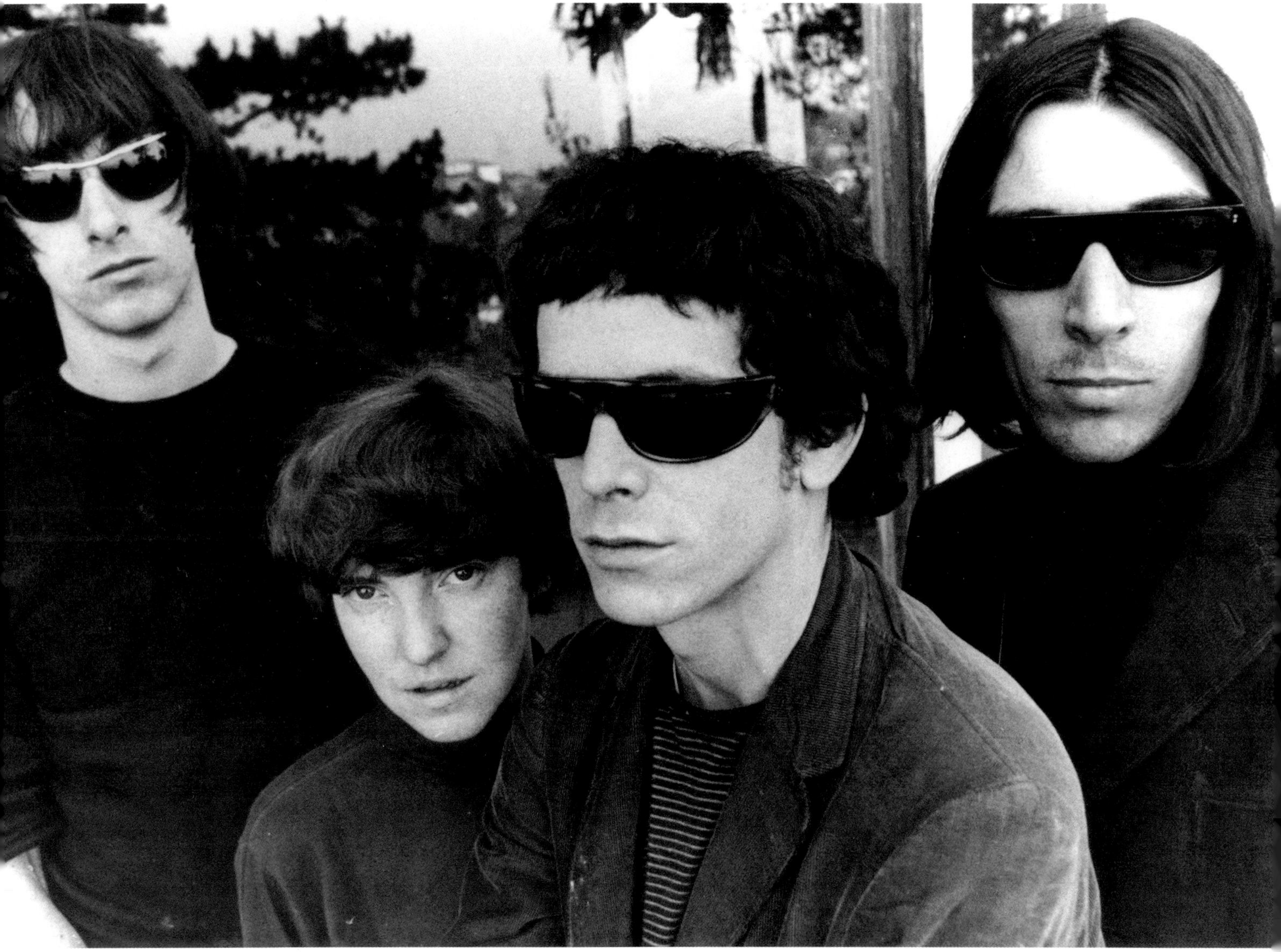

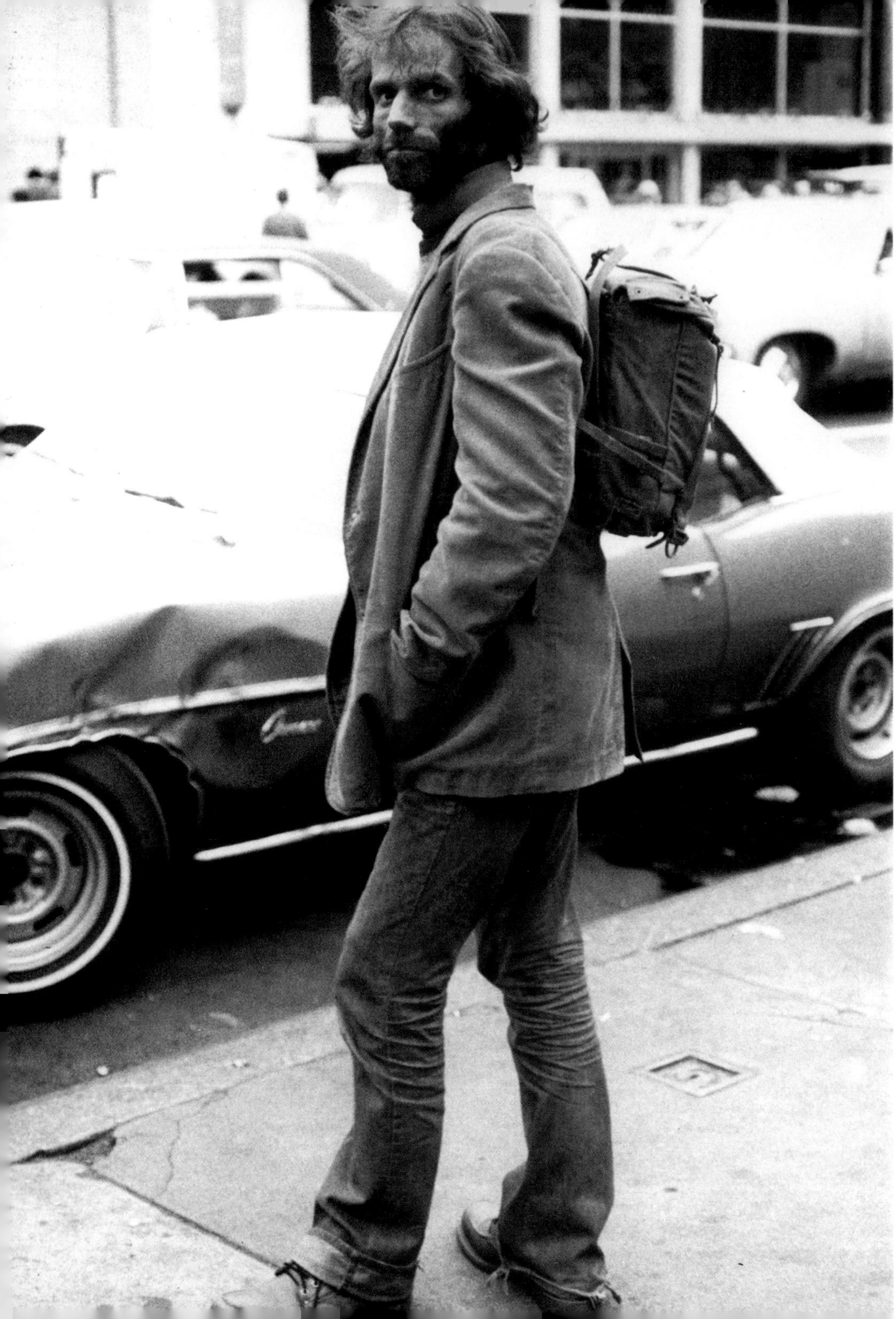

ten

this photo may not be – etc.

1963. The year is shortly coming to a close. Billy is living in the Lower East Side with a group of young people, aspiring artists and dancers, who are all into amphetamines and one of the things about taking amphetamine it makes you talk a lot or you obsess with doing something and you keep doing it without stopping, and what happened to Billy was that he started tin-foiling his entire apartment – the walls and ceiling. The wooden floor was sprayed silver too.

Andy and I enter. Here is Billy and Freddy Herko and Johnny Dodd and Soren Agenoux and Ondine... several others flit through the rooms. It's an afternoon get-together... a haircut party. (I had already known Ondine and Soren – at least a year before I met Andy – through parties given at a loft on Bond Street that John MacDermott and "Mr. Clean" were renting.)

When Andy and I moved into the Factory, January 28th, Billy arrived one day to visit and Andy said, "Well, maybe you'd like to paint the place silver?"

On a grey, chilly morning 1969, Billy Name is seen at the Factory writing a note for Warhol, which reads "ANDY – I AM NOT HERE ANYMORE BUT I AM FINE, LOVE, billy." He then locks up, descends by elevator, leaving behind a place and people he called home for five years. He mingles with the morning rush-hour traffic, not to be seen or heard from again.

SLOW FADE-OUT

CUT to black & white. Billy, in headshot close-up, looks directly into the camera. He begins reminiscing on his past life living at the Warhol Factory 30-seconds into the shot and then a slow fade-out, synchronized to a voice-over dissolve, begins to merge with a muted color FADE-IN, flashing back to

Opposite: Billy Name, 1971, two years after he vacated the Factory.

October 1966. Billy, with aerosol in hand, is spraying an empty factory space silver, wrapping the support-columns with silver tinfoil. Splintering sunlight adds to the already thick, dusty atmosphere. In the background, a record of a Maria Callas aria from Puccini's *La Bohème* mingles with street noises. The camera slowly swivels on a 180° pan, taking in the entire width and depth of the space. Off to one side, a beautiful fashion model in Khadejha print dress – Benedetta Barzini – is seemingly lost in concentration applying make-up in front of a stained and cracked mirror fixed above a seedy wash basin. In a far corner, Andy and Gerard, uninterrupted by a sudden outburst of conversation off-camera, are preparing to silkscreen a canvas.

CUT to close-up of the work at hand. The Factory is a buzz of seemingly disconnected activities. Everything appears genuinely mundane on the surface, but beneath lurks an incredible surge of creative energy that will change the course of American culture. A new history of art is in the making. These people are unaware of the consequences.

Michael Katz, a photographer living on East 7th Street in the Lower East Side, has arranged to make a group portrait of some of his friends and their friends. As I recall it was at Ondine's urging that I be included in the picture. I had hung out with a few of those present, shared their amphetamine, was welcomed into their group – what I referred to at the time as the "dawn patrol".

I'll attempt to identify as many as I can remember of those present, starting with the back row and working my way forward. From left to right: John Daley, this writer, Michael Smith, Ron Gronhord, Jack Champlin, Gregory Darnopuk, Ken Wollitz (obscured). Second row: Dale Joe, Ondine, Norman Billiard Balls, Billy Name, Charles Stanley, and Dorothy Podber. Seated directly in front: Binghamton Birdie, Freddy Herko, and Dino. Today there are only a few faces to join past and present. First Freddy died. Hallucinating that he could fly, Freddy took a balletic leap through the window of Johnny Dodd's 4th floor flat on Cornelia Street in the West Village, landing on the hood of a parked car. Charles Stanley also a suicide. John Daley has since died… Norman Billiard Balls… Ondine… Johnny Dodd; Jimmy Waring, conspicuously absent from this picture, also dead. I never knew what became of John MacDermott or Mr. Clean.

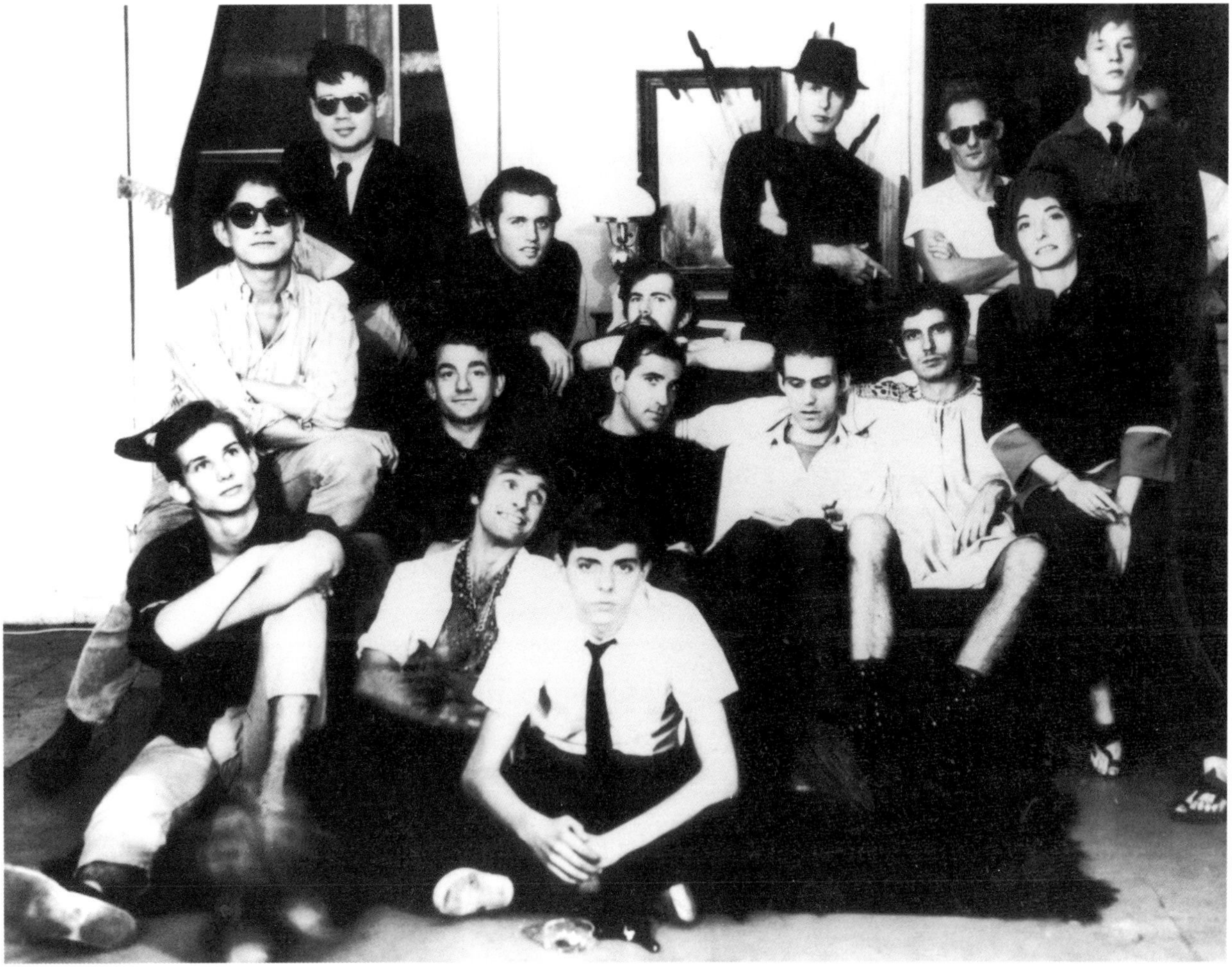

January, 1992, Billy comes to visit. We're now "country neighbors" he says. Poughkeepsie, Great Barrington, about 45-miles as the crow flies through distance and time – a reality "separate" from New York's misty white, predawn light. Over dinner Billy confesses that he – not Andy as I'd always assumed – had, "out of jealousy", crossed out my name on the photo-ready mechanical for the *Index Book* title page 1967, at which time I'd been living in Rome.

And I'm thinking Goethe: *Not everything that history offers us has actually happened. And what has actually happened has not happened the way it is presented, and what we know to have happened is only a very small part of what actually happened.*

This photograph may not be – etc.
This photograph, like so many others, dissolves.
Other photographs take its place.
A whole trunkful.
Other times, other faces.
The future looms.

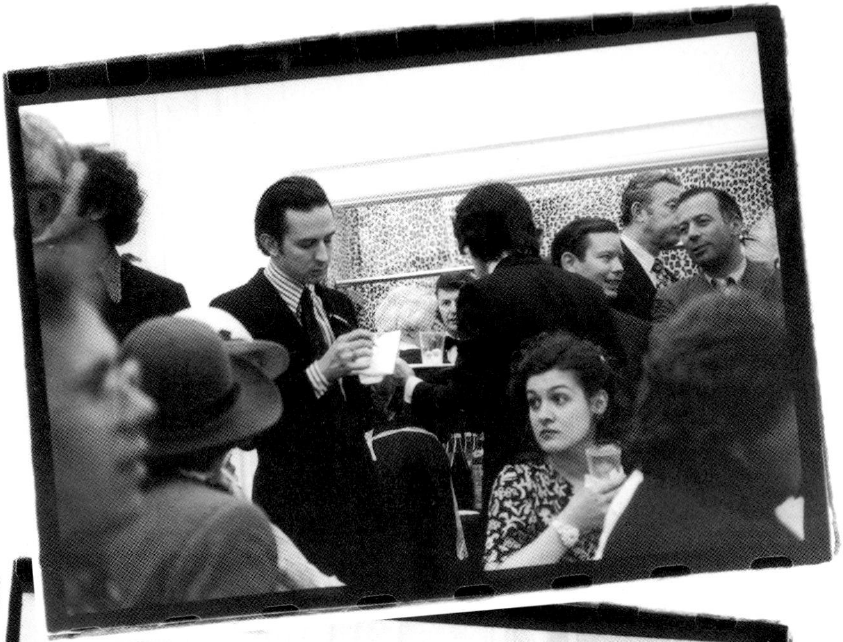

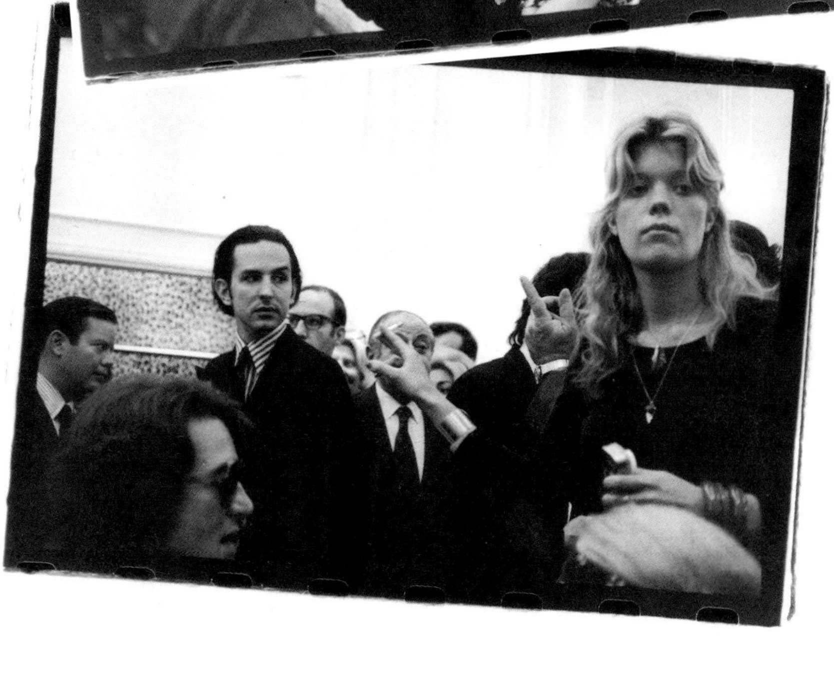

eleven
fritzy, 1969

When Fred Hughes half-jokingly remarked to a friend in my presence one afternoon at the Factory that his "biggest ambition was to go to bed with one of Gerard's girls", he wasn't kidding. *Read any good books lately?* is what I wanted to say to Fritzy in a campy pitch.

Fred was always tailgating me in those days – he'd be lurking, waiting for the intro – as if I somehow possessed a magic inexplicable to his notion of life, like "How does Gerard do it?". I could have told him if he'd only asked. The secret, if you could call it that, that Fred so desperately wanted to possess, was no secret at all. Simply by rising above the superficialities, being true to one's nature in life, is all that's required if one has the patience and discipline. But Fred would have none of it, ah-ah, too intellectual for his taste, his sense of sartorial splendour, and besides he hadn't the time. He was a man about town, like they say, a cosmopolite obsessed with social vanity but lacking social conscience – a calculating opportunist when it came to girls, pure and simple, turning on the charm, more or less, especially if they were beautiful – "well-bred", as it were – coming from affluent stock. Never mind the lack of monetary wealth. You could be as poor as a church mouse so long as you donned the plaid of your clan, or had a title attached, like *donna* – a modest one at that. I'd had my fair share – so, too, to some extent, I was in awe. Class aura does have an edge in the sexual ritual and when combined with beauty is combustible.

I had just begun dating a young Swedish girl, Agneta Frieberg, a Ford model, really the girlfriend of Jack Youngerman, the painter, but it was made apparent their longstanding relationship was soon winding down for whatever reason I did not ask.

Opposite (top): Fred Hughes taking notes at Fernando Sanchez's REVILLION runway show, 1971. Seated, lower right: Paloma Picasso.

Opposite (bottom): Fred Hughes at REVILLION. Lower left: Halston in sunglasses; upper right: Berry Berenson.

Agneta was truly a "babe". A good-natured girl, adventurous in spirit, though seemingly uncomfortable with her whole sense of self. She was in appearance about 5'91/2", long-waisted with hair pure as a Kansas wheat field in August and nearly touching the small of her back. Blonde blonde blonde in three words. She'd been photographed by the great Louie Fauer, had gone out with him for awhile, was the Breck Beautiful Hair image you'd see on placards, packaging and shampoo labels in drugstores, beauty counters at Macy's. You couldn't help but notice: Agneta stared out at you with the warmth of her big blue eyes. In a sense, she had it all, which allowed her to slow down a bit from the agency calls. She was by then twenty-three. She was beginning to discover the underground art scene. She discovered me.

Anyway, rumour had it Fred was planning a dinner party at his new flat, but as yet he hadn't invited me, that is until hours before the occasion. The note he placed on my desk read:

> Dearest,
> You are
> invited to
> a small
> dinner
> at my house
> around
>   8:30 9:00
>
> Fred

I'll *dearest* you. It was already 4:00. This hardly gave me time to primp, seeing as I would no doubt want to bring Agneta along, but when I called I discovered that Fred had already gotten to her. *My, this guy works fast!* I said to myself, as Agneta and I talked about when we'd arrive. "See you at the party," and I hung up the phone. What did Fred hope to gain, I wonder? I don't suppose it would have occurred to him to simply say, "Please bring Agneta along."

This was the kind of typical behaviour Andy encouraged with those close to him. I guess it kept us on our toes. He was always being mischievous like that, playing his friends off one another, then stepping back to see what ensued. A real faggot mentality. That's how he got his kicks I suppose, always being the voyeur. I played it close to the vest when around him, never letting on who I'd be dating at any given time. As much as I tried not to allow all this intrigue to affect me, it wasn't always that simple. Fred's desk directly faced mine, 15 feet apart at the most, so when I'd get a call from a girlfriend I'd find myself speaking in whispers.

The party, I might add, was a smashing success. I was happy for Fred, it was his first at his one-bedroom flat. There wasn't a prettier bunch of people in all New York that night. They were all here in Fred's living-room, collected by Fred.

It was considerably late – the party beginning to wind down. The Smith sisters – Geraldine and Maria – locked in conversation in a corner, silhouetted by a floor lamp draped with some of Fred's art deco ties. Someone nameless passed out in the bedroom. Fred in the kitchen cleaning up. "Good night, Fred and thanks" we called out, halfway out the door.

Agneta and I decided to walk the entire way to her apartment up at East 54th on the 21st floor. It had rained earlier. There was a chill in the air now. Up and down Fifth Avenue rain-reflected street lights still glowed; yet in all this far vista shone the lights of only one automobile. A patrolman on night duty stands guard over a silent side street. Office buildings, their last lights quenched, stand dim against the night sky. Clouds, fewer still, break away, revealing some stars. No-one up yet. For a moment we caught our reflection in the Tiffany's window and stood still, hands in each other's pockets. Huddled together. I whispered in her ear, "You're now an official member of the 'Dawn Patrol'." It was getting to about that hour. The city bathed in a rosy hue before sunrise. We laughed and bolted out into the middle of Fifth swirling in a couple of circles, hailing a cab which circled round the rest of the way home – manhole covers steaming as we passed. Her head in my lap now.

A year later – Winter 1970 – while in the crosswalk, 15th and Park South – Union Square – on my way somewhere I happened to glance over my shoulder and caught a glimpse of Fred across the way – not more than 30 feet distant – ushering a young girl into a cab. I thought it curious to see Fred up at this ungodly hour, 8:00am. Though I couldn't quite make out who he was with – Fred's shoulder blocking my sight-line – she suddenly turned to give him a kiss. Lo and behold, it was Loulou de la Falaise quickly stepping into the cab which spun around into the rush-hour traffic heading uptown. I just stood there motionless, silent, feeling invisible like a deer holding still. Now I was being the voyeur. At first it seemed totally unreal, like something happening on a big movie screen. But I needed to keep this real-life movie going – not disturb its separate reality by my physical presence – so I traced my sight on Fred those few last precious seconds as he quickly made his way up to 16th Street. He abruptly turned the corner and was gone. His flat not more than two short blocks distant.

I was amused and felt strange at the same time that I should bear witness to this, but then it had significance for me and for no-one else. My reality – the one now logged back in memory – had been usurped by Fred's foolish phantasy even though Loulou and I never had chance to continue the second time round. I couldn't "call" him on that. I was no longer part of the Warhol circle or on Fred's team for that matter. I was cast adrift, on my own now, but I had my wits about me and wasn't going to let this incident get me down. No need to carry old baggage on head, as don Juan aptly made clear. My photography was pretty much in high gear, intent on learning about how far I could transform it into artistic experience. Pity though, I never got around to photographing Fred in the best light.

For a moment there I'd forgotten where I was. A passerby bumped into me and I lurched forward a little into conscious vision. People going every which way. Street noises. Long moving shadows cast on the pavement. I then disappeared into the morning rush.

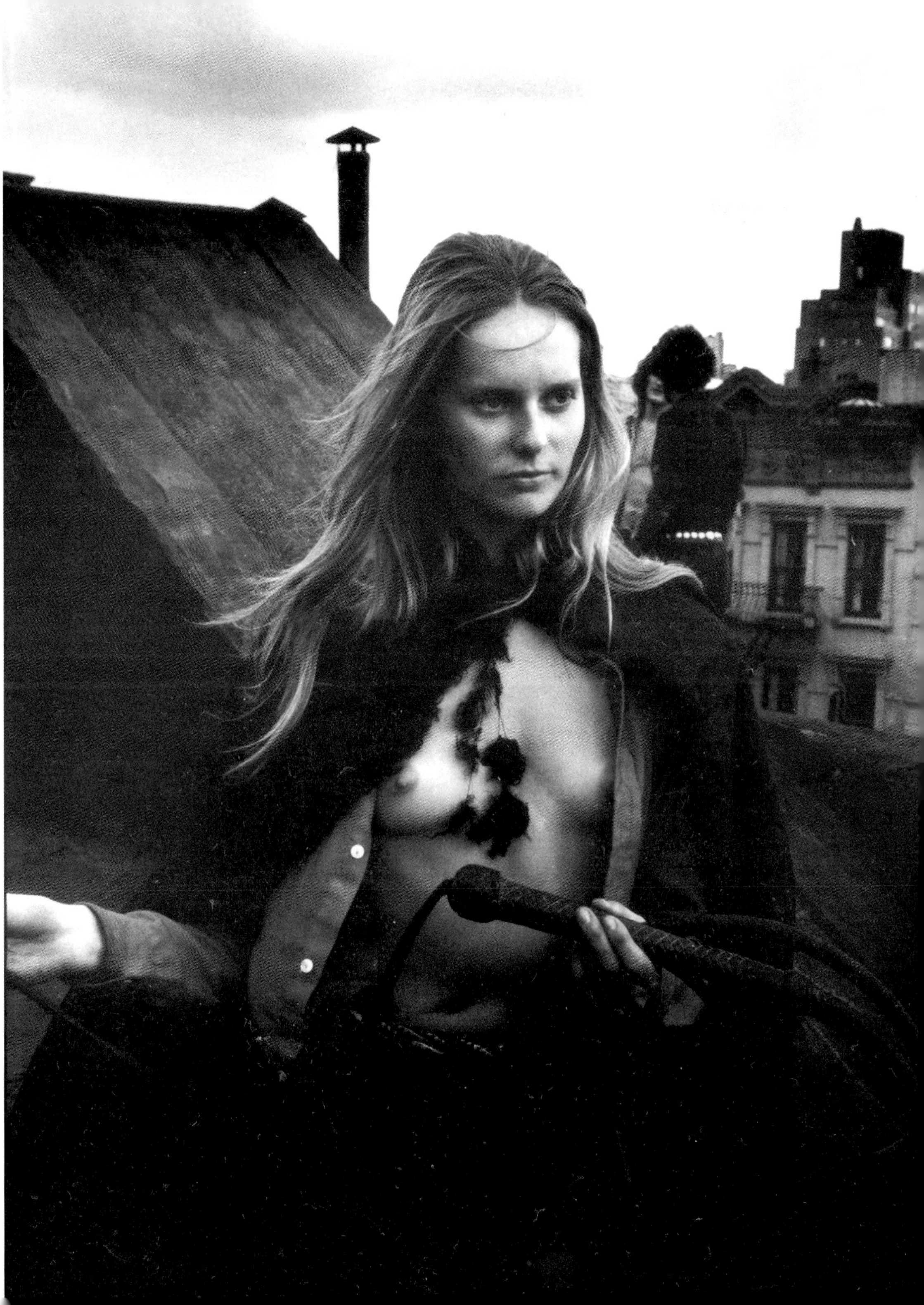

Agneta Frieberg, 1969.

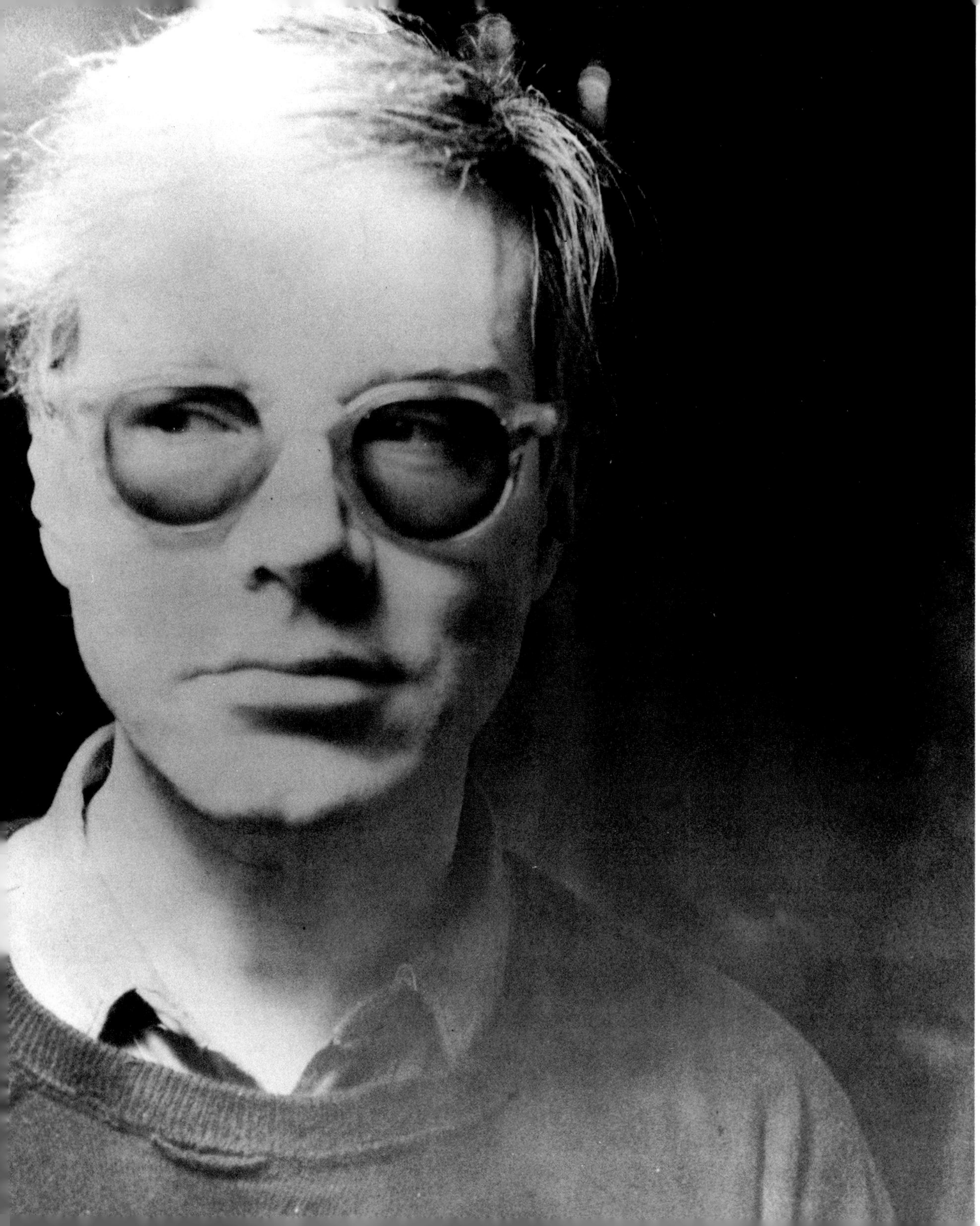

twelve
a conversation with andy warhol

I was introduced to Andy Warhol in the Fall, 1962, at a party given by the underground filmmakers, Willard Maas and Marie Menken. I recall Andy's silver hair, white skin, dark shades, and outright nervousness. I didn't pay much attention to him at the time.

Several months later, June 9, 1963, to be exact, Charles Henri Ford was aware that Andy was in desperate need of an assistant to help with production of his silkscreen paintings. Charles, knowing that I had previous silkscreen experience, presumed rightly that this would be the perfect match and was the catalyst in bringing us together.

On June 11, I began working for Andy at what was then his studio, a condemned hook & ladder company located on 87th Street between Lexington and Third Avenues. The city had sold the building to a real estate agent at an auction, and Andy was renting the entire building for $150 a month until such time as he would be given notice to vacate the premises.

We began working almost immediately on silkscreening a portrait of Elizabeth Taylor on a canvas that had been prepared with a background of silver spray paint. The job was not too difficult, but became messy later when the screen had to be cleaned with Varnolene.

We printed four or five 40 x 40 inch canvases, after which we returned to Andy's home which was two blocks away where I scrutinised Andy's photo collection while "Sally Go Round The Roses" spun. The photos were an odd assortment of car crashes, people being tortured, and tabloid shots of movie stars. Several of the glossies in this collection were used for the actual subject matter he reproduced in his silkscreens. He was a Social Realist in reverse; he was satirizing the methods of commercial art as well as the American mythos. But instead of satirizing the products

Opposite: Andy Warhol at the Factory, ca. 1964.

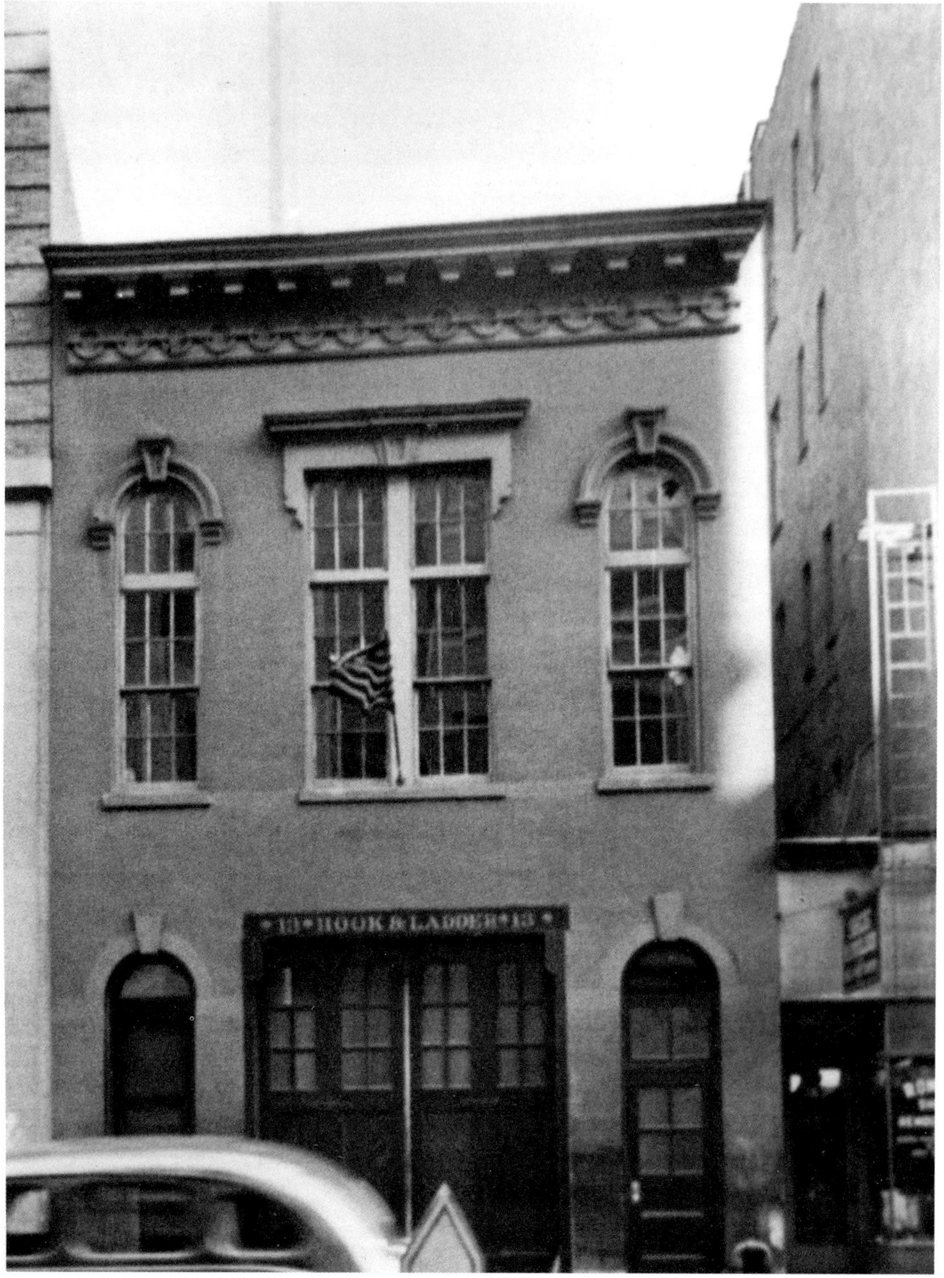

Hook & Ladder Co., #13, where Andy Warhol and Gerard Malanga first worked together on the silkscreen paintings, 1963.

themselves, he had satirized the “artful” way they were presented.

Andy had many pitfalls to overcome with his art, and on many occasions we resolved these problems. It was always impossible to make an exact copy of his paintings. It was always accidental, a new element or a new emphasis, either manual or psychological, would crop up in the work. Andy wanted to keep the human element out of his art, and to avoid it he resorted to silkscreens, stencils, and other kinds of automatic reproduction.

But still the Art of Accident would always creep in. A smudge here, a bad silkscreening there, an unintended cropping. Andy was always anti-smudge. To smudge is human. He wanted to blot out blots. When we took up screenprinting, it was not to get away from the preconceived image, but to more fully exploit it through the commercial techniques of multiple reproduction. Unlike Rauschenberg, Andy never destroyed his screens after they were used, and for this reason he has always been worried about the possibility of a forgery. If somebody faked his art, he could never hope to identify it.

Andy has always felt his work to be vacuous, but at the same time he felt he couldn’t tell how someone would react to one of his paintings until the person actually saw it. He thought someone had to see his painting in person to realize how vacuous it really was. Too many people who say it’s vacuous have never experienced the vacuousness of it all. They are judging it either as a reduced illustration or just an abstract idea. They say who’s interested in a can of soup? We know what it looks like because we eat it. They say we’ve seen pictures of it in magazines. So Andy reproduced a can of soup as it appears in an advertisement, and then they think he’s changed something. People just don’t know how vacuous something is until they see a copy of it. Maybe somebody will have to imitate his work before it looks as vacuous as it really is.

The following is a discussion we had of what we’ve been feeling about during the past seven years.

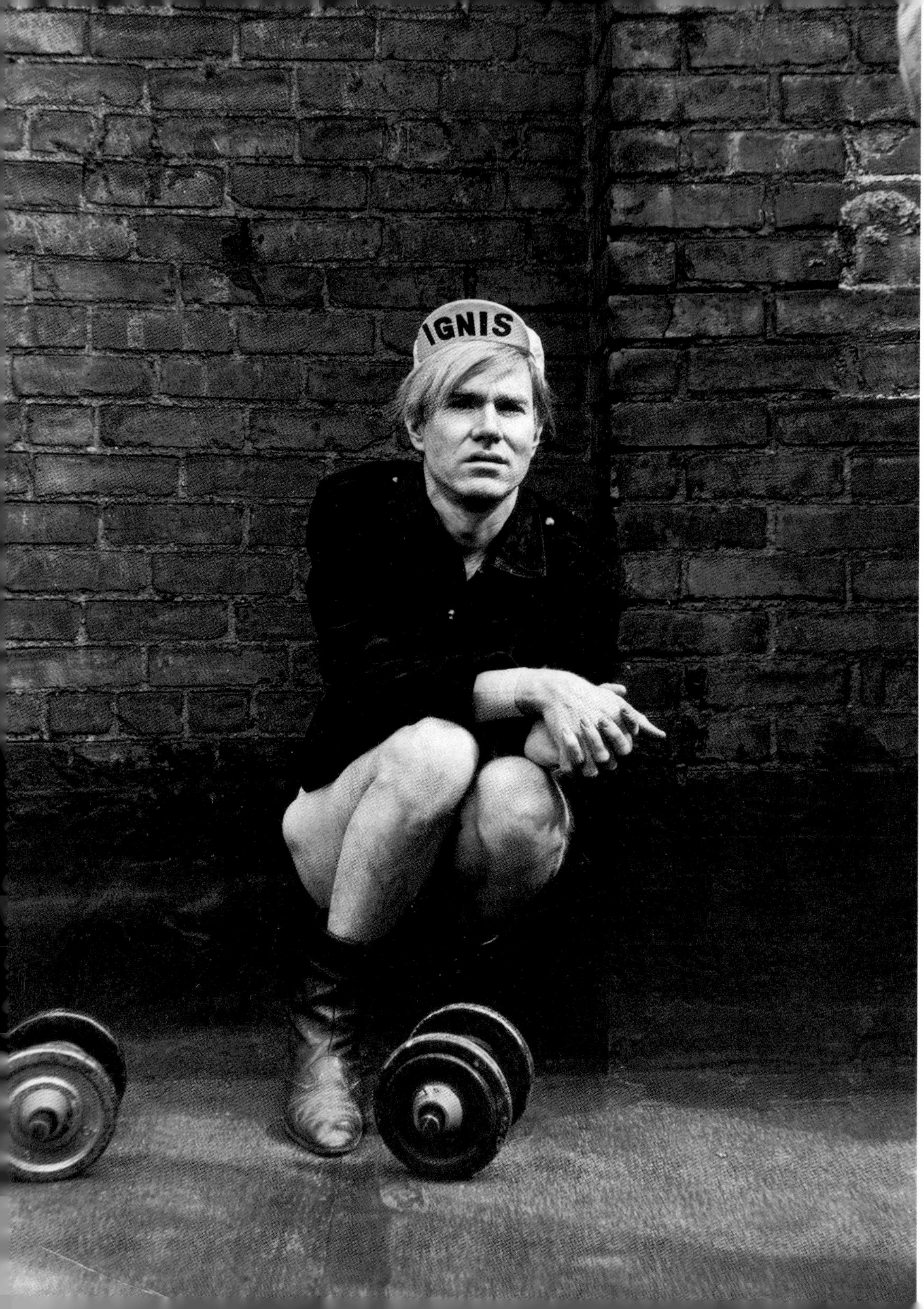

Andy Warhol as he appears in Piero Heliczer's underground film classic, *Joan Of Arc* (1966).

GM: Andy, when did you make your first print?

AW: Don't you remember? It was the print in three colors of the Liz Taylor portrait.[1] Actually, I didn't silkscreen it myself. Leo [Castelli] had it printed up in a limited edition which I signed. It was in the format of a poster and unlike the current *Campbell Soup Can* portfolio. If I remember correctly, I felt that if everyone couldn't afford a painting the printed poster would be available.

GM: What was the motive behind repeating the same image over and over in a painting?

AW: I don't really know or remember. I think, at the time, I started repeating the same image, because I liked the way the repetition changed the same image. Also, I felt at the time, as I do now that people can look at and absorb more than one image at a time.

GM: Gathering from what you've said I feel that the idea of the repetitive image ties up with the split-screen experiments incorporated into the film, *Chelsea Girls*.

AW: Correct, but that was a divine accident. The idea of the split/image in *Chelsea Girls* only came about because we had so much footage to edit, and I wasn't into editing at the time, and the film would have been too long to project in its original form time-wise. By projecting two reels simultaneously, we were able to cut down the running-projecting time in half, avoiding the tedious job of having to edit such a long film. After seeing the film projected in the split/screen format, I realized that people could take in more than one story or situation at a time.

GM: How random is your randomness in choosing the images you work with for the paintings?

AW: Ah, what do you mean? I don't choose images randomly, but make a careful selection through elimination. This was the same approach we used with *Chelsea Girls*, although we did eliminate two to four 35-minute reels. As for the paintings, the images I've used have all been seen before via the media. I guess they're media images. Always from reportage photographs

1. Documenting Andy Warhol's graphic work is difficult as he has consistently employed the graphic media to make things other than prints. No documentation was kept on Warhol's early graphics as many of these works were only considered prints after the fact. For example, the first *Flowers* print was a photo offset poster, signed but not numbered, for a 1964 exhibition at the Castelli Gallery in New York. The *Elizabeth Taylor* print Warhol refers to here was not his first print. Warhol's first signed and numbered print was probably *Cooking Pot* (1962). The print was made from an engraving of a newspaper advertisement and was signed on the verso with an embossed blind stamp of the artist's signature and numbered in pencil in an edition of 60. It was included in the portfolio *International Avant Garde*, Volume V, published by the Galleria Schwarz in Milan.
—Paul Cummings, Editor.

or from old books, or from four-for-a-quarter photo machines.

GM: Do you feel you've changed the media?

AW: No. I don't change the media, nor do I distinguish between my art and the media. I just repeat the media by utilizing the media for my work. I believe media *is* art.

GM: At what point did you stop painting and start using screens to print your paintings?

AW: Around 1962, though the backgrounds to the paintings have always been painted by hand before the silkscreen is applied. Silhouette-shapes of the actual image were painted in by isolating the rest of an area on the canvas by means of masking-tape. Afterwards, when the paint dried, the masking-tape would be removed and the silkscreen would be placed on top of the painted silhouette shape, sometimes slightly off-register. I wasn't too careful about making a perfect register. I used to be concerned about this, but it would never come out perfectly registered anyway, because it was hard to see through the silkscreen once I'd screened one image and moved it over to the next piece of canvas, so I would approximate the area upon which the silkscreen would be placed, and nearly 100% of the time the image would reproduce an almost perfect register.

GM: What distinguishes your prints from your paintings?

AW: I suppose you could call the paintings prints, but the material used for the paintings was canvas. The prints, if they were silkscreened by us, were always done on paper. Anyone can do them. Why, even now, there's this boy in Cologne who has printed us slightly smaller versions of my *Marilyn Monroe* paintings. But his versions are also done on paper and with more color combinations.

GM: Is there a relationship between your prints and your involvement with film?

AW: At the time I wasn't aware of any relationship. They were for me at that time and still are two distinct expressions. But you did point out to me the similarity in the repetition of image in both media. I'm speaking here in regard to the early films, like *Sleep* and *Empire*.

GM: Yes, I remember holding up to the light a clip from *Sleep* and noting how each frame was exactly alike; each frame was static because the film was static in its actual projection. What percentage of influence do friends or people you speak with have over your work?

AW: I don't know. I always get my ideas from people. Sometimes I don't change the idea. Or sometimes I don't use the idea right away, but may remember it and use it for something later on. I love ideas.

GM: Do you reuse the same screens for later paintings and editions?

AW: The screens I used for the *Flowers* and *Campbell Soup Can* paintings were never reused for the portfolios. First of all, they were never the same size. Second, the portfolios were never screened by me. They were always manufactured. I chose the different colors for them.

GM: Why do you use a rubber stamp?

AW: I don't always use a rubber stamp for my signature; but I turned towards the idea of a rubber stamp signature because I wanted to get away from style. I feel an artist's signature is part of the style, and I don't believe in style. I don't want my art to have a style.

GM: Do you think of yourself as media?

AW: Media influences everyone. It's a very powerful weapon. Didn't you tell me once that George Orwell prophesied the potency of the media when he spoke of "Big Brother is watching you" in his novel, *1984*?

GM: What plans have you for the near future?

AW: To do nothing.

—ca. 1970

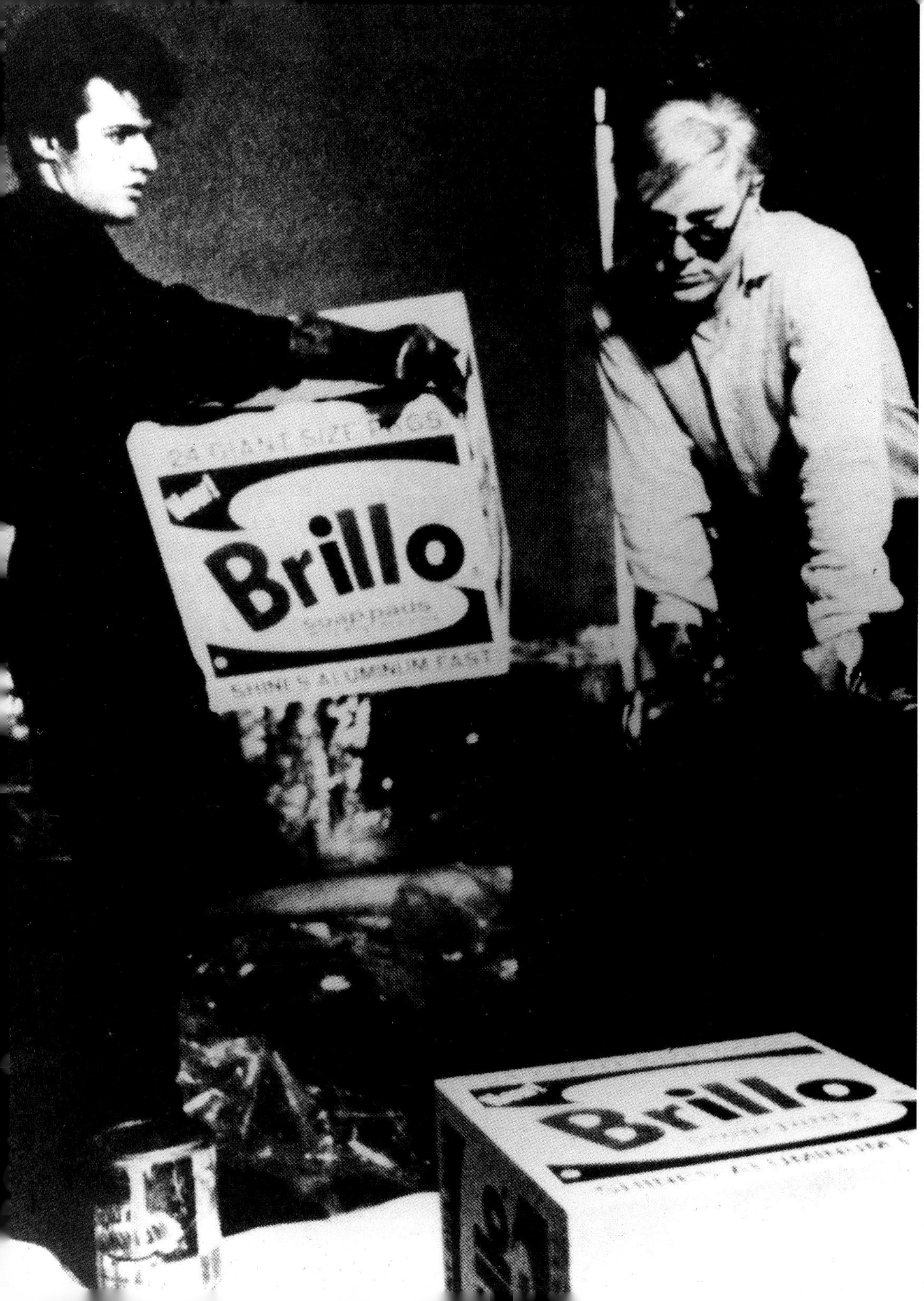
24 GIANT SIZE
Brillo
soap pads
SHINES ALUMINUM FAST
Brillo

thirteen
how we made the brillo boxes

Paper delivered at the International Symposium for Andy Warhol's Brillo Boxes under the auspices of the Akademie der Bildenden Kunste in Nürnberg, Friday, 19 November 1999.

On a cold, blistery day in early December, 1963, I found my way to a stepdown storefront at 409 East 70th Street between First & York avenues. The Havlicek Woodworking Company, Inc. New snow mixed with old snow piled high in the gutter. Cars whizzing past – their tail-lights flashing in a red afterglow. A dog barking. It was already late afternoon. Sky of pink and orange hue with a cloudfront coming in. The wind had died down.

Mr. Havlicek, his first name escapes me, a burly guy in his mid-forties, complexion flush from the winter spell, took my order and gave me a smile: "Several hundred boxes, please!" Boxes cut from pine and cut to size, fitted together with tiny wood nails. 17 x 17 x 14 inches, to be exact was one such size, I recall.

I look around. Sawdust scattered on the floor. The scent of hewn wood. An assortment of woodworking machinery, large and small. A rack of hand tools. A step ladder hung from the ceiling. A pin-up calendar marking the last month of the year. The holiday was nearing. Andy and I were in the midst of packing up the old firehouse where we'd worked these past six months. We'd already silkscreened 60 paintings or so. Shipped most of them out.

A few days after the move to our new workspace, January 28th, a truckload of wood boxes arrive, individually wrapped and taped in clear plastic sheeting. And so would begin the arduous task of taping the floor with rolls of brown paper and setting out each box in a gridlike pattern of

Opposite: Gerard Malanga and Andy Warhol preparing to silkscreen the *Brillo Box* series at the Factory, ca. February 1964.

eight rows lengthwise.

Billy Name and I would take turns painting with Liquitex all six sides of each box – which numbered nearly 80 – the Campbell's tomato juice for starters, by turning each box around on its side. We waited until the paint dried.

Andy and I repeated this process silkscreening all five sides again down the line. The sixth side – the bottom side – remained blank. We'd talk from time to time while working. At this particular time he provided no specific interpretation to why he thought up the boxes in the first place. When I asked, he said merely that he liked to go shopping. For a guy of 20, I took his shopping for granted.

Completing the work took nearly six weeks, from early February well into mid-April. Andy's show ambiguously titled "The Personality Of The Artist", would open April 21, 1964 at the Stable Gallery on the upper East Side. The opening was a festive affair. The boxes took over much of the floor space turning a gallery into what now seemed a warehouse with little room left over for the onlookers and press.

The following night, Ethel and Robert Scull, *nouveau riche* collectors of Pop Art, threw a party in Andy's honour at our workspace which by now took on the name, "The Factory". It was a *Who's Who* guest list, though I don't remember *who* exactly. It's been a long time.

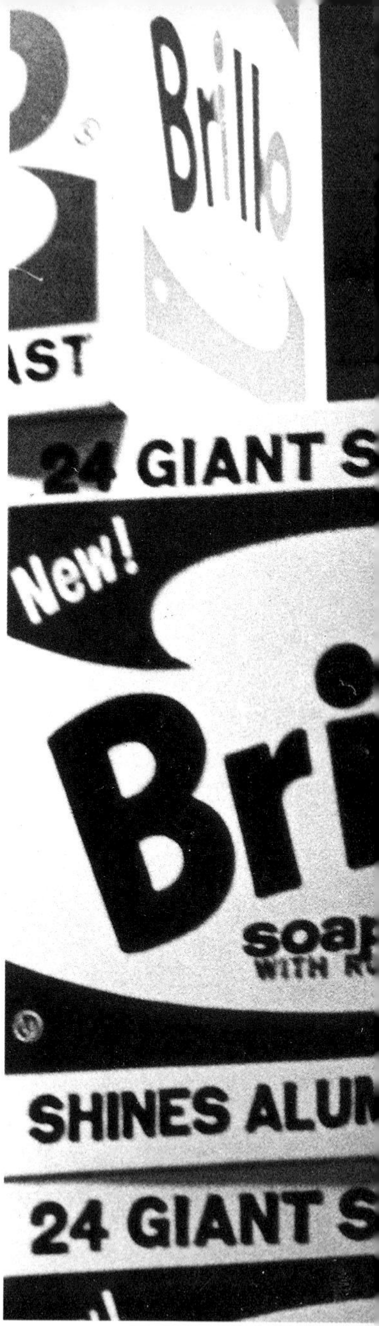

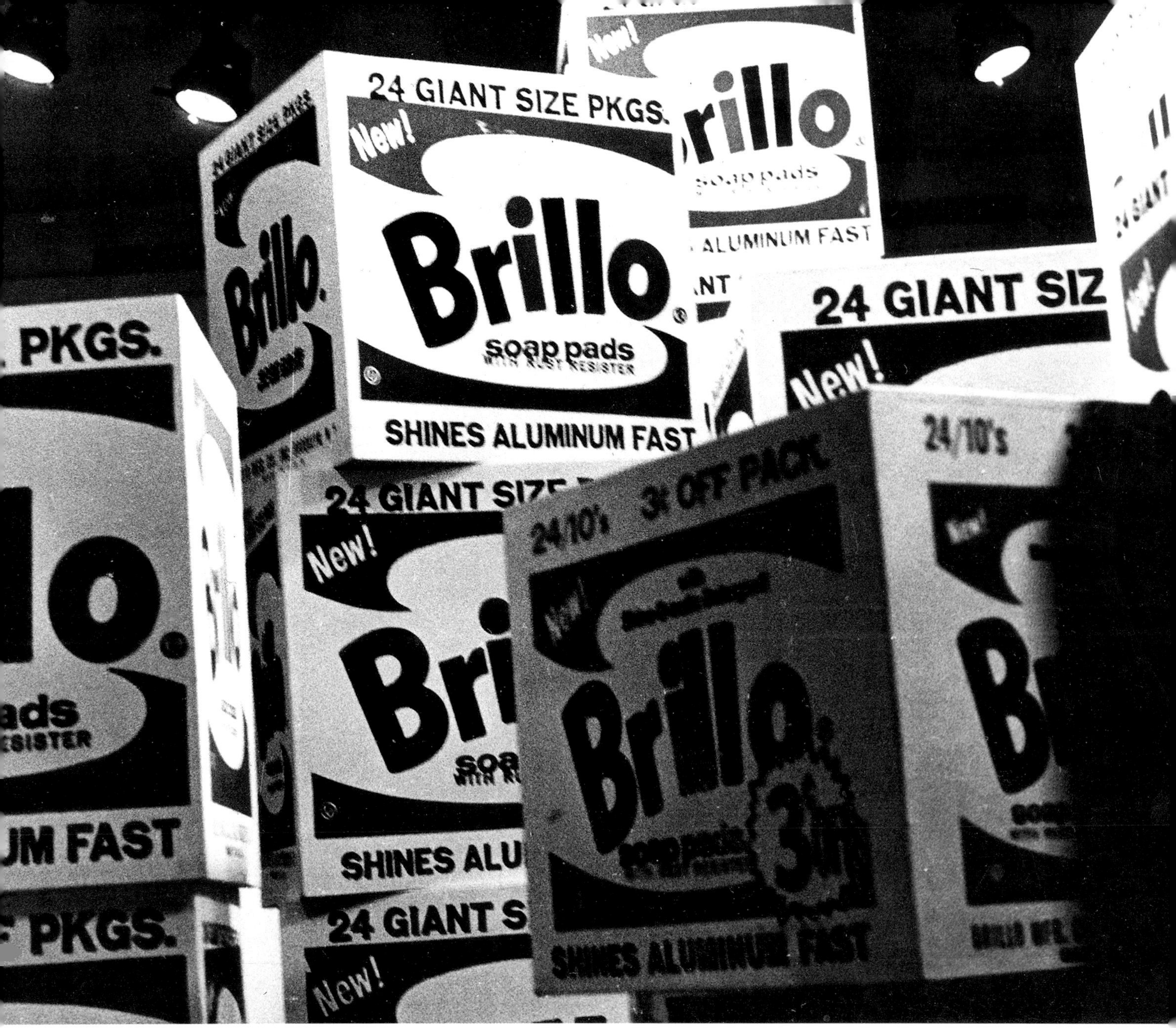

Andy Warhol: "The Personality Of The Artist", exhibition at Stable Gallery, April 21–May 9, 1964. Installation photo of grouping of Brillo Boxes.

The great trouble with art in this country at present, and apparently in France also, is that there is no spirit of revolt – no new ideas appearing among the younger artists. They are following along the paths beaten out by their predecessors, trying to do better what their predecessors have already done. In art there is no such thing as perfection. And a creative lull occurs always when artists of a period are satisfied to pick up a predecessor's work where he dropped it and attempt to continue what he was doing. When on the other hand you pick up something from an earlier period and adapt it to your own work an approach can be creative. The result is not new; but it is new insomuch as it is a different approach.

This statement is as relevant now as when first articulated by Marcel Duchamp for the Eleven Europeans in America catalogue, the MOMA exhibition of 1944 curated by James Johnson Sweeney.

Basically, Duchamp had a knack for anticipating all kinds of art, including the kind of machine-like art that Andy Warhol would execute exactly 30 years later: The wood boxes of various shapes and sizes. Del Monte peaches, Heinz ketchup, Mott's apple juice, Campbell's tomato juice, Kellogg's corn flakes – and, of course, Brillo – products for daily consumption or use, packaged as such to project a kind of corporate image akin to the popular culture Pop Art would recontextualize, repackage in "making it new". And so, when Andy and I created the assembly-line grid for how the wood replicas would be painstakingly screened, the concept of the "original" was substituted for an original copy reflecting the idea of a corporate assembly line. Rather than consider the original a readymade in the Duchampian mode, Andy created a copy of the original that became an original in itself – the original of the original – and didn't sign any of them. The object became a signature in itself.

When I refer here to the Brillo Box we must regard that as generic to the entire series comprising, as it were, two distinct versions in combinations of blue and red on a yellow field and the one we've come to know – the red and blue on a white background. We also have in this series the 5 brand-name boxes I've already mentioned. I think the reason the Brillo Box is the most remembered is the association we have for the name. What is "Brillo" anyway?

The word is invented – that is, it didn't exist as such before the product was invented. It was conceptualized to give the product an identity, a corporate image, if you will. The word "Brillo" in itself connotes a kind of Pop Art-like word, rooted as it were, in the word "brilliant", meaning that this steel-wool product will clean your pots and pans to a brilliant shine. The funny thing is, as a word enters into the lexicon, we know instantly what it means and what it's meant to do. It becomes like a cereal that goes "snap, crackle and pop". It's like Almond Joy. It's like Spam. It's easily recognizable, easily understood.

The product itself is made of what's described as steel wool – small steel threads intricately woven to form a pad both in thickness and size fitting snugly in the palm of your hand, and there you are off doing the dishes. Getting a steel splinter caught in your finger can be nasty business.

The first thing to remember is that the six grocery cartons Andy chose to replicate are disposable, intended to be trashed or recycled after being transported or stored. The contents within these oversize boxes also contain disposable packaging of the product most often seen, consumed or used by the consumer. They are designed to be emptied, and are made to hold fixed or measured quantities of goods. Five of the six brand-name boxes contain food. The only box to contain something other is the Brillo Box. The only element of design appears on five of the six sides as I've said in the form of corporate logo and weight product certification, etc.

The six box types have their own package identity through the application of specific graphics and color. It is no accident that initially there was a designer involved. It was his job to make the product recognizable, not only to the customer but to the retailer as well.

Looked at individually the original boxes were three-dimensional objects, although designed and printed flat. The designer had the opportunity to treat one or more of the surfaces with printed words applied directly to the cardboards either by offset or stencil. The original boxes were not designed to create an aesthetic effect. They were designed in a way merely to enhance product-recognition. They were meant only to transport and store. And yet when duplicated as hollow wood shapes, they instantly reveal a sudden pronounced aesthetic dimension. Nothing has changed and yet everything has. What was once a simple, disposable corrugated cardboard box is now a beautiful object – or a banal one, depending on the eye of the beholder. What was once Pop Art in all its artifice has taken on the aura of an authentic antique. So the boxes have acquired a sort of aura with the years. The paint has faded in places, the corners chipped. At their unveiling brand-new they did not shock as has been alleged, but put smiles on people's faces. The spirit was both playful and subversive. A Pop Art painting may not look at all "Pop" in 50 years. Already the Brillo Boxes are beginning to show signs of cultural fatigue. In other words, they've aged well.

To paraphrase one of the great creative thinkers of modern art, Harold Rosenberg: the effect is to convert the original cardboard box into something which affects the imagination in the manner of a work of art but with the weight of its actual existence intact. So the integrity of the original was maintained throughout.

If what Jean Arp says is true, that his sculptures ought to be come upon as one comes upon a stone polished by a stream, then the same would be for a consumer in a supermarket coming upon a group of Brillo Boxes stacked in random or orderly display. What is the real? What is the made up? In other words, as Rosenberg claims – and it's true –"a work of art ought to be a thing added to the world of things rather than a reflection of things that already exist. In short, while the work of art today is not illusory in the sense of being a representation, it is of a nature to give rise to new forms of mystification through drawing the spectator into an invented realm not unlike that of his everyday life."

And what better way of being reminded of this added dimension than with the everyday consumer goods of everyday life... with Brillo, a highly recognizable and useful product.

Having been transformed, Andy's Brillo Box is neither the real box in all its tactility nor its replica that at first glance seems real. I would say, it's a combination of both. But since it creates no lasting illusion, it is logically, just what it is, that is, a reality – but with a twist: it does not look like art. But looks can be deceiving as we well know. Had they been "readymades" they simply just wouldn't cut it.

It's now exactly thirty-six years from when I first stepped down into a little woodworking shop on the upper East Side. Mr. Havlicek is an unsung hero. So when I look back, the period named for Pop Art, where people like Andy and John Ashbery and me were trying to find each in our own way a new way of expressing ourselves, was really from 1963 to 1967.

That was it and yet it felt longer. When I hear "Pop Art is dead", I think "It was a long time dead". It was killed by the media holding a mirror up to its face.

There never was, and there never can be, a tradition of Pop Art, but popular culture is never dead. So much has radically changed within the culture or been transformed in the years intervening as to make repetition seem obsolete... and so much more change lies ahead. It's kind of scary.

In the early '70s onward Andy, by turning his sights to classical genres after developing a radically new style and approach, had failed to recognize the consequences of his own discoveries. What he attempted to do, by definition, involved mimicking every conceivable idea or subject-matter in the history of art, but he was unable to justify those choices as "making it new". The Brillo Boxes, nonetheless, aged well because they can at least be placed in perspective, then and now.

In Pop Art there is always something to see because what we see we are seeing all the time. It is, of course, years later.

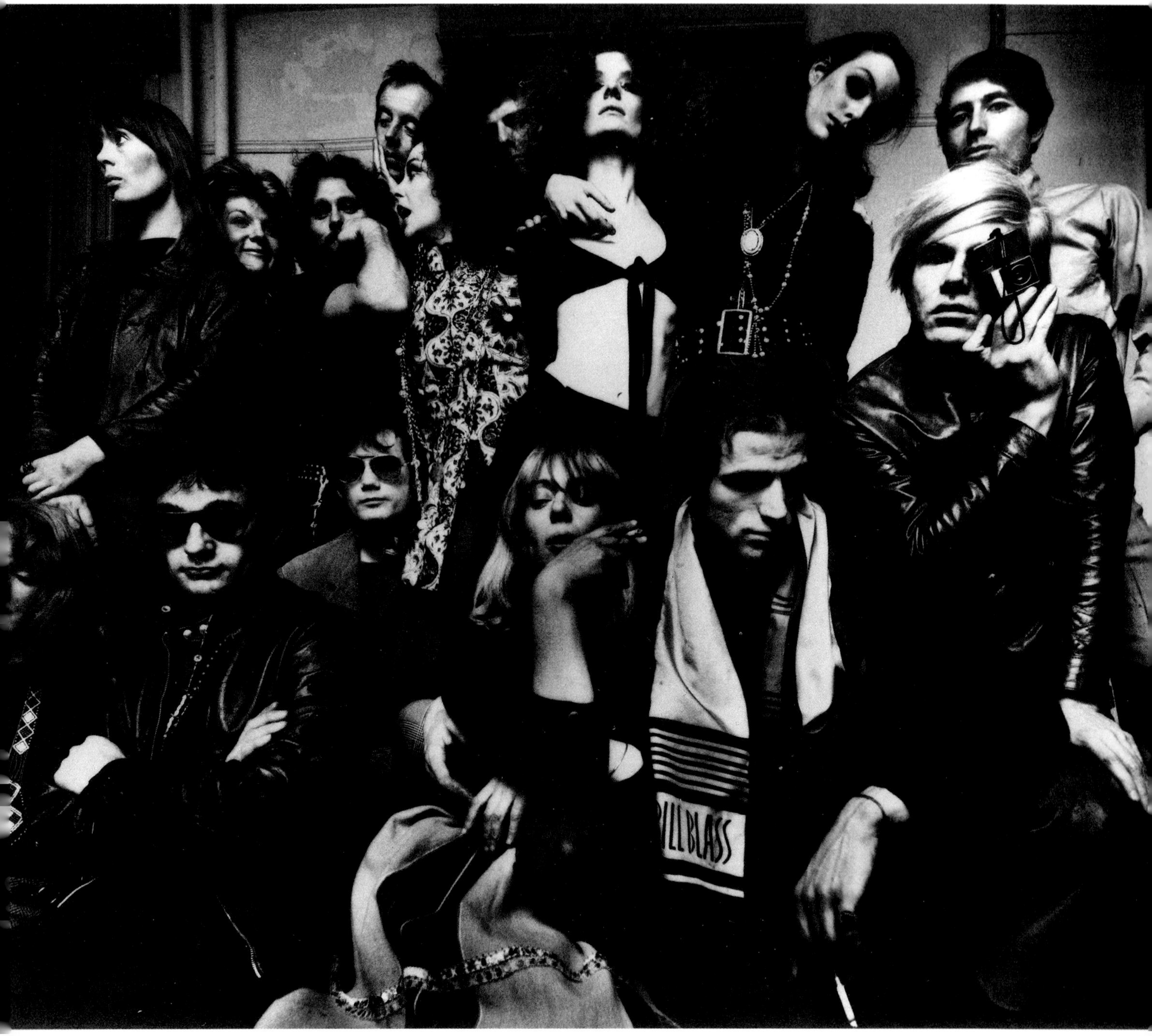
ILLBLASS

fourteen
dead warhol

Paper delivered for the symposium "Andy Warhol's Posthumous Reputation", at the State University of New York (SUNY-New Paltz) under the auspices of Professor Reva Wolf and the Department of Art History, 11 November 1999.

Where to begin? Today I believe viewers are divided in their response to Andy Warhol's work – some for the right reasons; some for the wrong. The shock has been taken out of Pop Art because our psyche is completely saturated by a culture that's become more pop than Pop Art ever was. You simply can't do Pop Art now. It would be anachronistic.

So Pop Art is no longer new, whereas the culture has evolved to the point of being forever new. Hence, Andy's art is not timeless, but is an art of its time. That's good.

The early 1950s, for instance, were years of tumult in the art world. Battle lines were drawn up. Jackson Pollock seemed to capture the moment and the media as well, giving Abstract Expressionism a respectable profile. Yet the media was blind to Pollock's soul-searching, his sensibility, magic, his passion, his poetry. His untimely death in 1956 took some of the forward energy out of the movement, but he remains a culture hero nonetheless.

This unparalleled explosion in American art in the '50s helped create fertile conditions for Pop Art to emerge in 1962 with a spirit more radical still. For the first time since French dada, a new art movement found itself aligned with the culture from which its imagery sprung, but with the distinction that it was more a celebration than a revolution.

Andy was controversial for his time because he did not paint what

Opposite: Group portrait at the Warhol Factory, 33 Union Square West, NYC, February 1968. From left to right (top row): Nico, Brigid Polk, Louis Waldon, Taylor Mead, Ultra Violet, Paul Morrissey, Viva, International Velvet, and unidentified man. From left to right (bottom row): Ingrid Superstar, Ondine, Tom Baker, Tiger Morse, Billy Name, and Andy Warhol.

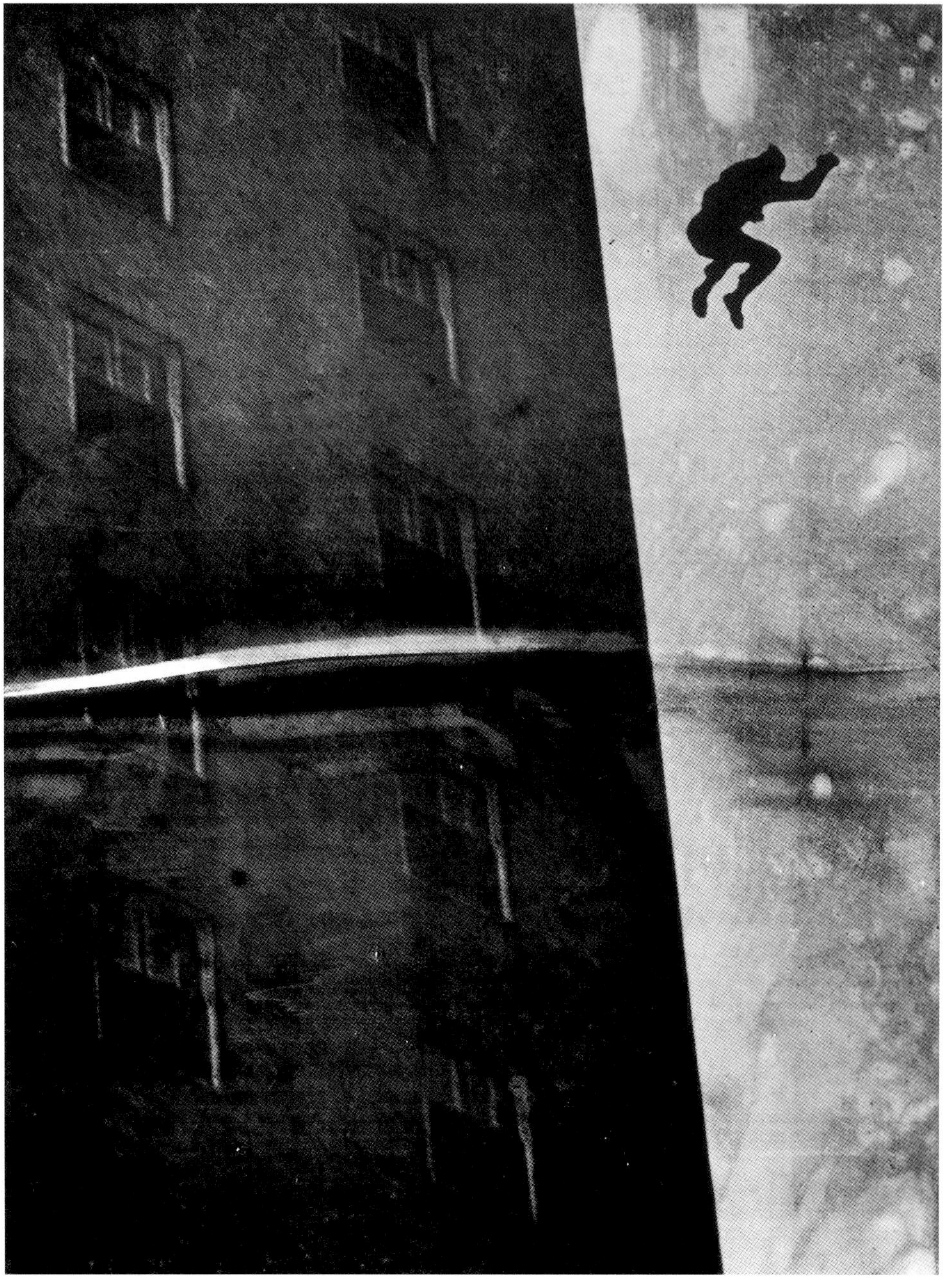

Suicide (1962).
Silkscreen ink on paper,
40″ X 30″.

an artist is supposed to paint and neither did the other pop artists. He "made" paintings about death and disasters, about race riots, about the mourning of JKF. His art reflected what the news media reported, comprised as it were of images we'd all seen at one time and then forgotten. Now we're seeing them again as if we'd never seen them before and this time we don't forget. Art has a way of referencing reality into new contexts.

Andy's art, in part, was the projection of what it's like being a fan. He had a love affair with culture – a culture consisting of landscapes littered with the dead, car crashes, accidents of one kind or another. One lone person hanging limp from a spike on a telephone pole. The silhouette of a body leaping into the dark grainy void, or completely covered over with a white sheet just moments after the leap. In fact, the two pictures might even be linked within one story. In fact, I know they are. It is a world in which death and disasters seem not to make a whole lot of sense.

You could say the photographers arrived at the accident scene ahead of Andy, but he remained after they'd all left. The eerie presence of the artist remains, reminiscent of Weegee. I suppose you could say Andy was in a sense reclaiming what the "photographer unknown" had already seen, leaving behind the photo as evidence. And already a distance exists. Andy is merely the observer of the observer – a bystander. He is thrice removed. His observation becomes the painting's focus and locus.

Braque once noted that "The painting is finished when it has effaced the idea". But there is something not quite finished about Andy's *Death & Disaster* paintings, fixed in time, as it were – as if what had occurred almost seemed staged. That it doesn't seem quite real. And yet real people died. The fate of so many lives sealed anonymously. Lives coming to an end abruptly and for no apparent reason other than someone made an undisciplined mistake. And so the people in these paintings, by being fixed in time, become timeless but with a catch: their timelessness is not fluid. It is dead time. They have no past to return to or future to move into, and few survive, as evidenced in *Five Deaths On Red*, for instance. Here one would think such bright coloration suggests possibility of deep meaning, but what that meaning is escapes me. Perhaps I already found the answer in the poems I wrote during the time working closely with Andy on this series. We just happened to choose red that day.

It is only in these paintings, aptly called *Death & Disasters*, that

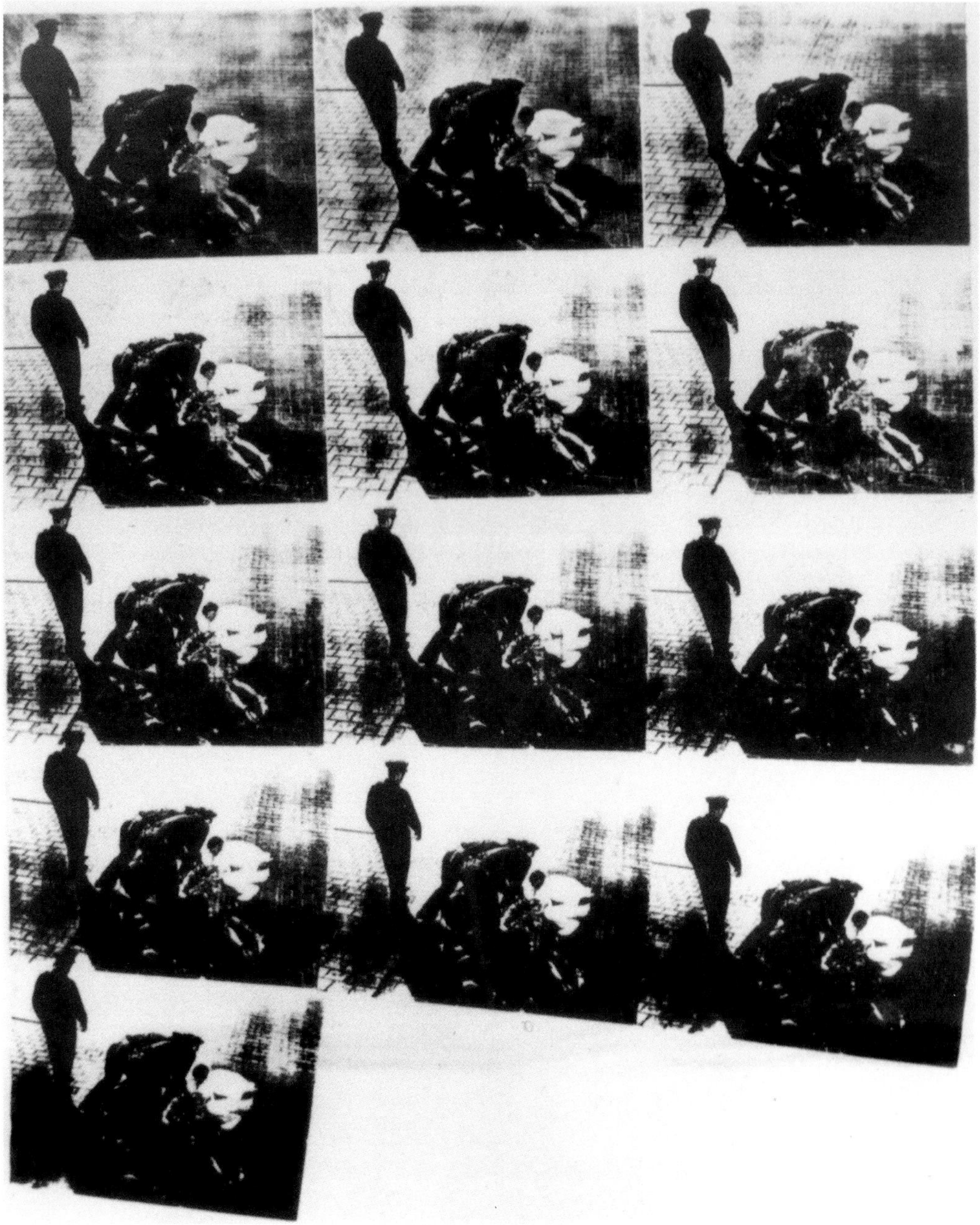

Bellevue I (1963). Acrylic and silkscreen ink on canvas, 106" X 83".

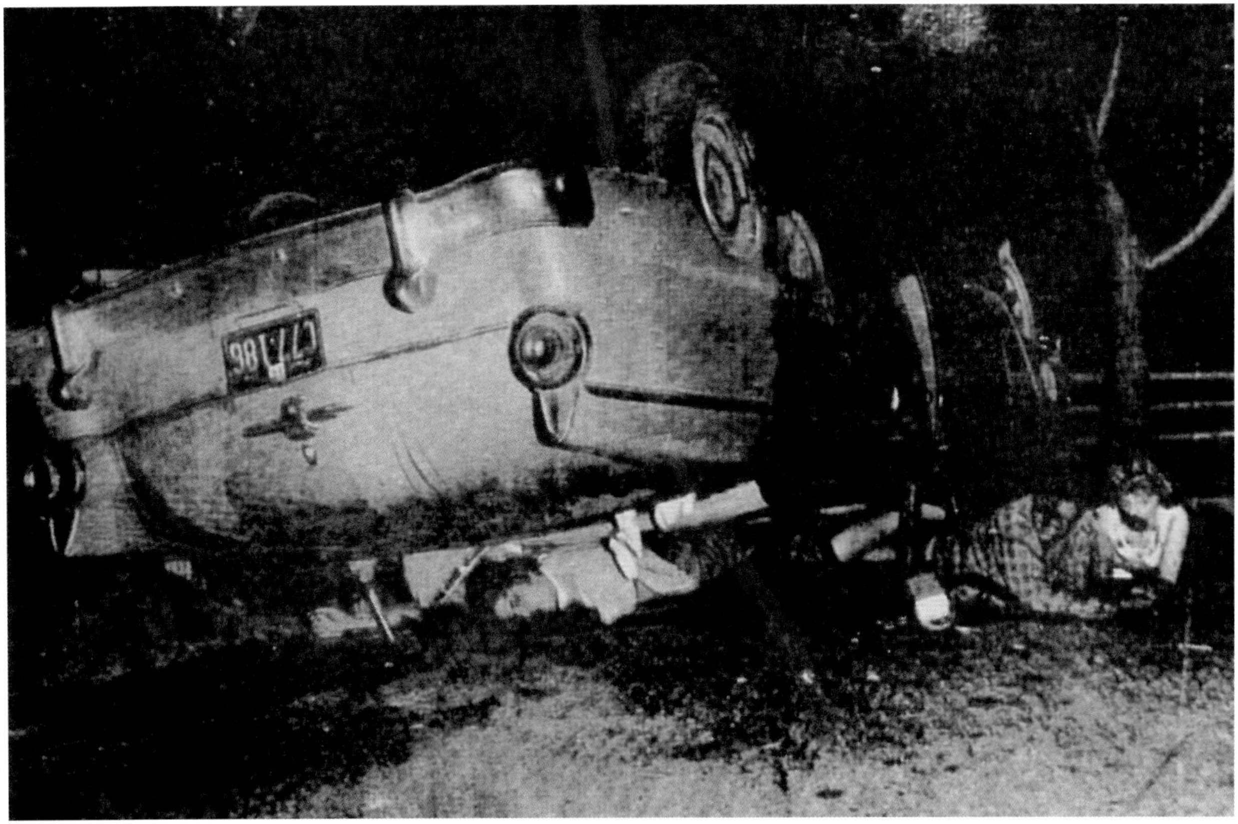

Detail from *Five Deaths On Red* (1962). Silkscreen ink on synthetic polymer paint on canvas, 30" X 30".

Andy might have been trying to communicate something of himself to the viewer, but what that is has never been fully revealed. Perhaps it was his way of staring death in the face. In any case, we worked quietly together. A few suggestions or a shift of the screen with some surprising results. We never rejected anything, we embraced the mistakes.

Does Andy deserve a place in the pantheon of 20th century art? Of course he does. Nearly 40 years after their creation, all of Andy's works covering the period 1962 through 1967 still retain much of their magic and power, because they were generated at a time when art was in flux and the camera-eye seemed more pervasive.

THE MOBS: A New Look

2—Power and Politics • Series by Anthony Scaduto • Page 49

WEATHER
Mostly Sunny, 80.
Tomorrow: Sunny, 80-85.
SUNSET: 8:2[illegible] PM
SUNRISE TOMORROW: 5:26 AM

New York Post

© 1968 New York Post Corporation

Vol. 167 No. 169 — NEW YORK, TUESDAY, JUNE 4, 1968 — 10 Cents — 15c Beyond 50-mile Zone

LATE CITY
Over the Counter Stocks

ANDY WARHOL FIGHTS FOR LIFE

Marcus Taking Stand

By MARVIN SMILON and BARRY CUNNINGHAM

Ex-Water Commissioner James Marcus was expected to be the government's first witness today in the bribery conspiracy trial that has wrecked his career and saddled the Lindsay Administration with its only major scandal.

His opening testimony follows a dramatic scene in U. S. District Court yesterday when Marcus, 37, changed his plea to guilty in a surprise switch which visibly jolted four of the five other defendants in the alleged $40,000 kickback plot.

The dapper former aide and confidante of the Mayor said he was in no way coerced or promised anything to change his original plea of

Continued on Page 2

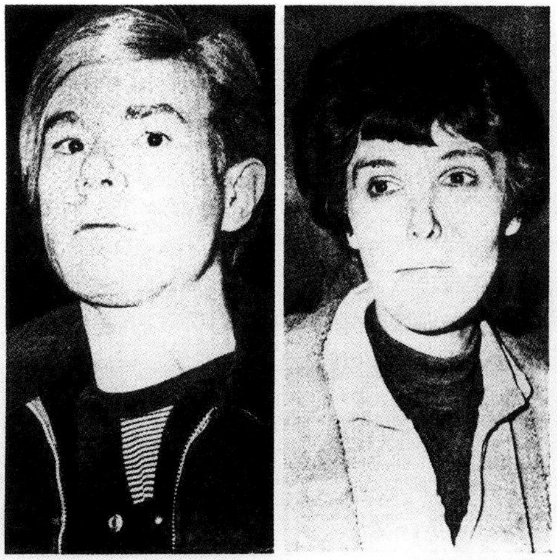

Post Photos by Boxer and Engel

Pop artist-film maker Andy Warhol makes the scene at a recent Long Island discotheque party. Valeria Solanis, who surrendered to police after he was shot and critically wounded, is shown as she was booked last night.

By JOSEPH MANCINI
With JOSEPH FEUREY and JAY LEVIN

Pop artist Andy Warhol fought for his life today, after being gunned down in his own studio by a woman who had acted in one of his underground films.

The artist - sculptor - film-maker underwent 5½ hours of surgery performed by a four-man team of doctors at Columbus Hospital late last night and was given a "50-50 chance to live."

Andy Warhol: Life and Times. By Jerry Tallmer. Page 3.

He remained in critical condition today and his chances for life had not improved.

At 7:30 last night, just three hours and 10 minutes after the shooting, Valeria Solanis, 28, a would-be writer-actress, walked up to a rookie policeman directing traffic in Times Sq. and surrendered.

She reached into her trench coat and handed Patrolman William Schmalix, 22, a .32 automatic and a .22 revolver. The .32 had been fired recently, police

Continued on Page 2

New York Post, Tuesday June 4th, 1968, after Andy Warhol is shot by Valerie Solanis of SCUM (Society for Cutting Up Men).

A new movement, Pop Art, had been born of a synchronicity among several artists working at first in isolation to each other. But within the close of that first decade, partly due to media hype, Pop Art was no longer news. Quietly, its members moved into other areas – evolving and exploring as they went along. In fact, Andy went through a transformation of sorts himself. After the near-fatal shooting of June 3rd, 1968, Andy stopped silkscreening on canvas altogether. He couldn't handle the physical steps involved. The rep work. The drudgery. The mixing of paints. As it is, he nearly became the subject of one of his own death paintings. And it would not be until the early '70s that he'd take up the screen again.

In the meantime, popular culture was radically changing and I believe it no longer held for him the sudden mystique arising out of the choice he made early on regarding subject-matter and ideas. What to paint? as it were.

Roland Barthes remarks that the artist has no power, but he has some relationship with truth. It is at the very heart of this notion where Andy strived for power – and I'm talking here of the early '70s – that he betrayed that truth and, I believe, his art suffered for it.

The kinds of paintings he made from the '70s onward – excepting, of course, the *Shadows* series – bear no connection to the early work – that is, the radical work from the '60s. Andy no longer stopped to look but stopped looking. He became a cash cow the more he turned out the same thing in different guises, based in part on a culture he had little or no connection with any longer – simply, that culture outpaced him. He was now dealing with the debris, with worn-out ideas. Rather than shake the pumpkin he was out to please – and was handsomely rewarded. He was part of a changing world that is, in fact, still changing, but he himself didn't change. He traded in his radical spirit for the glitz and glamour of transparent trends. He gave his blessing to 9th rate talent. He bowed to goddesses of fashion. He surrounded himself with people who contributed nothing creative towards his art. In effect, he was merely "bringing home the bacon", as he once said, burdened with the responsibility of several hungry mouths to feed. He allowed himself to be used. He was simply out-of-step with himself and he was afraid because he could not change from within. He was stuck.

He may have been an original, but he was no longer original. He

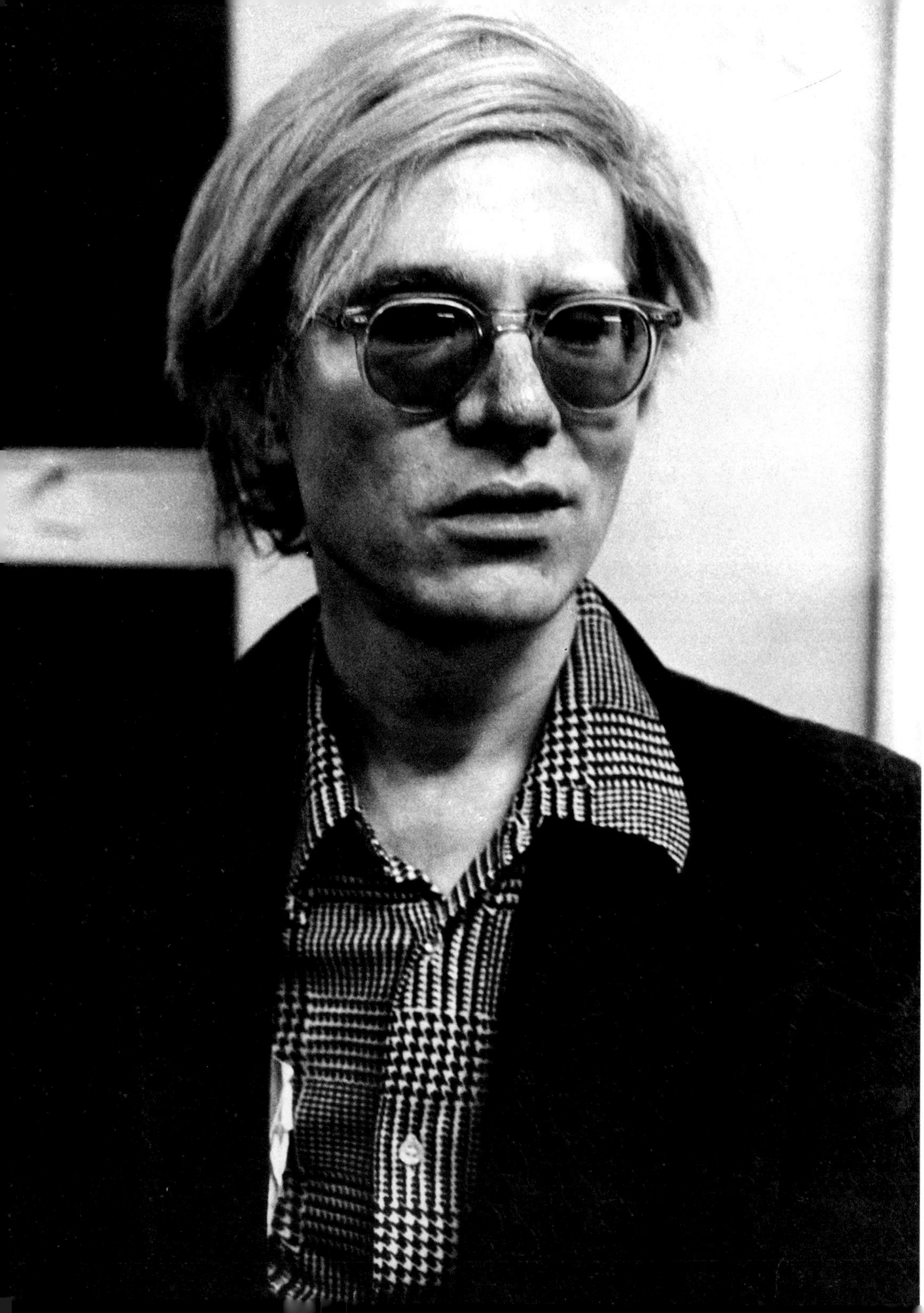

Andy Warhol at the
Union Square Factory,
1969.

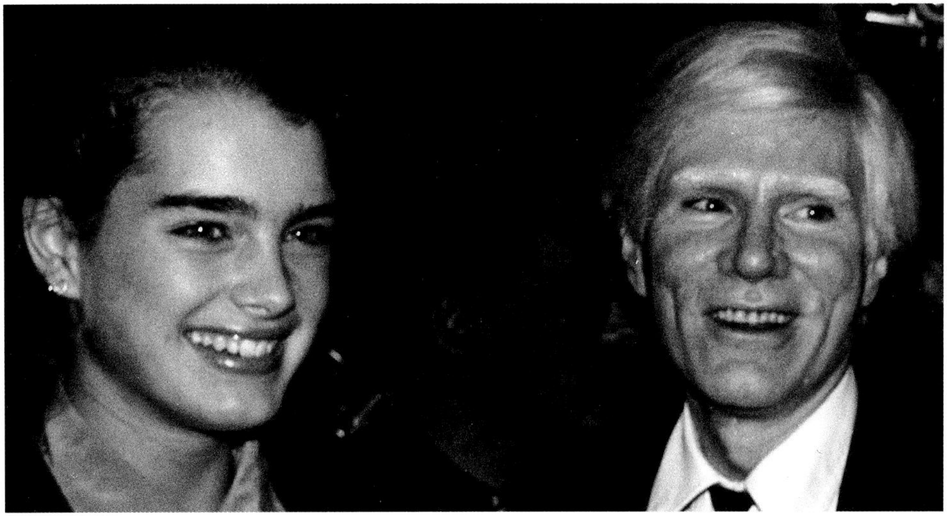

Andy Warhol and Brooke Shields at Studio 54, 1980.

merely replicated a lot of the old themes of power and wealth. The look became more decorative than the knockout punch. He seemed to be falling back on tradition, but on other artists' tradition. So what we have is an appropriation of certain set themes and genres. Art that already existed, either his own or someone else's, became the dominant subject for his new way of transforming ideas, for his new art. But is it art? Better yet, is it important?

The work is overly decorative, as I've said. A bit fey. But, then, some nincompoop of a critic will chime in, *Andy's got great color sense*... and so does Matisse. So what – it's an art that conveys no suffering whatsoever.

Recently, I was locked in a conversation at a party – I did all the listening – where this magazine publisher was going on at the mouth about a certain photographer's show, and I wanted to take this guy by the ears and give him the godfather kiss, but that's not done in polite society. I realized that power and money create the aura of acceptance and hype. That if you're poor, you're a nobody no matter how gifted you are. Suffering is not what art is about these days. It's about invention. It's about marketing. It's not about having a great deal of luck. If you're someone who has pretences to making art and also have wealth – well, you're taken seriously, so it seems.

Who knows what Modigliani would have created had he lived longer? I'm confident his soul would have never been corrupted. But even here, you can see the tinge of sentimentality seeping in through the cracks. Not his fault. Attitudes change. Today it's Basquiat's turn. His bones are being picked clean.

With Andy, on the other hand, his soul was corrupted. That might sound a bit judgmental, but maybe not. I personally feel his focus got shifted when he found little of anything to paint and merely fell back on familiar safe themes. "It's so easy," I can hear him say. Andy seemed prepared to sell himself to the highest bidder. He gained fame and fortune but lost his self in the process.

Andy was an intellectual painter in spite of himself and, perhaps, that's one of his more enduring strengths and an intellectual bonus besides. Something to think about. Just as no-one escapes the media, Andy will not escape us. We watch an AT&T TV commercial catching glimpses of computerized light-leaks, giving the impression of an underground movie when it's all digitized and now nearly every spot has to have the same kind of graphics. It's gotten corny in the extreme. Reality, as we think we know it, has succumbed to virtual reality. What was a technical flaw in Andy's camera became a "divine accident". Andy and I embraced the mistakes, like I said. Duchamp was my teenage hero. The media is a broken mirror.

The point being there are no visible mistakes in Andy's art after 1970. Too bad. Everything seems to fall effortlessly into place. The roughness of the paint's surface has been hewn to a slick, anal, constant look. Nothing reverberates. It just stands still. I'm certain a car crash can inspire a poem. I'm just as certain a cartoon dollar sign doesn't. There are other artists better qualified to the language of signs. I can think of Mimmo Rotella for one.

Andy was good at what he did. It shows in the carefully selected pop personalities, the deaths and disasters, the myriad flowers, the occasional portrait commission. Andy's late work from 1970 onwards impacted on the way his early work will survive and be appreciated and, I hope will be also inspiring. The early work will triumph over the later work in spite of the speculators. But for now we're witness to this millennium dance of death. There's a lot at stake here and the History train is nearly full to capacity. Who is remembered?

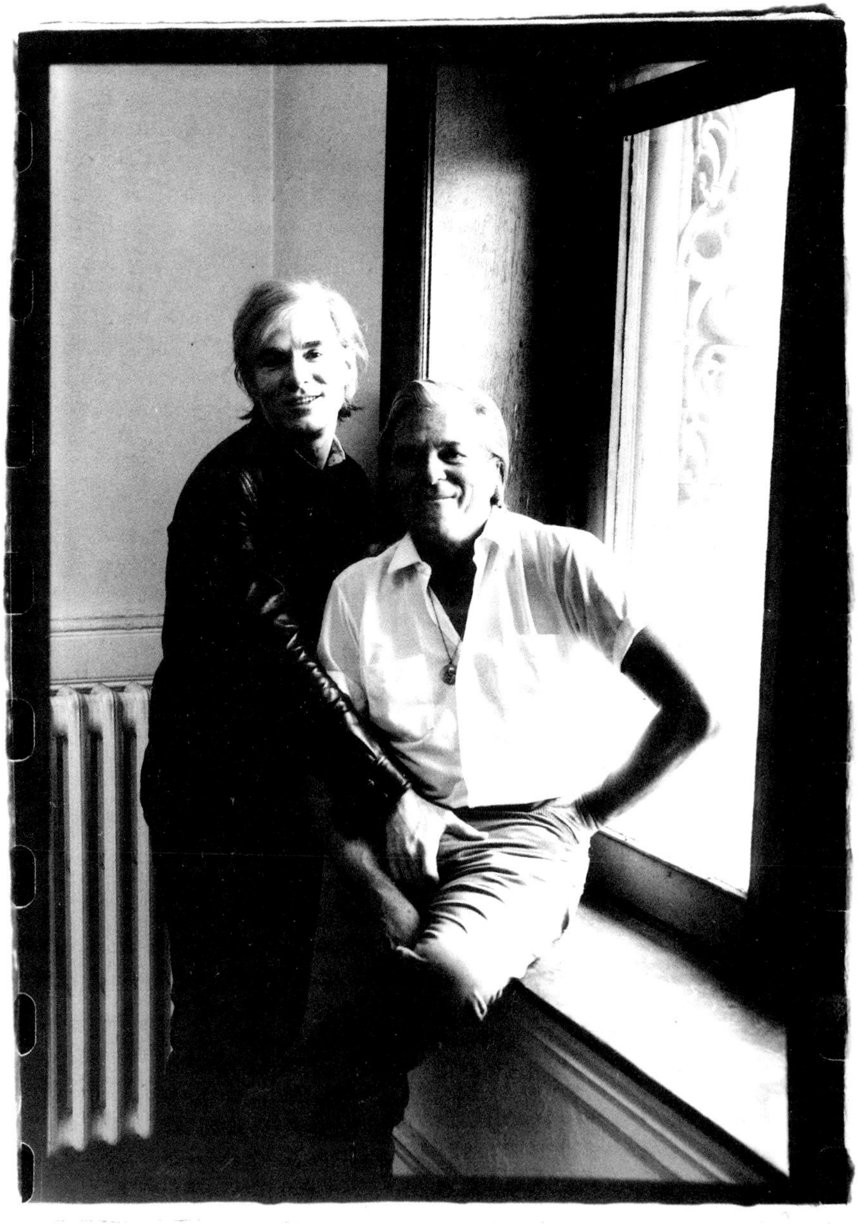

Andy Warhol gropes Parker Tyler on his first visit to the Union Square Factory, 1969.

credits/acknowledgements

ACKNOWLEDGEMENTS
Grateful acknowledgment is made to the following publications in which some of these pieces first appeared (some in somewhat different form): *Harbinger* #1 (**The Empire State Building is a Star!**), Stellan Holm Gallery catalogue (**Electric Chairs On Display For The First Time!**), *Kulchur* #16 (**Andy Warhol Interviewed**), *The Ant's Forefoot* (**People Places Food Art**), *The Print Collector's Newsletter* (**A Conversation With Andy Warhol**), and Christophe van de Weghe Fine Art catalogue (**The Kiss**).

The Assistant was, in part, originally adapted from an interview with Charles Guiliano and later incorporated into the much larger piece, **Notes From A Non-Literary Life** included in the *Contemporary Authors Autobiography* series, published as Volume 17 by Gale Research, Inc., Copyright © 1993 by Gerard Malanga.

This Photograph May Not Be – etc. and **Fritzy, 1969** were initially written as chapters for my unpublished memoirs, entitled *Memory In Progress*.

The remaining texts are previously unpublished.

To all those publishers and editors who took an interest seeing my work into print, many thanks.

PHOTOGRAPHY CREDITS
Aside from those works in the private collection of Gerard Malanga or in the public domain, nearly all the images reproduced in this volume are copyrighted by their makers, or by the respective families, estates, foundations, or representatives of the artists. Every effort was made to contact all such parties to obtain official permission to reproduce, and we are grateful for the kind co-operation extended by the artists included in this book. These are as follows:

Gerard Malanga: Photographs by Gerard Malanga, Copyright © by Gerard Malanga, which appear in this book include Billy Name (Chapter X, p.126), The Velvet Underground (Ch. IX, pgs.122 + 125), Agneta Freiberg (Ch. XI, p.137), Fred Hughes diptych (Ch. XI, p.132), Warhol/Union Square Factory groupshot (Ch. XIV, p. 154), Andy Warhol (Ch. II, p.30 & Ch.XIV, p.162), and Parker Tyler visits Andy Warhol at

The Factory (Ch. XIV, p.165).

Fred W. McDarrah: Photographs by Fred W. McDarrah, Copyright © by Fred W. McDarrah (Ch. II, p.52)

Billy Name: Photograph by Billy Name, Copyright © by Billy Name (Ch. XIII, p.149)

Andy Warhol: Movie stills of *Empire* and *Sleep* (Ch. V, p.84 & Ch. VIII, p.108 respectively) first published in *Film Culture*. Copyright © The Archives of the Andy Warhol Museum, Pittsburgh, PA.

Artworks by Andy Warhol:
Ch. II, p.36: *Triple Elvis* (Andy Warhol Foundation for the Visual Arts)
Ch IV, p.80: *The Kiss (Bela Lugosi)* (Private Collection)
Ch. VII, p.96: *Blue Electric Chair* (Private Collection)
Ch. XIV, p.156: *Suicide* (Collection Adelaide de Menil, New York)
Ch. XIV, p.158: *Bellevue I* (Private Collection)
Ch. XIV, p.159: *Five Deaths On Red* (Collection Stellan Holm, New York)
Copyright © by Andy Warhol Foundation for the Visual Arts/Artists Rights Society (ARS), New York.

Additional copyrighted artworks by Gerard Malanga include: *Screen Tests* by Gerard Malanga & Andy Warhol (Chapters II, V, III, VIII, pgs.48, 64, 68–79, 89, 112, 113), Copyright © 1967 by Kulchar Press. Renewed © 1997 by Gerard Malanga.

Untitled (The electric chair in a room made silent by signs) from the Thermofax Series by Gerard Malanga & Andy Warhol (Ch. VII, p.99), Copyright © by Gerard Malanga.

With Love From Andy "Pie" And Gerry "Pie", photo-mixed media (Ch. II, p.18), Copyright © by Gerard Malanga.

The *Third Avenue El* series (Ch.II, p.21, 22), Copyright © by Gerard Malanga.

Edie Sedgwick Photobooth Portrait (Ch. II, p.45), Copyright © by Gerard Malanga.

Benedetta Barzini Photomaton Portrait (Ch. II, p.55), Copyright © by Gerard Malanga.

Andy Warhol 16mm Film Portrait (Ch. VI, p.92), Copyright © by Gerard Malanga.

Andy Warhol Assemblage (Ch. I, p.17), Copyright © by Gerard Malanga.

Andy Warhol photobooth fragment (pgs.174–175), Copyright © by Gerard Malanga.

Gerard Malanga's *Film Notebooks* (Ch. II, pg.44 & Ch. VIII, p.111), Copyright © by Gerard Malanga.

Andy Warhol and W.H. Auden portraits by Charles Henri Ford (Ch. I, p.10 & Ch. II, p.25), Copyright © by Gerard Malanga.

Unless otherwise indicated, additional photographs in this volume have been provided by Gerard Malanga from his own personal collection. The photographers and artists of works are listed alphabetically below.

Ira Cohen (Ch. IX, p.124)
Lorenz Gude (Ch. II, p.35 & Ch. XII, p.138)
Michael Katz (Ch. IX, p.129)
John Palmer (Ch. VIII, p.116 & Ch. XII, p.142)
John D. Schiff (Ch. II, p.33)
Indra Tamang (Ch. XIV, p.163)
Edward Wallowitch (Ch. VIII, p.104)
Barbara Waterston (Ch. II, p.60)

If we have omitted a photographer's name or were unable to locate a photographer in question for permission to reproduce photographs included in this volume, it was unintentional, and corrections will be made in any future editions.

A personal thanks to Ira Cohen and Eric LaPrade for their expedient and meticulous photo research.

index

Page numbers in bold indicate an illustration. Entries in italic indicate an artwork or film by Andy Warhol.

Overleaf: Andy Warhol ca. 1964

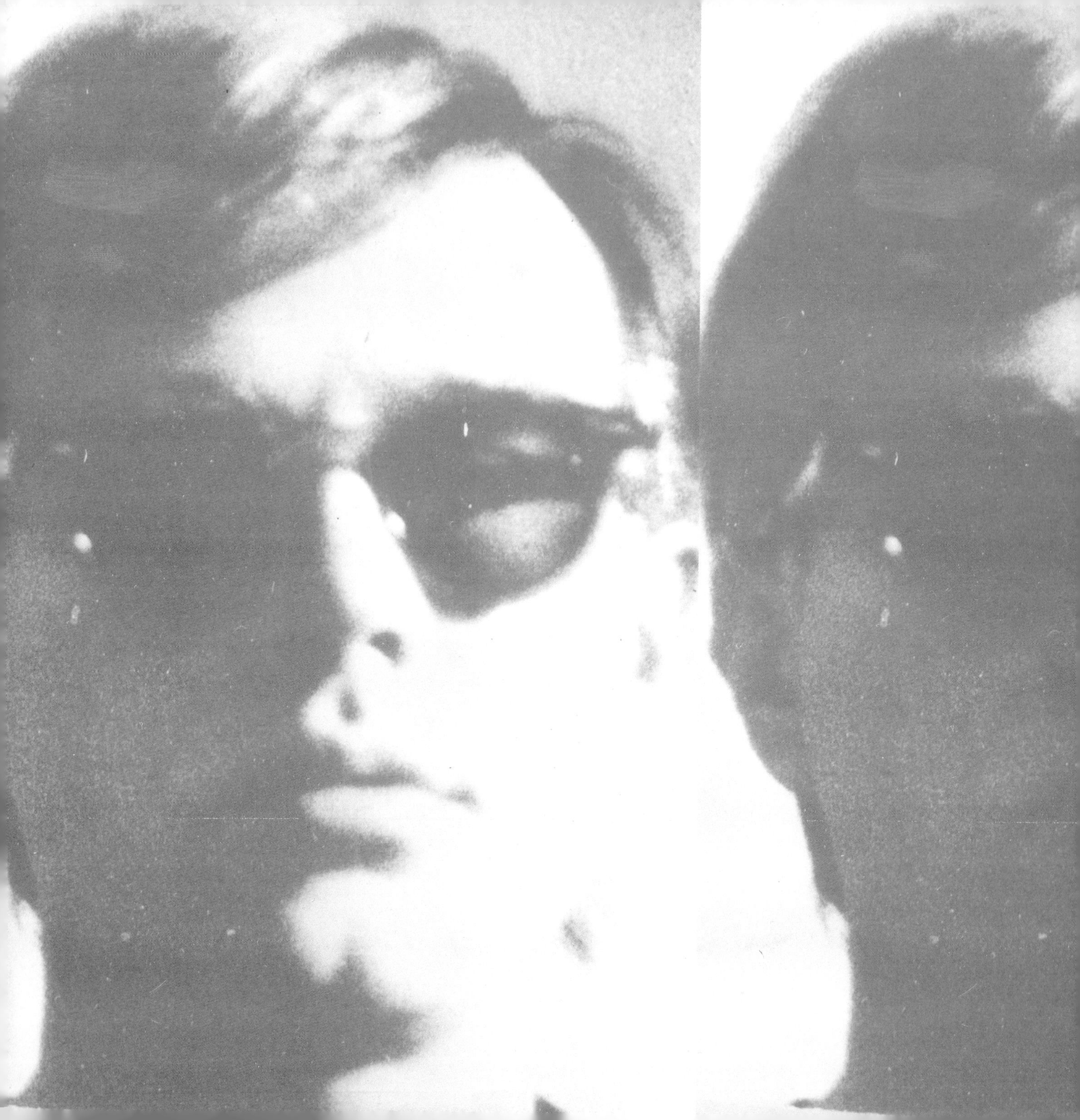

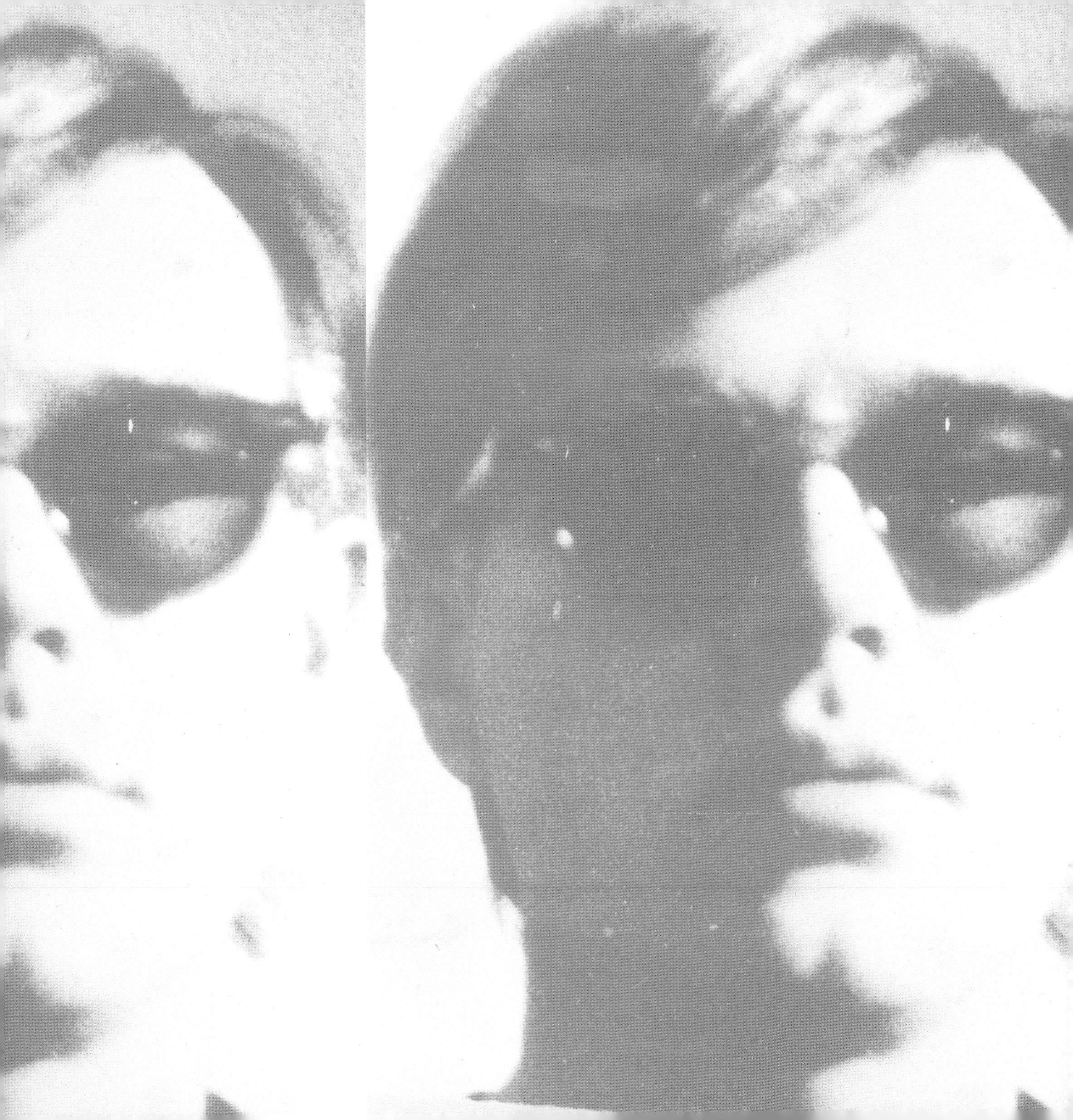